THE TECHNIQUES OF SMALL BOAT RACING

THE TECHNIQUES

OF SMALL BOAT

RACING

By

The International 14 Sailors of North America

Edited by STUART H. WALKER, M.D.

Illustrated by DAVID Q. SCOTT

W · W · NORTON & COMPANY · INC · New York

To our designers—Charles Bourke, George Corneil, Uffa Fox, Clarence Farrar, Ian Proctor, and the many others who continue to demonstrate how much we have yet to learn about sailboat racing.

And (from the Editor) to my father who taught me to sail and to study—and so to study sailing.

Library of Congress Catalog Card No. 60-5950

PRINTED IN THE UNITED STATES OF AMERICA
FOR THE PUBLISHERS BY VAIL-BALLOU PRESS

56789

Contents

Part IV Race Management and Rescue

Illustrations

Photographs between pages 128 and 129

Planing in Hamilton Harbor, Bermuda
Reaching plane—note lift of hull
George Corneill design on the Severn River
Awaiting the start in Round Bay
Reaching plane—note boat kept bolt upright
Reaching plane—note flat wake
Stopped by sea on a broad reach—note severe stress on rig
Spinnaker run—note level clews, horizontal pole
Reaching in Round Bay
Charles Bourke design—note adjustable jib fairleads, hiking straps,
centerboard hoist
Uffa Fox design—note boom vang with winch in thwart
Capsize in the Potomac—righting technique
Righted—lack of buoyancy will prevent self rescue
Before the squall on the Severn

Line drawings and diagrams by David Q. Scott

Endpaper photograph by Morris Rosenfeld

Foreword

Racing sailors compete for many different reasons and with many different convictions as to the purpose of the race. Some feel that it is a test of speed which should be won by the fastest boat. Some feel that this is unjust, that the skill and experience of skipper and crew should be the deciding factor. One day experience in judging wind conditions provides the winning strategy; another day sheer "seat of the pants" ability in a breeze gets the boat to the weather mark ahead of the pack; and another day starting tactics or the clever application of an overlap proves decisive.

All factors are important; none can be disregarded in any class. But only in an open or restricted, rather than one-design, class is a full evaluation of the factors related to boat speed available. And only when boats are functioning at peak efficiency can the significance of the crew's ability be assessed. The International 14 Class as the major small restricted class of the world has provided the optimum testing ground for factors related to boat speed for many years. In addition, because the 14 is a demanding boat raced in top flight competition, it has produced some of the world's outstanding helmsmen. The refinement of the 14's has made them sensitive to minor variations in rig, sails, and sailing technique so that the significance of many factors ordinarily little recognized becomes evident.

From these vantage points the International 14 sailors of the United States, Canada, and Bermuda have pooled their knowledge in the production of this book. Each chapter is written by a recognized expert in the field under discussion who has collaborated with many others and drawn from all the available literature on his subject. The book has been correlated to avoid repetition and conflict, but fresh individual approaches are presented throughout. The material is presented for the experienced racing sailor who is interested in developing the maximum boat efficiency and the highest refinement of strategy, tactics, and technique. However, it is felt that the principles presented apply to all small sailboats (and usually to large ones) and that novices and experts, planers and nonplaners, engineers and tacticians all will find it to be the best available source of advanced knowledge in the field of small boat racing technique.

Stuart H. Walker

Introduction—The Development of the International 14-ft. Dinghy in North America

By CHARLES W. BOURKE, Toronto

I feel that an introduction to a book such as this should have only one form—a brief history of the early development of dinghies and of their evolution into the International 14-footers as raced in North America today.

Where the first sailing dinghies originated is controversial, but it has been suggested that they were developed from the towing dinghies of large yachts. In a recent letter, Dr. Alfred Delaney of Dublin (who represented Ireland at the Olympics in monotypes, 1947 and 1952) states that Dublin Bay Water Wags were built and sailing as early as 1887. These were an open type of boat from a Club Committee design, adapted from 1878 shapes and built by Fife of Farley and Atkinson of Dublin. Fifty were built at this time. Another forty, built in 1900, were one-design, very close to the dimensions of the early 14-ft. National. It is interesting that these boats carried spinnakers.

Canada gives credit to Mr. J. Wilton Morse of the Royal Canadian Yacht Club, Toronto, for designing, in 1897, the first Canadian 12-ft. sailing dinghy. This became very popular and was quickly followed by a 14-footer, clinker-built, half-decked, with centerboard and gaff-rigged. A good description of Canadian dinghies may be found in *Sailing Craft* by Schoettle. The 14-ft. National Dinghy (English type) by Bruce Larkins Atkey, also is well covered by Schoettle—and as well by Uffa Fox in his *Sail and Power* (1936).

Canadian 14-ft. dinghies were built in great numbers after 1897 by Ackroyd Bros., Toronto. It is claimed that these builders constructed 3,000 before retiring. Their beautiful sailing boats were found all over the Great Lakes, in the United States and Canada. And when the Canadians took Genoa in 1944, some sail enthusiasts discovered three Ackroyd dinghies there. Mr. George Corneil contributed in a large way to dinghy sailing, having built hundreds of 14-footers which still star in regattas. There were many, many other builders—Peterboro Canoe, Lakefield Canoe, Art Grew, Gravette, Thompson Boat Works, William Ogle, to mention a few.

There has been international competition on Lake Ontario in 14-footers since Mr. James Douglas of the Toronto Canoe Club presented the Douglas Cup in 1914. The Genesee Club, Port Charlotte, Rochester, was the first to challenge for this cup. Even before this, Rochester and Toronto clubs raced for the Emerson Cup in 12-footers. The last 12-footer to win the Emerson Cup at Toronto was *Ouija,* owned by W. G. Reilly—a keen sailor in both 12- and 14-footers. *Ouija* was the first Marconi-rigged dinghy with Ratsey City Island sails seen on Lake Ontario. She was designed by Professor George Owen of M.I.T. The Emerson Challenge Cup is now competed for in a three-boat team race series in International 14's.

Rochester was not successful in Douglas Cup challenges until 1921, and the appearance of the famous *Gloriette,* designed by Mr. Ward of Tonawanda, N.Y., for Mr. A. Sharp of Rochester. *Gloriette* was radical in design, being built on the wave-form theory, which gave her a hollow bow, hard bilge, and slack run. She was Marconi-rigged and proved very fast in our average 8- to 10-knot breeze on Lake Ontario. George Roat and Bert Sharp sailed her to victory in the early twenties against a gaff-rigged dinghy piloted by Doug Addison and Bill Walker of the R.C.Y.C. *Gloriette* successfully defended the Douglas Cup until Tom Turrall of the National Yacht Club, Toronto, won it off Port Charlotte in 1924 in a strong wind with a gaff-rigged Ackroyd boat. Tommy Turral, known as the Storm King, was a great dinghy sailor and loved a good breeze.

By the middle twenties nearly all 14-ft. dinghies in Lake Ontario had changed from gaff rig to Marconi (Bermuda). It was generally accepted that the Marconi rig was best in light to moderate winds, but many still favoured a gaff rig for a breeze. Some sailors took both rigs to regattas and swapped them about, depending on their own forecasts of the weather. In trial races for the Douglas and Emerson cups, Toronto clubs allowed time out to change rigs.

The Marconi spar at this time took many shapes. Some had a fair curve from gooseneck to peak; others curved like a coachman's whip; a few were straight. All were heavy, 30 lb. or more. Sail track was heavy too, not being designed for small boats. The smallest procurable was the standard ⅝ in. of today. Some used brass strips, set on wooden battens. Others used aluminum, which had to be cut from sheets. Slides had to be adjusted to suit tracks. This was one of our biggest problems with the early Marconi masts. Screw heads in the track would work out and prevent slides from moving. Screw drivers and files were always a part of our sailing kit.

The Marconi masts were heavy in our cat-rigged dinghies because all the area was in one sail, which gave hoists from gooseneck to peak of up to 23 ft. 6 in. Goosenecks were from 6 to 12 in. above deck. Booms were about 12 ft. and mainsails varied as to hoist length and aspect ratio. (I doubt if we knew then what aspect ratio meant.) The masts were placed about 24 in. aft of the stem, and the width of the bow at this position was about 36 in. The crew had to have snake hips to get past the rigging and spar—and the skipper had to do a balancing act in the stern while the crew pushed away from the dock. Coming in was even worse, especially if the boat was wet and slippery, with a well varnished, crowned foredeck to deal with and long wet pants dragging under your heels. We didn't wear Bermuda shorts then except for soccer.

The dinghies up until 1932 were influenced by the *Gloriette* shape (the wave-form theory), so the bows kept getting finer and the spars not any lighter. You had to be a close relative of Hercules to step the spar alone on a dock and you needed a lot of foot room. After launching, someone had to hold the mast or the dinghy easily blew over at the dock.

In 1930 an incident took place which had far-reaching effects on dinghies. The Canada's Cup Races were on off Port Charlotte (Rochester Y.C.'s 8-meter *Thisbe* against Royal Canadian Y.C.'s *Quest*) and the famous C. D. Mallory was there judging. One afternoon, when the 8-meters finished early, Mr. Mallory proposed a dinghy race. A stiff northeasterly breeze had stirred Lake Ontario into a sizable sea, so the dinghy race was run between two piers jutting out into the lake—an area of about half a mile by 150 yards. The dinghies were provided by the Rochester Yacht Club—cat-rigged Marconis of *Gloriette*'s breed, but with even finer bows.

Because the contestants were internationally known yachtsmen —C. D. Mallory; T. C. Ratsey from Cowes; Herbert Stone, editor of *Yachting;* and Peck Farley, Rochester R-boat sailor—the race created great interest and drew a large crowd. The race itself was keen, tough, and terrifying. The word "terrifying" is used advertently, as there was a beat to the mouth of the piers and a run back in the most cork-screwingest of seas, caused by rebounding between the north and south piers. Peck Farley won, C. D. Mallory came in second, and Herb Stone and Chris Ratsey sailed a dead heat for third. All four have gone now to that special Valhalla which surely must be reserved for dedicated sailors such as they.

One of the results of this race was that Mr. Mallory asked if he could buy one of my boats for his son. This was sent to him from Toronto. It arrived at Martha's Vineyard just as he was leaving for Newport to sail as a guest on *Enterprise* during her practice run before the America's Cup. Mallory loaded the crated dinghy on board his boat *Bonnie Dundee* and took her along to Newport. There he left her with Starling Burgess, designer of *Enterprise,* who was interested in the dinghy.

This was the America's Cup Race in which *Enterprise,* sailed by Harold S. Vanderbilt, defeated *Shamrock V,* sailed by Captain Ned Heard, in four straight races. One morning during the series there was a fog off Brenton Reef and the big race was postponed. In Newport Harbor it was clear, and Mr. Mallory sailed the dinghy through the fleet, causing much interest as she could go very fast in the light conditions. He sailed her over to the English camp of Charlie Nicholson. Here Chris Ratsey, Heckstall Smith, and others who had sailed International 14-footers designed by Morgan Giles and Uffa Fox got into a rousing debate over the relative merits of the two types of dinghies.

After the series Mr. Mallory wrote me about these discussions and asked what I knew about the International 14-footers. Strange as it seems, I knew nothing. We did not get the English yachting publications then as we do now, with articles by writers such as Ian Proctor, John Westell, Uffa Fox, and the like. I suggested that there was one certain way of discovering which type was best, and that was to race them. Mr. Mallory was very keen on this and before Heckstall Smith left New York he suggested writing Sir John Field Beale of Y.R.A. to arrange a match. C.D. got right on to it and was all for races in Florida during the following winter. We felt that would not be the right time. However, our commodore, George H. Gooderham, always interested in promoting yachting, kept in close correspondence with Mr. Mallory to work out a time suitable to us all.

Meanwhile interest was building up from another direction. In the early thirties John Barnes, a keen sailor from Henderson Harbor, New York, decided to start building Ackroyd-type 14-footers at Skaneateles Boat Works. Barnes got in touch with Herb Stone of

Yachting and through him met C. D. Mallory and learned of the proposed races between English and Canadian fourteens. Commodore T. K. Wade, R.C.Y.C., was in New York, joined the discussions, and brought us back the latest reports. Barnes wrote an article for *Yachting* on the speed of the Canadian-type dinghy and this was replied to by Mr. G. Prout of England. I also got into the argument with an article in *Yachting*. All of which ended up with definite plans for an international competition. Mr. Paul Hammand and Commodore Henry Morgan of the Seawanhaka Corinthian Yacht Club in conjunction with Sir John Beale of the Royal Norfolk and Suffolk Yacht Club arranged a match to take place at Seawanhaka in September, 1933.

In 1932 I had rerigged my cat to a sloop and won three races in a row. I was protested on the grounds that dinghies had always been cat-rigged. I argued that as long as my sail area was within the contemporary limit of 140 sq. ft. I could use it any way I wished. The protests were disallowed. By this time I was convinced that the sloop was the fastest rig; and in the winter of 1932, when Kingston built three dinghies to my design, I urged that they be sloop-rigged. The Lake Sailing Skiff Association had a regatta at Kingston in the summer of 1933; and Rochester, planning new boats to meet the English, sent Mr. C. D. Mower of New York, famous yacht designer, to Kingston with John Barnes to see our boats. We had much discussion as to cats versus sloops. Rochester finally had three dinghies built, more or less like the Canadian types, to conform to L.S.S.A. rules, with half-decks, but sloop-rigged.

The races were finally scheduled for Saturday, September 16, 1933, at the Seawanhaka Corinthian Yacht Club. On our arrival we were greeted with the amazing sight of an International 14-footer *lying at mooring*. Our dinghies, as I have already said, were mast-heavy and could not possibly stand at mooring. The International's spar was small in section, with three sets of spreaders, a parrot perch, a jumper, and (this was the age of ocean racing and baggy wrinkle) her three side-spreader ends were wrapped with tape to the size of golf balls. This was only the beginning of the many innovations at which we marveled. She was smooth-skinned, entirely open, with built-in buoyancy tanks. Her heavy bronze centerboard weighed about 150 lb. and was raised and lowered on a hoist winch. She was sloop-rigged and had 125 sq. ft. of measured sail area with lapping jib and carried a large spinnaker. Our boats were clinker-built cats (except mine, which could be rigged cat or sloop), carrying 140 sq. ft. of sail. They were half-decked, with finer bows, heavy spars, and with centerboards varying from 50 lb. of steel, through aluminum, to wooden boards held down with shock cord.

So the races got under way. The British and Long Island teams sailed International 14-footers. The Canadians were sailing cat-rigged boats and my cat-or-sloop. And Rochester sailed boats similar to ours, one cat-rigged, the other two sloops, with the jib on a boom attached to the mast which could be swung aft off the wind. The British team included Colonel and Mrs. H. C. S. Richardson, Alan Colman, Peter Scott, David O. Beale, and Oscar Browning; the Long Island team: Henry Anderson, Charles F. Havemeyer, Porter Buck, and Roderick Stephens; the Rochester team: William Calkins, Harold Christy and Phil Farnham; the Canadian team: Atwell Fleming, Reginald Dixon, and Charlie Bourke.

We started out on a windy morning with the New York papers headlining a hurricane expected hourly. And I must say we went out with misgivings—we were not hardened to hurricanes then. I had never seen one, let alone sailed in one, and we had expected light weather, which is supposed to prevail on Long Island early in September. It was blowing 20 knots as we started, all reefed. I sailed my dinghy as a sloop with jib lowered and a very high narrow sail which could not be reefed and was badly balanced. The first leg was a short beat and our two cats got round first, then started rolling "Down to Rio" style. I rounded closest to Alan Colman and Peter Scott. They set spinnakers and started planing. Those British dinghies simply flew away from our cat-rigged boats in a cloud of spray! The hurricane moved out to sea but left us lots of wind for the week. We never left dock without reefs. We had to do our reefing at the dock, but the Internationals were able to reef while sailing.

We had a week of great racing, won by the British team, and all were convinced that the sloop, properly rigged, was the only thing for 14-footers. At a large meeting and farewell dinner, Mr. Van Merl Smith presiding, our views were thoroughly aired and discussed. Olin and Rod Stephens, Uffa Fox, C. D. Mallory, and many other prominent yachtsmen were present. Some of us were against the use of spinnakers on small boats, feeling that they would add to our problems running before the wind. Next morning Mr. Clinton Crane came out to Seawanhaka to talk to us about spinnakers. He had heard we were against them and felt we were wrong. His theory was that modern yacht racing depended on the spinnaker work of the crew. (How true this is today!) Mr. Crane helped us change our minds.

Mr. Norman Gooderham, R.C.Y.C., who was at the Races as one of our staunch supporters along with Jerry Snyder and G. E. Macrae, suggested buying one of the English Internationals to take home. His kind offer was turned down, however, as we could not have sailed the boat then in L.S.S.A. races. Our rules called for Scantlings, and the Internationals were built to a weight rule. On our return home we immediately had a meeting at the National Yacht Club, Toronto, to tell the many dinghy sailors what we had seen and learned and our views on sloop rigs, spinnakers, and the other new ideas of the International 14's.

Next the Royal Canadian Yacht Club invited England to send out an International 14-footer team. In 1934 one came from the Royal Norfolk and Suffolk Yacht Club, Lowestoft. This team was captained by Stewart Morris, who with Roger DeQuincey sailed the famous *R.I.P.* Peter Scott and Charlie Curry were in *East Light.* John Winter and Tom Scott had *Lightning* and David Beale and Oscar Browning sailed *Canute.* Rochester sent a team of cat-rigged dinghies. R.C.Y.C. had two new clinker-built, sloop-rigged dinghies, designed to L.S.S.A. rules. These were *Judy* and *Riptide.* Our others were a 1928 catboat, sloop-rigged, and Harvey Bongard's new *Bonnie,* that could be rigged sloop or cat. This *Bonnie* was interesting, as she was, I think, the best cat ever built. She had a very light spar and as a cat could plane. However, she hardly ever raced as such, instead took on the sloop rig and was the last of the cats for a long time to sail with the sloops.

The British won this match impressively—also some races open to all classes—and helped to convince us all that the sloop was the best rig. Afterward George Ford purchased *R.I.P.* and she was the start of a 14-ft. One Design fleet at the Rochester Yacht Club. Rochester in 1936 sent a team to race in England and to sail in the P.O.W. Week being held at Hunter's Quay on the Clyde. This is discussed in Uffa Fox's book *Sail and Power.* Stewart Morris won the 1936 P.O.W. with *Alarm.* The design of this boat was very fast and was brought to the States to become the model for a large fleet of U.S. One Designs which spread over the country and out to California. Sandy Douglas built a great number of them. In Canada, the Royal St. Lawrence Yacht Club also adopted this type.

The Royal Canadian Yacht Club sent a team of four dinghies to Lowestoft, England, in August 1936. These Canadian 14-footers were smooth-skinned, built to L.S.S.A. rules (scantling). The British boats were built to Y.R.A. rules and weighed around 240 lb. Some used light wooden boards. The Canadian boats were lighter ashore. Two weighed under 220 lb. One weighed 250 lb. All carried 50-lb. weighted boards. The Canadian crews averaged heavier by about 30 lb. per boat, so displacement was actually very close. The Canadians scored in this match, which is also well described in Uffa's book. Following the match were good meetings, at which many rules and specifications were discussed, changed, and adapted —each side giving and taking ideas from the other. In 1938 a British team again visited the Royal Canadian Y.C., Toronto. Canadians and Britishers were now sailing to the same International 14-footer rules. Canada won this match. In open-to-all races, off the Exhibition Grounds at Toronto, Peter Scott, Charlie Curry, and Colin Chinchester-Smith gave a great demonstration of the International 14-footer's ability in hard weather and big seas. Canada intended going to England in 1940, but the war intervened.

After the war the molding of boats became popular through the development of new techniques. In England, Fairey Marine were hot-molding hulls to Uffa Fox's newest designs. In the U.S. 14-footers were being molded to *Alarm*'s shape. In Canada, however, we had no manufacturing source, as our production was small, and this technique is costly unless produced in quantity. The National Research Council at Ottawa came to our assistance in 1946 and gave its hot-molding facilities to some keen Ottawa sailors. Through the interest of Professor Parkin, head of the Research Council, and the ability of Mr. Jack Noonan, my 1946 design was molded there, and "Conneda" was built for me. This 14 set a fashion and was admired by all who saw her on either side of the border. Molded boats didn't leak and having no bibs were easy to clean. Hence Paul McLaughlin's remark about *Conneda*: "You don't take a sponge aboard, just a duster." Interest in molded boats developed in Canada, and in 1951 the Industrial Shipping Co., Nova Scotia, molded their first lot of International 14-ft. skins. These were finished by builders or by do-it-yourself methods. Hamish Davidson of Vancouver is also doing this hot molding; and Continental Yacht Sails, Toronto, are now cold-molding 14-ft. dinghies.

In 1949 a British team visited the Canadian Dinghy Association Championships at the Royal St. Lawrence Yacht Club, Montreal. Here, too, we had the pleasure of racing with Dick Fenton, Bill Lapworth, and Peter Serrell from Los Angeles and Shorty Trimingham from Bermuda. This was truly international racing. The British won the series as Charlie Curry put on a particularly good show in a new Uffa Fox design, the "Fairey Mark I" molded by Fairey Marine —a beautiful, powerful dinghy, at its best close-reaching. Curry won the Viscount Alexander Cup at Montreal, then went to Essex to win the Connecticut Cup, and from there to Bermuda where he captured the Princess Elizabeth Cup.

So over the years the process of development has progressed— from the international races and from the meetings, arguments, and discussions that followed the races—until a splendid type of small boat has been evolved to give the greatest of pleasure to the keenest of sailors. In Canada we have been lucky to have two enthusiastic dinghy sailors who have been very generous in sponsoring new boats to keep us up to date. I am referring to Mr. R. C. Stevenson of the Royal St. Lawrence Yacht Club and Mr. H. J. Bongard, R.C.Y.C. —both past presidents of the C.D.A.—who have given much of their time and funds to the development of sailing. In both England and North America, as well as in Bermuda, the International 14-ft. Dinghy has produced exciting competition and developed keen sailors. This was pointed up in dramatic fashion by the results of the Mallory Cup, held in September 1957 at Marblehead. This cup, dedicated to the memory of C. D. Mallory, who did so much for all types of sailing, is raced for annually and is emblematic of the North American Men's Sailing Championship. Contestants are selected after trials in their own localities and through elimination series in all areas of North America. International 14-ft. Dinghy sailors were elated over the number of them (six of the eight finalists) who won the right to skip boats in the 1957 series, over the showing they made during the series, and over the fact that a well-known 14-ft. dinghy sailor, George O'Day, captured the cup itself. I have sailed or crewed on most types of modern boats, even been aboard the famous old "Bluenose"—but of them all, for sheer thrill, give me a 14-footer running with spinnaker in a fresh breeze and long sea.

Now that I, a senior in this art of sailing, have given you the history of the evolvement of the International 14-ft. Dinghy in North America, I shall leave it to the younger generation to give you in the chapters following their ideas on the skills of sailing today.

PART I

The Elements of Racing

Preface

Sailboat racing is one of the most complex of sports. Its variations attract individuals for countless different reasons. Athletic prowess is often of value; but even in dinghy racing, where this might be considered the prime necessity, men over fifty are regular winners. Engineering knowledge is essential to the production of an ideally effective and light rig, but youngsters with nothing more than sailing experience in their backgrounds often take the prizes. The fastest boat with the best sails may be beaten by the proper application of a tactical maneuver at the starting line, and the daredevil expert may capsize after taking one risk too many.

Many of these facets remain almost unexplored by the majority of sailors, each limiting himself to the sphere of his initial interest. However, top-flight racing ability nowadays demands a thorough knowledge of all the elements of sailing and racing. The chapters included in Part I present a complete coverage of the essentials which are prerequisite to racing technique. The presentation is designed to demonstrate the significance of the scientific principles which underlie the development of speed under sail, the behavior of the wind and current, and the utilization of the regulations governing racing.

Fast boats win most races, and it is the hours spent ashore in development and preparation for racing which are often the most significant. The engineer sailor finds much to interest him in sailboat racing, but it is hoped that an understanding of basic principles will help all sailors toward an interest in and the production of a faster boat. To reassure those who recognize sailboat racing as more than sail making and sandpapering and race winning as more than boat speed, the chapters presenting the principles of wind and current demonstrate the significance of strategic planning and execution. For the aggressive competitors out to beat the other boat at all costs, the chapters on the racing rules and race management present the tactical principles involved in close maneuvering. For those whose main interest is sailing technique, the chapters on crewing and

3

rescue serve to introduce the major portion of the book concerning the technique of small boat racing.

The essential elements of this sport are:

a) *the production of a fast boat,*

b) *the application of strategic principles concerning wind and tide to sail the optimal course,*

c) *the application of principles of technique to produce the maximum boat speed under all conditions, and*

d) *the application of tactical principles to prevent harmful interference from other boats and to interfere with other boats to one's advantage.*

There is constant variation in the relative significance of the various elements concerned, so that a major requirement of racing skill is the ability to distinguish the significant from the insignificant. In light air the acquisition of increased boat speed, through the strategic discovery of increased wind strength, is the prime consideration; in moderate air the skipper must be chiefly concerned with tactical interference; and in heavy air the ability of the skipper to handle the boat in the presence of overwhelming thrust usually becomes the determinant of winning. All elements and all techniques are operative to some extent in every race, but the ability to choose the significant action between alternative requirements imposed by conflicting elements distinguishes the great helmsman. Recognition of relative significance comes only through experience, but an attempt is made herein to indicate the probable significance of both elements and technique in the particular conditions discussed in each chapter.

A major element of success in small boat racing is the constant effort to evaluate one's own boat and one's own abilities in the light of competitive action. Unfortunately, it is difficult to progress significantly beyond the level of available competition. Conversely top competition breeds great sailors and should be sought continually. Learn to recognize the superiorities and defects of your boat and your techniques (as evident against the best available competition)—capitalize on the superiorities and work to overcome the defects. If your boat points high, start to windward and tack early for the mark, but strive harder to improve your ability to drive the boat further off the wind; don't idly capitalize on your good fortune. If you are a great downwind sailor, try to find a great upwind boat. If your boat and abilities don't develop, someone else's will—and the level of competition is improving every day.

1. Wind

By ARTHUR W. BESSE, JR.,
Boston

The wind is the flowing of air masses. Sometimes the flow is smooth and steady, at other times the flow is turbulent and full of eddies. The flow may be the rushing tearing torrent of the gale, or it may be the gentle drift of a light breeze. Or stagnant pools of air may form, leaving the sailor becalmed on a glassy sea.

From long experience a helmsman may learn the winds in a particular harbor and be able to predict the shifts with reasonable success without ever understanding why these shifts occur. This same skipper is lost in an unfamiliar harbor. However, the helmsman who understands the causes of wind changes can race successfully in strange harbors and can apply observations made in one harbor to another. The ability to sail well in strange harbors has become increasingly important as more and more helmsmen have moved into the various light, high-performance classes which are easily trailed to a great many away-from-home races.

PREVAILING WINDS, WEATHER SYSTEMS, AND LOCAL BREEZES

The wind at any particular point may be regarded as the result of the superposition of a prevailing wind, a weather-system wind, and a local breeze. In norther latitudes, including most of the United States, the prevailing wind is west or southwest. (Southern Florida, however, is on the edge of the trade-wind belt and has a prevailing easterly wind.) If it were not for the weather systems that sweep across the country and the various local breezes, all our races would be sailed in a southwester.

The weather systems consist of low-pressure areas around which the wind rotates counterclockwise (in the northern hemisphere) and high-pressure systems around which the wind rotates clockwise. The systems in general drift eastward with the prevailing westerly wind. It will be assumed that the reader is familiar with these weather systems and keeps himself posted of their movement during the sailing season.

The wind direction in a weather system is readily predictable by the direction of rotation. However, it must be remembered that the pressure system is drifting in from the west with the prevailing wind. The actual wind is a combination of the prevailing wind and the rotating wind. For example, the easterly flow of air around the northern side of a weak low tends to cancel out the prevailing westerly and may result in a flat calm. The westerly flow of air around the southern side of the same low reinforces the prevailing wind. The greater the variation in pressure, of course, the greater the force in the weather-system winds.

In addition to the prevailing wind and winds due to pressure systems, there are local breezes associated with shore configurations. In some areas these local winds are strong enough to overcome the prevailing wind. In other areas these local breezes are important only when the other winds are extremely weak or are canceled out. High- and low-pressure systems cover large areas (100- to 500-mi. diameters) and require a day or more to pass. These pressure areas, therefore, have an essentially steady influence over the small area and time involved in small boat racing. An exception is the arrival of a front, especially a cold front, during a race.

The race is to the next mark, and the small boat skipper need seldom consider weather changes more than a few miles or an hour away. More frequently his interest in weather is confined to wondering whether there is a favorable slant or a dead spot 100 yd. nearer the beach. Or, on a reach, he may wonder whether he should fall off momentarily to keep the spinnaker drawing during a momentary header, or whether the wind is permanently shifting and the spinnaker should be doused and every effort made to work out to windward before the wind shifts still further.

SEA BREEZE

Local variations in the wind are affected by temperature differences between land, sea, and air. Local winds are also influenced by the difference in resistance to air flow over land and over water. Deep water remains cool throughout the summer; off the coast of Maine the water remains too cold for comfortable swimming all summer. The land, on the other hand, on a sunny summer after-noon is hot, beaches and pavements frequently too hot for walking with bare feet. The hot surface of the land heats the air, the hot air rises, and the cool air over the water flows in to replace it. Thus is the sea breeze created. The surface of the land reaches its highest temperature in the middle of the afternoon, and it is not until well into the afternoon that some sea breezes appear. Sea breezes are not independent of other air movements. In Buzzard's Bay, on the south-west side of Cape Cod, the prevailing wind (s.w. in the area) rein-forces the sea breeze and produces the fresh southwesterly winds for which the bay is famous. A hundred miles farther north in Massachusetts Bay, the coast has an easterly exposure. Here the prevailing southwest wind works against the easterly sea breeze, and the sea breeze is generally moderate. On many a summer day this section of the coast has a cool sea breeze while five miles inland the wind is southwest and the temperature 10 to 15 degrees F. higher. My experience has been that *when becalmed on an early afternoon, you can count on a breeze before long if it is sunny, but if it is overcast the air may well remain stagnant the remainder of the day.* Sea breezes do not always blow from the same direction. The island of Martha's Vineyard is located off the south side of Cape Cod. The Cape frequently creates a southerly sea breeze that affects the entire island of Martha's Vineyard. Reinforced by the prevailing southwesterly wind, a fresh southwester results. How-ever, on some days, when a pressure system discourages the south-wester, the Cape fails to create its own sea breeze. On these days the island creates its own sea breeze, which blows from the south-west on the southwest end of the island, but from the northeast on the northeast end of the island.

VERTICALLY STABLE AIR

If the lower air layers are colder and hence heavier than the upper air layers, the atmosphere is said to be vertically stable. Under these conditions the light upper air will float above the heavier lower air without significant mixing. Even if the lower and upper air layers are at the same temperature, the atmosphere remains vertically stable. However, if the surface air is much warmer than the overlying air, it will rise through the cooler upper air, in columns, with the cooler air sinking down between the columns. The columns may rise far enough to cause condensation and cumulus clouds, or even thunderheads. Under these conditions the atmosphere is said to be vertically unstable.

There is virtually no resistance to the flow of the upper layers of air, and they are in constant motion. The lower layers of air, however, are not infrequently stagnant, the sea a glassy calm. The friction between the air and land and between air and sea slows or stops the movement of the lower layers of air. At first thought, it would appear that the wind could blow across the surface of the water with little loss of energy. But if we consider the energy the wind transfers to the creation of waves, it becomes obvious that the surface of the sea must offer considerable resistance. The sailing yacht utilizes the movement of the bottom 50 ft. of an atmosphere many miles deep. This bottom 50 ft. of air owes its movement to being dragged along by the constantly moving upper air layers. The ability of the upper air layers to drag along the lower layers varies widely.

Warm air is lighter than cold air; and when the two meet, the warm air slides up and over the cold air. If the temperature difference is great, the warm air slides over the top of the cold air smoothly, with very little turbulence or mixing, and exerts but little drag on the cold air. This condition, when the temperature increases with altitude, is known as temperature inversion. The cold lower air is apt to hang heavy and stagnant over the sea or land. This condition is common during winter storms, when warm air sweeps up from the tropics and overrides cold. On the surface the condition may be marked by the phenomena of calm in spite of a rapidly falling barometer and rain in spite of freezing temperatures. Cold air is particularly apt to remain stagnant under a flow of warm air if high land blocks its movement. The well-known Los Angeles smogs are due, in part, to stagnant cold air trapped by the prevailing westerlies between the coast and the mountains. The cold air is too heavy to flow up and over the mountains.

The phenomenon of cold stagnant air also occurs on a much smaller scale. Cold water cools the air directly over it. This cool air may lie stagnant over the water and a warm breeze may slide right over the top of it. There may be a breeze blowing ashore when you throw the sails into the back of the car, but none when you arrive at the club float. The cool air may remain stagnant all day; or, more likely, the warm air will slowly warm the upper layers of the cool air, penetrating downward and reaching the surface during the middle of the afternoon.

In a stable atmosphere, winds are apt to be light and steady or there may be no wind at all. This latter sad state of affairs is fairly common over both Long Island Sound and Massachusetts Bay. High hills render it particularly difficult for cool heavy stagnant air to escape. The prevailing southwesterly, even reinforced by the sea breeze, may blow for many hours above the cool stagnant air of the Sound before the sun heats the surface sufficiently to permit mixing of the layers and wind on the surface. If the weather is overcast or raining, the whole atmosphere is often very stable and the calm may be of long duration.

An onshore breeze that has blown over many miles of cool water is generally composed of cool stable air. For this reason, *an onshore breeze is generally steady in strength and direction, until it flows over land where the heated surface air, rising, creates turbulence.*

VERTICALLY UNSTABLE AIR

An unstable atmosphere, with air aloft cooler than that below, is conducive to fresh, puffy, and shifting surface winds. Although surface winds are generally lower in velocity, due to surface friction, than the winds aloft, the updrafts and downdrafts in an unstable atmosphere mix the surface and the upper air currents, accelerating the surface wind. Downdrafts of the fast-moving upper air cause puffs. The downdrafts spread outward as they hit the surface, causing the wind to blow outward from the center of the puff. Therefore it is common to be headed on entering a puff and let up on leaving it. If the upper wind is blowing from a somewhat different direction than the surface wind, the puffs will also come from a different direction.

On a summer's afternoon the sun heats the surface of the land until it is hotter than the air. The hot land heats the surface air, which rises in pockets and is replaced by the cooler upper air. Since the upper air is generally moving swiftly, it appears as sharp puffs when it reaches the surface. This thermal turbulence over hot land mixes upper and lower air and causes the surface winds to be stronger and puffier than normal. The effect may extend a short distance over the water in the lee of the land. An exception, of course, is when the land is high enough to have a blanketing effect. I have raced in Vineyard Haven Harbor for many years. Here, on the northeast side of Martha's Vineyard, the typical summer southwester is fresher, sometimes much fresher, than on the south shore of the island. The temperature is also noticeably higher. The wind moderates in the late afternoon as the sun drops. More striking, within about ten minutes after the arrival of a cloud bank, the wind moderates and becomes steadier, less puffy. Once, cruising off Maine, we had a graphic demonstration of the effect of land. During the course of the day we passed from under the lee of the land into open water and back again three times. Each time it was warm, sunny, with a fresh southwesterly breeze in the lee of the land; each time it was cool, foggy, and with only a moderate breeze in open water.

The ability of hot land to create thermal turbulence and mix slow-moving lower air with fast-moving upper air is particularly marked when the land is very hot and the air cold. The International 14 dinghies have twice raced at Manchester, Massachusetts, on bright sunny spring days with a cool northwester blowing offshore. Blocked from the northwester one minute by a column of hot rising air off the land, the fleet might be struck the next minute with the full force of the cold air sweeping down to replace the hot. Decalmed one minute, on a wild plane the next, or, for some, in the drink! Turbulent conditions such as these in the lower atmosphere cause sudden variations not only in wind velocity but also in wind direction. Under such conditions the wise skipper will take advantage of each momentary shift and not try to follow any preconceived plan. The favored shore the first time around may be the disfavored shore the next.

Nighttime cooling, on a clear night, chills the surface air and tends to produce stability, stagnation, and calm. The sun's heat during the day on the land creates instability and tends to

    a) bring upper level winds down to surface level, and

    b) create a sea breeze.

It is sometimes difficult to predict which effect will predominate. The larger and colder the body of water, the more a sea breeze is favored. The stronger the upper level winds are, the more apt they are to penetrate to the surface.

The ability of the sun's heat to create thermal air currents in the form either of thermal columns with local surface drafts or of a true sea breeze is dependent upon the surface of the land along the shore. Buildings, streets, cultivated fields, and similar homogeneous surfaces tend to reflect heat and increase thermal air currents; while forests, hills, swamps, and other heterogeneous surfaces tend to absorb heat and dampen thermal air currents.

FRICTION AND REFRACTION

Land also has a very local effect on wind direction. Land offers more frictional resistance to air flow than does water. As a result, the upper air currents drag the surface air more slowly over land than over water. When the surface layers leave the land and pass out over water they accelerate, leaving an area of slightly reduced pressure behind. *If the shore line runs diagonally to the wind direction, this region of reduced pressure tends to draw the wind directly off the beach* (see *Fig. 1*). However, this applies only to relatively low-lying shore lines. Close under a high bluff, the land blankets or blocks any offshore breeze, and any breeze there is will tend to be parallel to the shore. The shift in wind direction under the lee of the land appears to extend for a variable distance of from 100 yd. to a quarter mile, generally extending farther under a large land mass than under a small. Edgartown's outer harbor (Martha's Vineyard Island again) is separated on the east from Cape Poge Pond by a narrow strip of sand. Beating out in a northesterly breeze, there frequently exists a favorable easterly shift under this shore. The shift is so local, however, that to remain in it the skipper must short tack, perhaps as often as every ten boat lengths. With a large fleet this involves some extremely close maneuvering.

Hills and valleys have varying effects upon shore-line winds, depending upon their vertical stability. In vertically stable air the winds tend to follow surface contours, rolling vertically down hill surfaces and following valleys. Cold rapidly moving upper air may roll down a valley and rush out with increased force at the mouth of a stream or along an avenue of a city. In Toronto Bay they give the name of the street in question to each of the many alterations in strength and direction produced along the city shores. In vertically unstable air thermal columns may follow hill contours, be aided in their rising by the rising warm land, and eventually burst off the hill crest in giant "bubbles." *Thus, in vertically stable air maximum wind strength may be present in the coves along a hilly shore, while in vertically unstable air the maximum breeze will be picked up at the end of the points.*

THREE TYPES OF WIND SHIFTS

When a helmsman encounters a wind shift, or sees a competitor encounter one, he must distinguish between three possible causes:
  a) *a general wind shift that will soon spread over the entire area, is permanent, and is due to the over-all weather pattern;*
  b) *a shift due to local topography, which is permanent but limited to a restricted area; or*
  c) *a local temporary shift due to vertical instability or turbulence.*

If you are headed by a temporary shift due to turbulence, an immediate tack is required to take advantage of the shift while it lasts. However, if you are headed by sailing into an area with a more favorable slant (for the other tack), due to shore-line configuration, it is wise to sail well into the new slant before tacking. Otherwise you will be tacking right back out of the favorable slant. Similarly, if some of your competitors receive a temporary favorable slant in a vertically unstable northwesterly, it is fruitless to waste time chasing it. On the other hand, if a competitor finds a favorable slant peculiar to a particular section of the harbor, it is well to follow his example. In case of a general wind shift, usually affecting all competitors, it is wise to consider the possible effect of a further shift and to adjust your course to receive the maximum subsequent advantage.

PLANNING THE RACE

All race planning starts with a knowledge of the local prevailing wind, the weather forecast, and the weather map showing "highs," "lows," and "fronts." From this information, the amount of sunshine, and the land formation, an estimate of atmospheric stability or nonstability can be made. From all these, as well as a knowledge of the temperature of the land and water, the possibility of a sea breeze developing later in the day can be predicted. From an examination of the chart, favorable slants due to topography often can be predicted. The weather map will indicate the major wind shifts which can be expected. From the height of the land, the degree of the sun's heat, and temperature of the water, an estimate can be made of whether the strongest surface wind will be close to the land, with its thermal currents, or far from its blanketing effect, whether the sea breeze or the prevailing wind aloft will predominate on the surface. By comparing the experiences of one race with other races and analyzing the similarities and differences, a better understanding of the wind can be gained.

AN EXAMPLE: GLOUCESTER HARBOR

All of these principles can, on certain days, be observed in action in Gloucester Harbor, located to the northeast of Boston, Massachusetts. Figure 1 shows an east-west cross section of the harbor and the

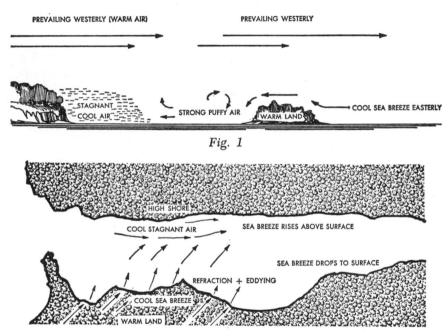

Fig. 1

Fig. 2

surrounding land and sea. The warm prevailing southwester is shown blowing over the land. Counter to this warm wind and blowing in under it is the cool sea breeze. To seaward of Eastern Point the easterly is moderate at mast level, fresh higher up. The surface wind is heated by the warmth of the land while passing over Eastern Point and, rising, is replaced, in part, by the fresher upper breeze. The lowest layer of air is most thoroughly cooled by the water and is too heavy to rise over the high land to the west of the harbor. Along the west side of the harbor is a stagnant pool of cool air. It is not uncommon to reach across the harbor on a fast plane in the vertically unstable air of the sea breeze to the east, only to be suddenly becalmed just before reaching the finish line in the vertically stable air

to the west—with the boats behind coming up like express trains!
Figure 2 is a plan of the harbor showing the shift more perpendicular
to the shore in the lee of the land. The diagram also shows how the
surface wind, being unable to climb over the high land on the west
shore, blows, at much reduced velocity, parallel to the shore.

An understanding of the wind is fascinating in its own right. More
than this, without such an understanding much of yacht racing is
luck; with such an understanding it becomes a game of calculated
strategy. Without an understanding, the winds in each harbor and
from each direction must be learned from experience; with an understanding every observation in any harbor helps predict the variations of the wind in the next harbor.

2. Tide and Current

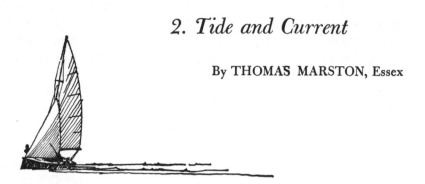

By THOMAS MARSTON, Essex

Few of us can travel in advance to study conditions in an area where a regatta will subsequently be held. In most cases our boats are hurriedly rigged a few moments before the race, amid hasty greetings to friends and with only half an eye cast to the weather. Perhaps somebody mumbles something about the direction of the current in rather vague terms, or hints that it will change during a subsequent race. You can bet the local boys know (or they should!).

PREPARATION

A few preparations are essential prior to racing in areas subject to current conditions. First to be consulted (if available) are the current charts and tide tables obtainable at agencys for U.S. government coastal charts. The current charts are available in small scale for a limited number of areas and are of value to show general current trends at various periods of flood and ebb only. The tide tables give times of maximum flood and ebb and indicate strengths of current—the essential considerations. Times of high and low water are only significant to predict the intervening times of maximum flow.

Of greater assistance in racing particularly in confined areas are the regular U.S. government charts. (The smallest-scale charts are of course preferable.) The cost is slight and as far as small boat racing is concerned the charts will remain good for a considerable time. Examine the variations in depths and widths of the body of water in the racing area and keep in mind as you study the chart that the flow of water is retarded by any ground whatsoever, whether it be the bottom or the banks. A short time spent looking over the charted channels and depths before you leave for a regatta will be well re-paid. Instead of having to watch the local boys for a few races until you "catch on," you will be able to start out on an almost equal foot-ing. Look to the depths for the maximum current but at the same time find out where you can't go. I've seen an entire fleet (myself included) sail onto a sandbar covered with 9 in. of water. If anyone had consulted a chart beforehand it wasn't apparent, and what a dif-ference it would have made had but one skipper done so!

Remember when evaluating local geography that the cross-sec-tional area (width × depth) of a given location is inversely propor-tional to the rate of current flow. Current is thus stronger wherever the *total* body of water becomes narrower or shallower. Current will be particularly strong off a point projecting perpendicularly into the current stream and will be reduced and may even eddy in reverse in widened areas such as coves adjacent to points. However, *the greatest current through any given cross-sectional location will be in the position of greatest cross-sectional area.* The friction of the bottom retards the flow in shallow and/or narrow areas, so that if alternate routes are available the water will seek the outlet of least resistance, *i.e.,* the location of the least surrounding land surface per unit cross-sectional area. In general, this means that the current will be maximal in the deepest channels, and least over the shoals and along the banks, yet will be increased in any area where the total water body shoals or narrows.

In general, current will flow parallel to the long axis of a water body, changing direction with major alterations in the course of the shore line. In a narrow-current stream maximum flow will be deviated to the outer side of a bend in its general course where the shore and bottom will be scoured out. Unless the inner bank has a particularly protruding point which narrows the total width of the stream, the current will be least along this shore. Where additional current streams from rivers or where bays enter the major stream, the general flow will be deviated for a variable distance, depending upon the rate and volume of the additional streams. Thus, off the mouth of a subsidiary stream the current will be deviated at an angle to the course of the major river determined by the relative strength of the two streams.

The strength of the current on the surface—the water in which we race—is often significantly modified by the wind. A strong wind opposing the current will reduce its strength considerably, while a strong wind will produce a current when it blows down the long axis of a narrow body of water. A rapid increase in reverse flow will appear immediately after the cessation of a strong wind, to compensate for its temporary effect upon water distribution. Combinations of wind and current will also modify the surface waves, decreasing the wave development when both are acting in the same direction and increasing their development when they are in opposition. With wind and current acting in the same direction, the surface ruffling produced by the current may be dampened by increased wind strength, so that in light air the patches of smooth water may harbor the most wind!

The last and best source of prerace information you have should be the member of the race committee officiating at the skippers' meeting before the start. Here is a golden opportunity. Instead of delaying your departure to the meeting for some last-minute touches in tune-up, leave early and obtain the committee man's opinions on the rate and significance of current flow, the exact time of tidal change, and the characteristics of local current behavior. Ask about anything, even the choice of course. You may get laughed at—or you may get the "inside story." These men are not infallible, but you should at least evaluate their information fully.

Look over the actual sailing area from the shore and then from the boat in relation to probable current flow. Pick up the landmarks and buoys noted on the chart, and picture the suspected current in its actual setting so that it can be remembered in the heat of battle. Note the effect of the current on buoys and boats in various locations, and correlate this information with the expected behavior and the time of tidal change.

GENERAL STRATEGY

The effect of current must always be considered in relation to other ever-significant strategic and tactical factors. In general, the less effective the other factors, the more significant is the current. Usually current is considered to be a major factor in light air only. Although it is certainly most important under these conditions, it actually has an equal effect at all other times.

Current, being a function of time and distance, is obviously significant in direct proportion to the duration of exposure. In lighter air and in slower boats the duration of exposure is increased and therefore the effect of the current is increased. Increased exposure when tacking to windward makes current more important on such legs. The slower the sailing angle, *i.e.*, on broader reaches and runs, the more significant is the effect of the current. Thus, the less rapidly the boat is moving, the more consideration must be given to the current; and the more rapidly the boat is moving, *i.e.*, a close reach or when planing, the less consideration is indicated.

In a steady wind, particularly when it is of sufficient strength to permit all boats to reach approximately equal maximum hull speed, strict adherence to the principles of current utilization is essential —and such adherence will often be the determining factor in the outcome of the race. With variable wind strength, however, current may sometimes better be disregarded in favor of sailing a course in areas of strongest breeze. It is of no value to get inshore out of the current if you are blanketed without wind. And it can prove equally worthless to bear off on a slow broad reach in order to take advantage of a slight increase in favorable current in mid-channel if the straight course is a fast reach.

Tactical considerations may also influence course alteration consequent to current conditions. The leading boat may more adequately cover a following fleet all subject to the same current conditions by remaining directly ahead rather than risking a major course deviation to acquire more favorable current. On the other hand, for a boat behind in the same situation a course alteration to take advantage of the current would certainly be indicated. To windward in variable winds, tacking with the headers may be essential even though the lifted tack may be out into an area of more adverse current.

Try to evaluate the relative significance of all pertinent factors for each leg of the course in advance, and periodically review the evaluations with changing conditions. Consider the strength of the current in relation to the duration of exposure, and the wind- and boat-speed variations to be expected with the course alteration indicated by the current. Don't overrate the significance of the current, but when in doubt don't disregard it. It may account for many of the mysterious losses of the past season!

RACING IN FAVORABLE CURRENT

When starting across a line with a significant current acting in the direction of the first leg, it is essential to keep well back of the line until the start. If the air is light it may be wise to anchor behind the line. In stronger winds try several passes to the point on the line at which you would like to start. Note the effect of the current and determine the initial position behind the line and the time involved in making the ideal run. Don't barge! Start the final run from a point well below the lay line if you plan to start at the weather end. Beware of being swept over the line or into a vulnerable weather or barging position. Plan to be a little late; a premature start in a favorable current is disastrous.

Generally it is desirable to tack into the main channel or region of strongest current as soon as possible after the start and to take short tacks to stay in the main channel until the windward mark can be laid. As it will be difficult to judge the exact effect of the current, approach the mark closely on the major tack before making the final tack to round. Be careful to take the final major tack significantly in advance of the lay line to avoid overstanding. If you find that you are overstanding, bear off early, aiming well below the mark in order to sail the shortest distance at the greatest possible speed. Tack as indicated on the weather leg; the favorable current will carry the boat to windward even while you are tacking.

The presence of favorable current increases boat speed through the air and therefore increases apparent wind. This means that the boat will not be able to point quite as high but in light to moderate air will acquire a speed increase beyond that produced by the current alone. The tack which is most closely parallel to the current will receive the most favorable apparent wind increase, while the tack most across the current will receive the greatest lift to windward. Try to take the tack most closely parallel to the current in the region of maximum current, as this tack receives the greatest benefit.

It is possible to sail a straight reaching course across a current and this should be attempted (see *Fig. 1*). However, as the current will often vary in strength from place to place it is essential to establish a transit between the mark ahead or behind and another fixed point which can be constantly checked. If such a transit is unavailable, keep a constant check on the relationship of the boat to the marks ahead and behind, adjusting course as necessary to keep the boat on the shortest course. It is desirable to sail at maximum speed (best possible sailing angle) across the area of maximum current to reduce to the minimum the exposure to the deviating force. Although current acting from abeam does not decrease boat speed directly, it may require an undesirable alteration in sailing angle to compensate and always increases the actual distance sailed even though the boat appears to remain on the rhumb line. Sometimes the sailing angle alteration required to achieve the shortest

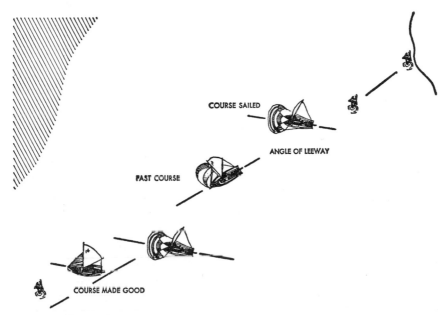

Fig. 1. When sailing across a current, the course must be adjusted to compensate for tidal set and constantly checked by reference to a transit astern (or ahead). The fastest possible course should be assumed in a limited section of extremely strong current to pass through it as rapidly as possible, i.e. a beam reach.

course is more favorable and partially compensates for the extra distance. In general, *try to determine the probable course deviation necessary to achieve a straight-line resultant course, modify this in terms of its harmful or beneficial effect upon the sailing angle, and constantly recheck to insure that the resultant course is actually approximating a straight line.*

When running in favorable current, course deviation will be benefited by the same current as that along the rhumb-line course. The current will decrease the duration of exposure to the deviating course and will tend to force the boat back toward the rhumb line. In addition the current will decrease the apparent wind, necessitating a lesser angle of inclination (closer reach) than usual to achieve a fast course. For these reasons an initial deviation to acquire clear wind or, if the current varies, to get into the region of strongest current should be attempted. *Tacking downwind is never more effective than in a favorable current,* because a significant speed increase can be achieved only by course variations from the rhumb line (due to the apparent wind increase) and the current constantly tends to correct the course deviation.

If the current flows at an oblique angle to the course of the run, assume the jibe most cross current as this receives the greatest apparent wind increase with the least course deviation. Be careful not to overstand the mark or finish line when tacking downwind. You may lose the ideal sailing angle and the shortest course, or in light air even be swept past the mark if the final tack is made too late.

RACING IN ADVERSE CURRENT

Adverse current increases the duration of exposure to its effects and therefore is of greater significance than favorable current. Every effort should be made to reduce this exposure time by keeping the boat moving at maximum speed and sailing the shortest possible course in adverse current. The outcome of sailboat racing is determined by relative speed differences between individual boats, and these relative differences are enhanced by adverse current and reduced by favorable current. When actual boat speed is reduced to 2 knots by an adverse current, a variation in boat speed of ¼ knot produces three times the speed differential of a boat-speed variation of ¼ knot when sailing at 6 knots in a favorable current. Thus a slightly faster boat, a slightly faster sailing angle, a slightly earlier acquisition of clear wind after the start, a change in course into an area of slightly reduced current, will be of far greater significance in adverse current.

The general principle of sailing in adverse current is then to "keep her moving." Increased duration of exposure consequent to excessive tacking, wind interference, pinching, etc., is far more harmful in adverse current and results in major differences in boat speed and major losses in distance gained over the ground.

When starting in adverse current, stay above the line (anchor in extremely light air) until a short time before the gun. Keep clear wind and keep the boat moving. Don't be caught blanketed below the line drifting helplessly away when the gun goes. If the wind is sufficient, try several practice runs to determine the course necessary to reach the desired point on the line in a known period of time. If the windward end is favored, barge from above the lay line sufficiently (but not excessively). Keep your wind clear; avoid starting in a crowded area even though one end may be greatly favored. The resultant slowing from blanketing and backwinding will be disastrous in adverse current and must be avoided at all costs. The boats which have clear air will have a tremendous speed differential over those subject to wind interference and will immediately work out an insurmountable lead.

If the current varies, take the end of the line most out of the current and stay in this area after starting (if this can be accomplished without excessive wind interference). If the difference is slight, if the wind is strong, or favors the strong current area, it may be sensible to disregard the current variation at the start.

While beating to windward in adverse current, keep the boat footing, avoid pinching. Take as few tacks as possible; every tack results in a significant loss.

One tack will usually be more directly into the current than the other. On this tack apparent wind is decreased and forward progress slowed, but if it is the major tack at least progress toward the mark is accomplished. On the cross-current tack, although boat speed through the air and over the bottom is less adversely affected, the boat is often moving away from the mark rather than toward it. The cross-current tack should be assumed in areas of least current and utilized as little as possible until you are in the immediate vicinity of the mark so that its necessary use may be determined as accurately as possible. When a group of boats approach the finish line in adverse current and are gradually set so that they are unable to lay the line, the winning boat will usually be the one which delays the longest in making her cross-current tack (see *Fig. 2*). She will sail the shortest distance cross current as the lay line is readily determinable from close aboard, while boats taking the cross-current tack from farther out may either greatly overstand or understand (particularly in light air). The time spent sailing cross current is usually the chief determinant of total time spent sailing to windward, as it results in the greatest losses. In very light air keep the boat on the most up-current tack, avoiding the excessive cross-current losses, until the wind finally arrives.

If the current varies as it does in a river, tack into shoal water immediately and take short tacks over the shoals until the mark can be laid. A few feet too far into stronger current may result in a major distance loss, particularly while tacking. But every tack produces a loss, so take as few as possible without getting into the stronger current. The time and location of tacking is, of course, influenced by the wind, its strength and its shifts. It may be better to sail on into stronger current in a major lift or to avoid tacking over the shoals if the wind is extremely light close to shore. The slower the boat and the greater the duration of exposure, the more consideration should be given to avoiding the current.

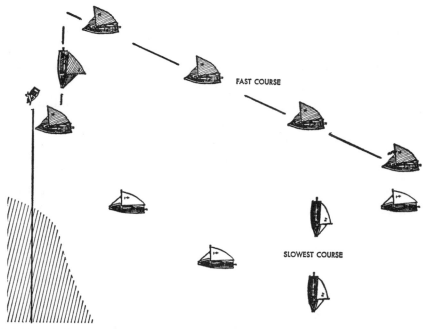

Fig. 2. Technique for overcoming adverse current when finishing.

Approach the weather mark closely, if possible on the up-current tack, so that the cross-current tack to round is made accurately from close aboard. Where a mark is located offshore in the strong current, it is best approached by extreme overstanding on a cross-current tack from the shore. It may be wise to delay the tack until the course becomes a beam reach, to permit the maximum possible speed and the shortest possible duration of exposure to the cross current. In strong current a misjudgment in tacking to cross the current may result in understanding and in the loss of many boats as one vainly tries to stem the current in mid-stream.

Take full advantage of local geographical conditions by sailing in the slack water behind a point or picking up the beneficial lift from a subsidiary stream. In strong streams there may even be favorable back eddies in the coves and along the inner banks of the bends in the shore. Give plenty of room to the mark as its anchor line may be stretched out at a reduced angle in the strong current. Be wary of tacking beneath or on the lee bow of another boat which is laying the mark, as wind interference may prevent rounding without fouling. Although the ground tackle is not part of the "mark," fouling of the anchor line by the centerboard stops the boat and permits the current to sweep her into the mark. It may be possible with good way on to raise the centerboard sufficiently to clear the anchor line and to swing the stern around rapidly, jibing, as you slip down along the mark—without fouling it.

The shortest possible route, usually the straight-line course, should be sought when reaching in adverse current. When crossing or stemming areas of particularly strong current, it may be best to alter course to the best possible sailing angle to get across as quickly as possible. If the current varies, it may be desirable to reach off into the slack current. This technique should be avoided, however, if the course deviation results in a significantly slower sailing angle, particularly if the strong current must be re-entered later in the leg.

The slow sailing angle produced when running is partially compensated for by the increase in apparent wind consequent to an adverse current. There is thus less reason to tack downwind, and the danger of excessive and unnecessary exposure by prolonging the course mitigates strongly against course deviations. If the strength of the current is variable, however, it may be desirable to broad reach into the nearest area of shoal water and to continue in the area of reduced current until the mark or finish line can be laid on the fastest possible course across the current.

SUMMARY

Prepare to utilize the current in the most favorable or least unfavorable manner by analyzing its probable effects throughout the entire course in terms of the geography of the area. Consider the relative importance of the current compared with the wind when considering course alterations. Plan to obtain the maximum duration of exposure to the weakest unfavorable current. Remember that adverse current is by far the more significant and keep the boat moving at maximum speed at all times when so exposed.

3. Sails

By E. COLIN RATSEY, Darien,
and STUART H. WALKER, Annapolis

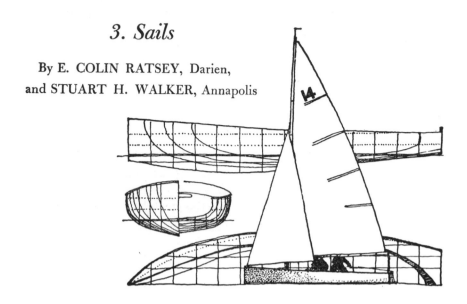

THE AERODYNAMIC FORCE

The aerodynamic force which propels a sailboat is the reaction of
the wind flow to being forced out of line and slowed by the airfoil
effect of the sails. This force is exerted on the sails at right angles to
a tangent to the surface at any point. The vector representing the
summation of all the perpendicular forces is always toward the
convex surface (or to leeward), but areas of undesirable reverse
pressure are produced on the leading and trailing edges because
of eddy formation. As the angle of inclination of the sail to the wind
is increased (wind more aft), the aerofoil suddenly "stalls," *i.e*,
eddies appear all over the convex surface and the aerodynamic force
or lift is markedly reduced. The maximum aerodynamic force is
probably produced just before this stalling point. In airplanes, increased lift with increased convexity of the airfoil without excessive
eddying and stalling can be achieved by the use of "slots" on the
leading edge, or intermediate "slats," or trailing edge "flaps." Sub-
division of the sailboat's rig, particularly the use of the jib, similarly
enhances the available lift by reducing the stalling tendency.

The aerodynamic force produced by airfoils is reduced by two
types of drag: profile drag, characteristic of the surface; and induced

drag, consequent to the lift produced. Profile drag is chiefly consequent to skin friction and the production of "pigtail eddies" at the
leading and trailing edges of the airfoil. Induced drag is chiefly
consequent to "wing-tip eddies" at the sides of the airfoil, *i.e.,* the
foot of the sail. Induced drag in the form of wind-tip eddies is reduced, per unit area, by an increase in the length in relation to the
width of the airfoil, *i.e.,* the aspect ratio. In addition, the loss of
force in the production of wing-tip eddies along the foot of a sail
is reduced by the presence of the adjacent sea and the boom, resulting in the equivalent of a 50 per cent increase in aspect ratio.

The vector summation of the aerodynamic force acting perpendicularly and toward the convex surface of the airfoil (or sail)
may be divided into two components: the thrust which drives the
boat ahead and the side force which acts to drive the boat sideways. These forces produce and are balanced by the resistance of
the water and air. The resistance of the water may be divided into
two major components: drag-profile resistance and induced (consequent to the hydrodynamic lift produced by the airfoil shape
of hull, centerboard or keel, and rudder) and wave-making resistance. Wave-making resistance becomes important only at near
maximal hull speeds (as the hull attempts to exceed the speed of the
wave which it has produced), so that throughout the usual speed
range the hull resistance is almost entirely due to drag, chiefly skin
friction; and this skin friction is directly proportional to the square
of the boat speed.

The sailboat is accelerated by the aerodynamic force until the
resistance produced by its movement through the water and air
becomes equal to the thrust of its sails. The boat speed, except
when accelerated or decelerated, is therefore that rate of forward
movement which produces a forward resistance equal to the airfoil
thrust. At low levels of thrust, moderate alterations in thrust result
in moderate alterations in resistance (due to skin friction) and boat
speed. However, at high levels of thrust, slight alterations in thrust
result in major alterations in forward resistance (due to wave mak-
ing) and therefore in boat speed. The accompanying diagrams
demonstrate the relative amount of boat speed which will produce
sufficient resistance to balance varying amounts of thrust. Conversely, the diagrams demonstrate the amount of forward resistance which must be overcome in order to produce an alteration in
boat speed at a particular level of thrust.

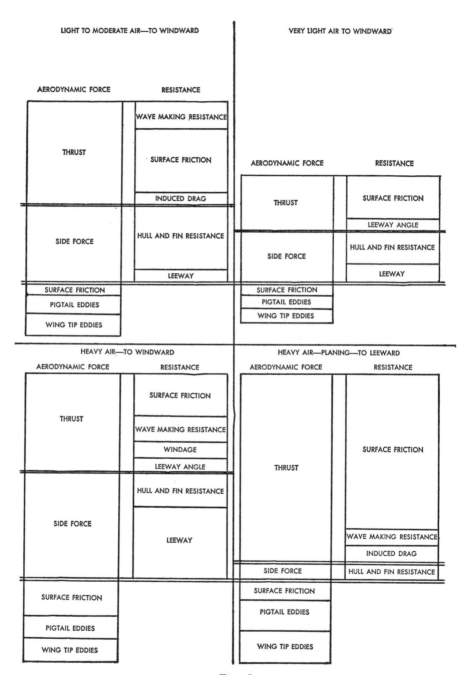

Fig. 1

Throughout the usual speed range, sail trim and other relevant factors being unaltered, the ratio of thrust to side force is constant. Consequently the forward/lateral resistance ratio is also constant. At low speeds the hull and centerboard (or keel) readily produce sufficient lateral resistance to balance the side force. At high speeds, however, the forward resistance is greatly increased due to wave-making resistance. Consequently to maintain the thrust/side force ratio equal to the forward/lateral resistance ratio, lateral resistance must (and does) increase. This is accomplished by an increase in the leeway angle from 1 or 2 degrees up to 5 degrees on a close-hauled course. Beyond 5 degrees, however, the forward resistance is suddenly and markedly increased by the oblique angle at which the hull moves through the water. A further increase in wind strength resulting in an increase in thrust and side force can only produce further and disproportionate increases in forward resistance, due to wave making and increased leeway, and an actual reduction in boat speed.

The maximum speed close hauled is therefore achieved at the time the increased angle of leeway becomes unable to maintain the forward/lateral resistance ratio. A rapid rise in forward resistance due to the increased leeway angle and an inability of the lateral resistance to prevent sideslipping with further increases in the aerodynamic force results in the often seen picture of a boat dead in the water and making rapid leeway despite a gale of wind! Boat speed in strong winds thus depends upon reducing the available thrust rather than increasing it! Increased speed may be obtained only by increasing lateral resistance in the presence of excessive thrust. Hulls are usually designed so that lateral resistance will provide an increased maximum speed under such conditions. Unfortunately this results in a potential lateral resistance in excess of that necessary to balance the slight side force at lower speeds. Overlapping headsails (with increased side force) may then be used without increasing leeway. Conversely, in high winds it is desirable to reduce excessive side force (which produces increased leeway) by using a small nonoverlapping jib. In very light winds, the thrust/side force ratio is decreased due to a disproportionate increase in side force and more lateral resistance is again needed if excessive leeway is to be avoided.

It is evident that each major force and resistance component must be considered as the summation of the various factors operative under any particular set of circumstances. Thus the forward resistance is equal to the sum of the resistance of the skin friction which increases as the square of the speed of the boat; the eddy making around the centerboard (or keel), rudder, and hull surfaces; the induced drag of the lift effect of these surfaces at various leeway angles; and the effects of wave making. In strong winds when the operation of hull sections at an excessive leeway angle and wave making result in great increases in forward resistance, boat speed actually may fall in the presence of increasing thrust. It is obviously as important to reduce the correlative factors which produce forward resistance to free energy for boat speed at it is to increase the factors which produce thrust. However, in this chapter only the production of aerodynamic force and improved facilities for increasing the resultant thrust will be considered.

OPTIMAL AIRFOIL CREATION

The force produced by an airfoil, or sail, is directly dependent upon the following factors:

1. The density of the air.
2. The speed of the apparent wind.
3. The speed of the boat.
4. The inclination of the airfoil to the apparent wind horizontally and vertically.
5. The shape of the airfoil (in section).
6. The plan of the airfoil:
   a) area,
   b) outline,
   c) aspect ratio,
   d) slope of the aerodynamic axis,
   e) bending of the leading edge.
7. The surface of the airfoil.

The force available and resultant is dependent upon the following additional factors:

1. The velocity gradient of the wind.
2. The heeling moment and the angle of heel.
3. The sail balance.

The Density of the Air

The density of the air, which is increased by a fall in temperature and/or an increase in atmospheric pressure, is directly proportional to the aerodynamic force produced. The winds of winter have more "weight."

The Speed of the Apparent Wind and of the Boat

The wind force in pounds is directly proportional to the square of the velocity of the apparent wind, and the force produced is therefore dependent upon the speed ratio between the boat's speed and the wind speed. This speed ratio and the density of the air must be considered in relation to each of the other factors affecting the aerodynamic force.

The Inclination of the Airfoil to the Apparent Wind

The optimal angle of inclination is chiefly dependent upon the aspect ratio rather than upon the shape or arch of the airfoil. At high speed ratios (boat speed high, wind speed low—moderate airs) a usual 3:1 aspect ratio produces the best close-hauled course at an approximately 45-degree angle of inclination, while at low speed ratios (boat speed low, compared to wind speed—heavy airs) a 3:1 aspect ratio produces the best close-hauled course at a lesser angle of inclination, *i.e,* higher on the wind. The greater the angle of inclination (wind more aft), *i.e.,* the nearer to the stalling point, the greater the total aerodynamic force produced but the less the thrust/side force ratio. The lesser the angle of inclination (the sails eased, luffing, or the boat headed), the lesser the total aerodynamic force produced but the greater the thrust/side force ratio. The above figures for angles of inclination from John Morwood's *Sailing Aerodynamics* represent the optimal compromises between loss of total force and loss of thrust with the usual aspect ratio of small boats —3:1.

The Shape of the Airfoil

An arch of 1:7 (maximum depth/length of chord), provided by a full sail, apparently produces the maximum thrust at all speeds and at all angles of inclination with a 6:1 aspect ratio. With a 3:1 aspect ratio an arch of 1:13.5, a flat sail, seems better to windward, 1:7 better to leeward. The position of the greatest arch apparently has little effect on the force produced but alters the location of the center of effort, *i.e.,* affects sail balance (Morwood—*Sailing Aerodynamics*).

The Plan of the Airfoil

Area. The greater the area, the greater is the resultant force. All other factors must be considered in relation to unit area.

Outline. An ellipse which produces negligible wing-tip eddy formation is apparently the ideal outline for an airfoil. The prevention of the full development of the boom eddy by the sea saves the triangular plan.

Aspect ratio. The greater the aspect ratio and the nearer the boom to the water (or hull), the lesser is the loss of thrust in wing-tip eddying. However, the greater the aspect ratio, the greater is the heeling moment and the lesser is the thrust per unit heeling moment to windward in strong breezes. Increased aspect ratio is more beneficial in light airs and fast boats, *i.e.*, at high speed ratios, and is more significant to windward than to leeward. In slower boats and in heavier airs lower aspect ratios may produce more thrust. Side force is only slightly affected by aspect ratio. At greater angles of inclination, downwind, thrust is increased moderately in proportion to aspect ratio in light winds but is greatest at an aspect ratio of 1:1 in heavy air (Morwood—*Sailing Aerodynamics*). The aspect ratio of the International 14, approximately 2-½:1 (effectively almost 4:1 when increased 50 per cent for boom-eddy reduction), is probably near optimal for a fast boat under a wide range of conditions. Lower aspect ratios, 2:1 or less, are probably better for non-planing hulls.

Inasmuch as the effective aspect ratio is determined by the height of the mainsail head above the jib tack (considering both sails as "slat" segments of a single airfoil), a sliding gooseneck on the main boom may permit aspect-ratio adjustment. In light air, at high speed ratios, the mainsail may be elevated to increase aspect ratio, while in heavy air the aspect ratio may be reduced for optimal effect and decreased heeling moment. This arrangement also permits the use of a lower aspect ratio mainsail which is optimal for downwind "stalled" sailing but which may be elevated for increased aspect ratio upwind.

Slope of the aerodynamic axis. The aerodynamic axis is the line joining the centers of pressure of the chords of the sail (roughly 40 per cent aft of the leading edge of each chord when close hauled). Unless a triangular sail is an equilateral triangle, its aerodynamic axis will not be at right angles to the wind flow, *i.e.*, vertical, and will therefore be aerodynamically swept forward (in mainsails) or swept back (in jibs). Sweep forward or back apparently decreases the lift before the stall but increases the lift after the stall. With the wind over the quarter or further aft the sails are stalled completely, and under these circumstances sweep forward or back seems beneficial (Morwood—*Sailing Aerodynamics*).

In the usual rig the mainsail is aerodynamically swept forward about 10 degrees to 15 degrees (chord lengths increasing aft at lower levels) and the jib is aerodynamically swept back. Increasing aspect ratio straightens the slope of both sails. Heeling causes the axis to sweep further back, increasing the sweep back of the jib and correcting the sweep forward of the main up to an angle of heel equal to the original slope of the axis of the sail. Further heeling increases the sweep back in both sails. As thrust with sweep forward tends to depress the bow, it may be desirable to rake the mast; conversely, when heeling is deliberate as in very light air, it may be desirable to trim the boat down at the bow to correct the excessive sweep back.

Bending the leading edge. The leading edge of an airfoil seems to be most effective when it is a portion of an ellipse (at right angles to the plane of the airfoil), with its convexity opposite to the convexity of the airfoil. Such a bending of the leading edge apparently increases the aerodynamic force and the stability of the airfoil. The topmast should bend to leeward and the midsection of the mast to windward to produce this effect. The arch of the sail would be distorted by excessive bending to windward so that this factor is of only negative significance, *i.e.*, no leeward concavity should be permitted. In any case, convexity of the leading edge of the jib is not possible when the jib is set on a jibstay, but no sagging whatever should be permitted, *i.e.*, the jibstay must be as taut as possible.

Surface of the Airfoil

Synthetic sails have completely supplanted cotton for small boat racing. Although a full understanding of their superiority may not yet be available, it seems certain that reduced porosity is the major factor. It is presumed that the synthetic sails reduce profile drag by preventing wind flow through the sail, thus decreasing eddy formation and resultant surface friction. The smoother surface may also reduce profile drag but this is probably of lesser significance. Water-resistant materials also reduce the weight aloft consequent to rain or spray—a major factor in stormy winds, which produce heeling. Dacron (or Terylene) is generally considered the most desirable sail material at this time because it provides the maximum strength, durability, water resistance, and reduced porosity together with sufficient flexibility to permit adjustment of draft on the boat.

If a synthetic sail does not set correctly the first time it is used, it should be returned to the sailmaker. There is no "breaking in" period for a synthetic sail, as the fiber strength prevents stretching, at least along the thread lines. However, despite the great strength of their fibers, all synthetic materials stretch on the bias. The stretch allowance for Dacron (or Terylene) is two-thirds that of cotton on the luff, very little on the foot, and nothing on the leech, as the leech is cut almost on the thread line.

Altering tension on the halyard can alter the luff, as this is cut along the bias of the material, and altering the luff will alter the location of the draft. The fullness usually should be about one-third back of the luff, but in the mainsail it may be pulled forward by tightening the luff rope and aft by easing it. Dacron sails seem to last about three times as long as cotton without losing the shape intended. However, they do deteriorate, as evidenced by the appearance of increasing numbers of fine cracks in the glazed surface. These cracks are associated with stretching along the bias. It is doubtful that folding or stuffing into a sail bag has any significant deleterious effect. However, flogging when hoisted at the dock or when luffing about before the start may seriously stretch and alter the shape of the sail and should be assiduously avoided.

MODIFICATIONS OF THRUST

Velocity Gradient

The velocity of the wind decreases downward from its true strength at 1,500–3,000 ft. altitude because of the friction of the earth's surface. Over water the pressure of the wind is three times as great at a height of 15 ft. as it is at 5 ft. The apparent wind, therefore, becomes nearer to the direction of the true wind further aloft, so that maintenance of the proper angle of inclination at each level requires a twist of the sail. At a boat speed of 4 knots the sail must twist approximately 6 degrees in the lower 30 ft., and at 8 knots approximately 8.6 degrees in the lower 30 ft., to be properly trimmed at all levels.

Heeling Moment and Angle of Heel

When a sailboat heels, there is a downward component of the aerodynamic force which reduces the thrust and the side force and decreases stability. As the righting force acts vertically through the keel, the greater the angle of heel the greater the disparity of alignment of the righting couple and the greater the instability or readiness to heel.

The effective angle of inclination of the airfoil to the wind is increased by heeling although this is partially compensated for by the shifting of the apparent wind aft as the true wind velocity increases. At any given wind velocity, however, the greater the heeling the greater the heading effect, *i.e.*, the more vertical the boat is kept, the higher she can point.

Sail Balance

The balance of a sailboat depends upon the moment turning the bow to windward produced by the forces acting in the long axis of the boat, the thrust, and the forward resistance, and the moment turning the boat to leeward produced by the forces acting across the long axis of the boat, the side force, and the lateral resistance. Inasmuch as the center of effort of the sails is always to leeward of the center of buoyancy, the fore-and-aft couple always produces a windward turning moment which is accentuated by heeling, easing the sheets, moving the draft further aft, or otherwise altering the angle of inclination to approach the stalling point. The lateral resistance is so designed that the moment due to the fore-and-aft difference in location of the center of action of the side force and the center of lateral resistance produces a leeward turning moment. This leeward moment is increased by any factor moving the center of side force effort forward, such as an overlapping, full, or eased jib or by any factor which moves the center of lateral resistance aft, such as raising the centerboard or operating at a decreased leeway angle. *When the boat is well balanced the windward turning moment of the thrust/forward resistance couple and the leeward turning moment of the side force/lateral resistance couple are equal and the boat holds a course without the use of the rudder.* The rudder, however, permits alteration of the center of lateral resistance; weather helm draws it aft, lee helm moves it forward. Thus the boat may be balanced by a precise adjustment and steered under a wide variety of conditions affecting the center of effort of the sails.

It is desirable for the center of effort of the sails so to correspond with the center of lateral resistance that there is a slight excess of the turning moment to windward. A turning moment to windward sufficient to require the rudder to be held at a 5-degree angle of attack will produce the maximum lift from the rudder surface and will tend to help the boat continually to windward. The sail plan and lateral resistance must be adjusted to each wind speed, not only to produce maximum thrust with the least forward resistance, but to maintain balance without excessive corrective rudder drag. A weather helm beyond the optimal 5-degree angle will cause greatly increased rudder drag (probably stalling), while a lee helm will produce a hydrodynamic force to leeward.

The center of lateral resistance at a 2-degree leeway angle—on reaching or running courses—is approximately 33 per cent aft of the leading edge of the chord of the airfoil surface of the keel, centerboard, or rudder. The center tends to move forward, however, as leeway increases on a windward course in heavy air.

The center of effort of the sails is dependent upon the line of action of the total resultant aerodynamic force of all airfoil surfaces. The center of effort of each individual sail is dependent upon the location of the maximum arch and the angle of inclination of the surface to the wind. To windward the center of effort is located about 40 per cent aft of the leading edge of the chord at any height but moves farther aft with increased angles of inclination until the geometric center of the sail is reached when the sail is stalled. In addition, as the sail is eased the resultant force line acting perpendicularly through the center of effort of the sail surface moves further and further aft on the hull. The turning moment to weather is thus greatly increased on reaches and runs and must be offset by movement of the center of lateral resistance aft (decreasing the leeway angle, raising a pivoted centerboard), by increasing the forward resistance to windward (heeling to windward), or by increasing the side force forward. The latter is the most effective technique and is readily accomplished by easing an overlapping jib, whose increased arch and more vertical aerodynamic slope will produce a major increase in side force (as well as thrust). In very light air with a minimal leeway angle, the center of lateral resistance may move sufficiently far aft that an overlapping jib is necessary to maintain weather helm (by increasing side force and leeway angle and shifting the center of lateral resistance forward again).

The location of the draft in the individual sails is dependent upon halyard tension, foot tension, and sheet adjustment; and variation in these factors may alter sail balance as much as alteration of mast position or rake, sail size, or centerboard hoist.

The use of a different sail will probably throw a well-balanced small boat completely off balance necessitating repositioning of the mast, the centerboard, and stays. Significant alterations in the position of the maximum arch in the main or jib may be produced by slight variations in vang or sheet tension and result in a major loss of balance. In sensitive boats like 14's this means that great care must be exercised when making known changes, and that, conversely, great care should be exercised to avoid even minor changes when "she's going well."

Sail and rudder balance is thus dependent upon multiple factors which may vary interdependently or independently so that the alteration of a single factor may produce opposing effects and reverse results. It is therefore desirable to have effective adjustment facilities for all factors available and functional during a race. Maximum centerboard lift or effectiveness to windward is obtained only when the board is lowered to vertical (or forward of the vertical). When sailing to windward in heavy air, in order to avoid raising the centerboard it may be necessary to move the entire sail plan forward to increase forward side force and maintain rudder balance. An adjustable mast partner permitting forward movement of the mast at the gunwale level and flattening of the mainsail arch may be an essential solution, but if this results in sagging of the jib stay with decreased aerodynamic force from the jib the result may be an increased rather than a decreased weather helm. Tightening the jibstay, to move the sail forward, may raise the boom, increase the sweep forward of the aerodynamic slope of the mainsail, and move the position of maximum arch aft, as the sheet lead now tightens the leech excessively, again resulting in an increase in weather helm.

JIB-MAINSAIL AREA

The relationship of optimal jib area to mainsail area has been extensively investigated in the English National 12-ft. Class. In this class, in which total sail area but not the proportional division of sail is restricted, sail plans with larger jibs and smaller mains have been evolved for optimal racing in the sea, while sail plans with smaller jibs and larger mains have evolved for sailing in the rivers. This is in extension of the principle of the cat rig's being optimal upwind (river sailing) and the sloop rig optimal when reaching. Cat-rigged boats were still leading the way to the windward mark in the 14-ft. class in the early thirties, but the reaching plane has demanded a jib and an interrupted airfoil for maximum efficiency at greater angles of inclination and higher speeds. Improved upwind ability is usually associated with small fore-triangles, but in heavy weather reduction in heeling moment and weather helm more than offsets the reduction in thrust (which is available to excess anyway) associated with a large foretriangle. In the International 14 ft. Class recent developments have shown the advantage of a large fore-triangle in heavy weather both upwind and down. A movable mast step and a movable centerboard (pin position) are necessary to take full advantage of these relationships.

APPLICATIONS

Jib

The jib is usually the most important sail on the boat, inasmuch as minor alterations in its setting result in major alterations in boat speed. The jib produces increased thrust to windward far in excess of that expected from its sail area as it increases the effective arch of the total sail plan, smoothes the eddies in the lee of the main, and increases the rate of flow over the leeward surface of the main, thereby increasing the negative pressure on the lee side of the main. In addition, the absence of a mast at the jib's leading edge makes it a much more effective sail per unit area than the main. The major drawbacks of the jib are evident to windward, however, when a sagging jib stay and variable arching reduce its efficiency.

A variety of techniques are now being utilized to cut jibs of proper and more lasting shape. Radial seams and parallel seams may avoid the bias stretch on the leech which is the great problem of mitered sails. Leech stretching is much less of a problem in equilateral overlapping jibs as the panels reach the leech perpendicularly. Nonoverlapping Star Class jibs seem definitely improved by the parallel (mainsail-like) seaming, however. Inasmuch as no alteration of vertical section is needed in a jib, they may be cut with the same flow throughout. A jib should not be cut full, since fullness can readily be provided by easing the sheet but cannot be completely removed by the sheet if built in. Maximum draft should be placed in the forward third of the sail but not so far forward that high pointing is prevented.

The jib should be set as low as possible, its foot closely approximating the deck or gunwale, to reduce the tremendous wing-tip eddy of the equilateral triangular plan. Increased tension on the boom vang will help keep the jibstay tight through the backstay effect of the mainsail itself (and this may be the primary value of the vang). The mast must be stiff enough and so confined at the gunwale level that its forward bend (due to the forward drive of the boom under vang tension) will not reduce the jibstay tension.

The usual aerodynamic sweepback of the jib may be reduced by constructing it more like an equilateral triangle, *i.e.*, with an overlap. The overlapping jib is an extremely effective improvement in sail plan and often furnishes untaxed additional area (dependent upon class rules). Although it increases side force, this is acceptable when excessive lateral resistance is available, as in light air. Even in heavy air the increased area is low and has little effect on heeling. Reduction in sail area for heavy air is effectively accomplished by setting a smaller jib, thereby reducing side force, which is poorly tolerated in these circumstances.

The low area of the overlapping jib, completely free of the mainsail, may be more effective, particularly when stalled. Such a jib requires a plastic window for adequate visualization to leeward, and most classes (chiefly planing types) using these large jibs now utilize windows. Transparent plastic sheets approximately 12″ × 18″ may be set into a panel a foot or so behind the luff for the use of the crew or further back and at a lower level for the skipper to observe under the boom. The plastic now in use is strong, retains it transparency well, can be readily and securely sewed in place, and does not distort the shape of the sail under usual circumstances. In cold weather, however, the plastic tends to hold any shape to which it has long been exposed, so that the window should be bagged carefully in a smooth flat position (on top of the folded sail) to prevent an accordion effect in light air. Stars and other boats which utilize small jibs, or which tend to heel, use windows in their mainsails. Wherever they are used, they not only prevent collisions and disqualifications, but provide readily available tactical information which may often make the difference between gaining or losing a competitor.

To leeward the jib reaches its greatest effectiveness. When eased, its arch increases, approximating the most effective arch for increased angles of inclination. In addition, an eased overlapping jib is particularly effective in controlling the weather turning moment of the eased main.

The greatest aerodynamic force is apparently produced when the jib is inclined at an angle of 10 to 15 degrees to the mainsail with a sufficient gap between the two sails to just eliminate major degrees of backwind. Exact information on the size of this gap (or slot is not available, but it is usually agreed that within the limits of the particular boat it should be as large as possible. The jibstay should be as far forward as possible, the mast bowed to windward, the jib led outboard, the head of the jib cut away or reduced, etc., so long as the boat is balanced and the sails are at the proper angle of inclination. The perfect jib should hardly backwind the mainsail at all except probably about 2 ft. above the boom near the mast. Moving the jib leads inboard or outboard to reduce backwind to this degree should indicate their ideal location. The desired fore-and-aft position of the jib leads is usually obtained by bisecting the angle of the clew, but this must be adjusted to avoid either excessive tension on the foot or the leech and resultant variable arching of the sail. The leech of the jib should never be tight or curled. A tight leech slows the boat by eddy production and distortion of flow in the lee of the main where it is most harmful. A fluttering leech probably does not reduce boat speed so long as it does not disturb the forward surface of the sail. *The lesser the wind speed, the greater is the possible deviation in the wind's course without eddying or stalling; i.e., the lesser the wind's speed, the greater the airfoil arch needed and possible to produce the same aerodynamic force.* Therefore, in light weather the jib leads may be moved inboard and/or the jib sheet eased to produce a greater arch in the sail without excessive backwinding of the main.

Mainsail

Optimal mainsail area is a compromise between that sufficiently large to produce maximum thrust in light air and that sufficiently small to prevent excessive thrust and heeling in heavy air. A sail with significantly less area than that most effective in light air will produce maximum speed to windward in heavy air without the reduction in speed due to excessive side force and leeway angle and consequently increased forward resistance. It is obvious that to provide adequately for the extremes of wind speed two mainsails must be available. A larger number is probably unnecessary and will likely result in poorer rather than better correlation of sail size to wind speed, inasmuch as it is often impossible to predict from the beach what the wind condition offshore will be during a race an hour or more later. A smaller heavy-weather main is essential to racing in planing sailboats which regularly race in particularly strong winds. Although larger sails may be successfully lugged upwind, their excessive thrust on a reach or run may be overpowering. Reefing is commonly practiced in such classes in England, where particularly severe wind and wave conditions are common; but this practice has never been utilized with success in North America, even when wind conditions were comparable. The time lost in reefing is not compensated for by improved performance upwind where excessive sail area is controllable or downwind where maximal thrust is essential to fastest planing.

Because sail area is limited by mast and boom measurements in most classes, increased area for performance in light air has been sought in larger and larger roaches. The synthetic sail materials have permitted major increases in roach areas with the same batten lengths. However, it seems probable that these large roaches cause excessive stretching along the bias of the material and more rapid deterioration of the sail shape. It has been considered necessary in most classes to limit roach in order to control area and to prevent excessively rapid deterioration.

The rig must be so tuned that the mainsail will have the necessary stability to maintain its shape. The mast must not develop any excessive lateral bends which will distort the draft but must permit the mainsail head to twist sufficiently to accommodate the altered apparent wind direction aloft due to the velocity gradient. The upper section of the mast must be flexible to prevent excessive shaking of the sail when the boat pounds in a seaway. Nothing stops a boat sooner than a tight mast tip in a heavy sea. In addition, it is desirable for the upper section of the mast to fall off to leeward when beating in heavy air, in order to reduce drive and heeling moment aloft. Many Canadians consider this to be the major advantage of the flexible rig in 14's.

It is probably more important to have two mainsails of different draft than of different size: a large full sail for light air and a smaller flat sail for heavy air. A great deal of effort has been expended recently to try to find methods by which full sails may be successfully used upwind in strong winds so that they may be available downwind when their greater arch is optimal or, conversely, to find methods by which flat sails may be successfully used downwind after they've served their purpose upwind. Alteration of tension along the foot seems essential to all of these methods, as alteration of halyard tension only alters the position of the draft. Additional draft may be provided by easing the tack or outhaul and excessive draft reduced by tightening the outhaul and tightening the boom with the boom vang or the mid-boom mainsheet lead, or by closing the zipper in a sail which has a zippered pouch along the foot. A full sail may thus be adapted to strong winds by reducing its arch and resultant thrust—usually through increased boom-vang tension— and with its side force reduced by easing the sheet may be feathered upwind without excessive heeling and leeway angle.

The use of a zippered pouch along the foot, which may provide many extra square feet of sail area and increased fullness along the foot when opened, seems an excellent technique but has not actually demonstrated much more than psychological advantages over the nonzippered opposition—and zippers do jam. Except for the extra area provided, the shape alteration can be as effectively accomplished by altered boom-vang tension. Actually significant alteration in the arch of the sail, except along the foot itself, necessitates alteration in the horizontal tension on the foot, *i.e.*, altered tension at tack or clew. Numerous devices have been tried for this purpose, the simplest usually being the best in small boats. Probably an adaptation of the Penguin's adjustable outhaul rig, now being used in Stars, permitting inboard outhaul adjustment under way, will prove most suitable.

Adjustment of the halyard provides adjustment of the position of the draft because of the significant stretch provided in the luff of even a synthetic sail. In stormy winds the halyard can be tightened, the draft reduced and moved forward, and the center of effort moved forward to counteract the tendency for it to shift aft with the apparent wind. The fullness should be about a third back from the luff for moderate air but may be moved even further aft in light air by easing the halyard.

In light air the "flaps down" effect of a tight leech is probably desirable, as the arch of an optimal airfoil section is greater at high speed ratios. It is therefore feasible and desirable to combine big roaches and tight leeches for light air mainsails and to avoid the necessity of keeping a tight boom vang to prevent the falling off of a big roach. The boom vang should be kept as loose as possible in light air to avoid reducing draft (only tight enough to prevent excessive twist aloft when the sheet is eased and to prevent jibstay sagging to leeward). A sail which needs a tight vang to control roach or leech in light air negates itself and should either have the leech tightened or the roach reduced.

Spinnaker

The spinnaker is usually used at the stall, its resultant aerodynamic force being consequent to the positive force of obstructed wind speed on its windward surface. A flat plate produces the maximum aerodynamic force beyond the stall so that in recent years spinnakers have again become flatter and flatter. Thus, nowadays, one sail may be used with equal effectiveness in both reaching and running. *The effectiveness of a spinnaker is determined by its ability to obstruct the flow of as much air as possible while disseminating the obstructed air as rapidly as possible so as not to interfere with the further obstruction of additional air.*

The larger the spinnaker, the more effective it should be. However, in very light air a smaller sail may be more effective as it may set better and in heavy air may be more effective as it produces a more controllable amount of thrust. Spinnakers, especially large ones, may be used more advantageously in planing boats in heavy air, as thrust can be dissipated in increased boat speed. Use of material with an absolute minimum of porosity is essential for spinnakers in order to produce maximal obstruction to air flow, and this difference in material is probably more significant than any other factor in spinnaker effectiveness.

Dissemination of the obstructed air is the major problem of spinnaker construction and a wide variety of shapes, seams, and holes has been created to achieve this end while still providing maximum area. The major factor here appears to be the positive value of disseminating a major portion of the air off the foot where the reflective effect of the sea provides increased propulsive force. Thus spinnakers must be designed to lift sufficiently and be sufficiently flat along the foot that they do not trap air flow in this area. If air is trapped and energy dissipated in eddy production, less force is applied to the surface and greater interference with the perpendicular flow of incoming air results, *i.e.*, less thrust is produced.

The other major factor in spinnaker effectiveness is stability. Instability undoubtedly increases eddy production and interferes with direct obstruction and dissemination of the air flow. Thus the large bell-shaped spinnakers with huge shoulders, although they may provide more area, are often less efficient because they tend to fall in and swing from side to side excessively. A sail which holds its shape in waves and wind variations, even if of smaller area, will often be more effective.

It may be desirable to set the mainsail moderately by the lee of the perpendicular to the wind when using a spinnaker so that there will be a forward flow along the windward surface of the main into the spinnaker. From this position a major portion of the lee surface eddy flow is also probably caught by the spinnaker. It is particularly important to avoid permitting the main to be backwinded by flow off the spinnaker. On a reach the spinnaker tends to be relatively stable, so that maximal area and flatness should be exposed to the wind by bringing the tack as far aft and down as possible while using the sheet to keep the luff "on edge." While running, on the other hand, the spinnaker should be flattened across the bow by tension on both the guy and sheet to prevent swinging and collapsing—the lighter the air, the tighter the sheet. The tack and clew should be approximately the same height and not too far above the water to gain the maximal reflective effect of the sea.

The pole should be sufficiently long and adjustable for height on the mast to permit optimal flattening and leveling of the spinnaker. Spinnakers in most classes have now outgrown their permitted pole lengths and are subject to increased side-to-side swinging and loss of effective area because of excessive arching with a short pole. Maximum girth or foot measurements may be desirable to keep spinnakers at optimal stability sizes in relation to pole lengths.

SUMMARY

Principles of Increased Boat Speed Through Sail Power

Factors Operative at All Times

1. Aspect Ratio: Increased aspect ratio because of the wind-velocity gradient and because of reduced "wing-tip" eddy drag produces increased thrust. However, in strong winds to windward high aspect ratios may reduce thrust by increasing heeling moment.
2. Bending the leading edge: A taut jibstay and a mast slightly arched to windward produce increased thrust.
3. Surface: A smooth nonporous surface reduces profile drag.
4. Heeling: The following harmful effects are consequent to heeling:
    a) Reduced thrust because of decreased effective aspect ratio and loss of the velocity-gradient advantage.
    b) Reduced thrust because of the production of a downward component of the aerodynamic force.
    c) Reduced thrust to windward because of the increased sweepback of the aerodynamic slope of the jib and of the main, if heeling is greater than 10 to 15 degrees.
    d) Increased forward resistance due to increased displacement (downward component of aerodynamic force) and increased wetted surface.
    e) Increased forward resistance due to increased weather turning moment (center of effort further outboard and convex lee bow surface in the water) with increased drag and increased weather helm.
    f) Decreased pointing ability due to lessened angle of inclination.
    g) Tendency to a progressive and disproportionate increase in heeling and its harmful effects due to increasing instability, increasing effect of weight aloft, and the shifting of bilge water.
5. Angle between jib and mainsail: The sails should be separated by a distance sufficient to prevent all but a minimal degree of backwinding and be inclined at an angle of 12 to 15 degrees to each other.

6. Forward resistance: The profile drag of the hull and fins should be reduced to the minimum and the centerboard (or keel) and rudder surfaces be shaped and inclined to provide the maximum lift with the least induced drag.

Factors Operative to Windward when the Speed Ratio is High
Light to moderate true wind velocity typically:

1. Inclination: Maximum thrust produced on a 45-degree course to the true wind with sails sheeted in to near stalling.
2. Shape: Maximum thrust produced by full sails with a loose foot and luff but a tight leech.
3. Slope: Maximum thrust produced by an overlapping jib, a high aspect ratio, and a vertical mast.
4. Lateral resistance: Raising the centerboard to decrease lateral resistance with an overlapping jib maintains the normal forward/lateral resistance ratio and improves thrust in the presence of a low side force.
5. Twist: Maximum thrust provided by optimal twist and eased vang.

Factors Operative to Windward when the Speed Ratio is Low
Very light true wind velocity typically:

1. Inclination: Maximum thrust produced with sails well eased and inclined 40 degrees to the true wind.
2. Shape: Maximum thrust with reduced side force produced by flatter sails.
3. Slope: Maximum thrust obtained by heeling rig to maintain sail shape and boat trimmed down by bow to improve aerodynamic slope.
4. Lateral resistance: Full lowering of the centerboard and use of a small jib maintain the normal forward/lateral resistance ratio and improve thrust in the presence of relatively high side force.
5. Twist: Maximum thrust provided by optimal twist and completely eased vang (velocity gradient high)

Heavy wind velocity typically:

1. Inclination: Maximum thrust produced on a course of 40 degrees to the true wind with sheets eased to decrease side force.
2. Shape: Maximum thrust produced by flat sails with a tight foot and luff but a loose leech.
3. Slope: Maximum thrust produced by a smaller jib (lower

aspect ratio—reduced heeling moment), raked mast, and minimal heeling.

4. Lateral resistance: Full lowering of the centerboard and the use of a small jib provide sufficient lateral resistance and dissipation of side force without excessive leeway, reduce forward resistance, maintain the normal forward/lateral resistance ratio, and improve thrust.

5. Twist: Maximum thrust produced by slight twist (velocity gradient reduced) and tight vang (which also flattens arch).

Factors Operative to Leeward

1. Inclination: Maximum thrust produced by sails at the stalling point—near perpendicular to the apparent wind.

2. Shape: Maximum thrust produced by full sails reaching (jib particularly effective to leeward due to increased arch when eased); maximum thrust produced by flat sails when running.

3. Slope: Maximum thrust improved by sweep back or forward with stalled sails (jib again particularly effective to leeward)

4. Lateral resistance: Unimportant to leeward as side force insignificant. Overlapping jib helpful in controlling weather turning moment.

5. Twist: Maximum thrust obtained by reducing twist with tight vang.

4. Hull and Rigging

By GEORGE MOFFATT, Barnegat Bay

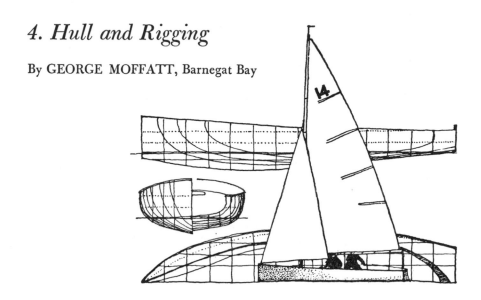

We know that a good sailor can make even a mediocre boat look very good. In competition among experts, however, where all fifteen or twenty skippers have the experience and ability to win, a boat which is a few seconds a mile faster will often make the difference. The very fast boat also has the ability to bail the skipper out of a tight situation. Remember the time you tacked under someone's lee bow only to find that you had called it too close and were in danger of dropping into the hopeless slot? A fast boat can get you out of this sort of jam. Later, as you describe the skill with which you extricated yourself, don't forget the old adage, "Nothing makes a skipper look better than a fast boat."

Essentially, everything about a boat can be considered as either lift or drag. By lift I mean force which tends to move the boat ahead; by drag, all the forces which slow the boat down. Thus the sails produce lift while the mast produces drag. The problem, then, resolves itself into an effort to make the most of all lift-producing forces while at the same time minimizing anything which produces drag.

THE HULL

Skin Resistance

Two completely distinct types of drag exist: skin resistance and wave-making resistance. Skin resistance results from the friction of water against the skin of the hull. In effect the hull drags an envelope of water around with it, the water next to the hull being dragged along by friction. Skene in his *Elements of Yacht Design* gives a table indicating the per cent of total resistance which is due to skin friction at various speeds. In a boat of about the displacement-length ration of the average small racing boat ($\dfrac{D}{\left(\dfrac{L}{100}\right)^3} = 100$, where

L = waterline length and D = displacement in tons of 2,250 lb.). The percentage of resistance due to skin friction varies from 85 per cent at a speed of .7 ($\sqrt{L}$) to 74 per cent at speeds of 1 $\sqrt{L}$) to only 25 per cent at speeds of 1.5 ($\sqrt{L}$). Obviously skin friction is most important in the lower speed ranges. *Friction, however, still amounts to 45 per cent of all hull drag even at a speed of 1.25 ($\sqrt{L}$),* a speed which is about maximum for many sail-driven hulls. The smoothness of the hull surface has a marked effect upon the amount of water it drags along.

The leading edge of any surface hits unmoving water and hence produces higher drag. Skin friction reaches its maximum on the short surfaces, such as the centerboard or rudder, which have friction coefficients of as much as 40 per cent more than the longer hull. Therefore, devote your best efforts to smoothing the rudder, board, and fore part of the boat. If nothing else, the mirrorlike bottom gives the skipper a tremendous psychological lift. Is the beautiful new-painted finish the fastest, though? Possibly not. Nature has a way of doing things the easy way, and she equips fish with a certain amount of slime. Tests indicate that a three-day slime on a boat helps to reduce skin friction somewhat, too. Graphite dissolved in paint or varnish also seems to produce a surface which is just a little faster than paint. The graphite finish works particularly well on centerboards, since it makes them very slippery, reducing friction on the trunk sides by over 25 per cent. The best method for applying graphite seems to be to mix as much microfine powdered graphite as possible into a good quality varnish. A quart of varnish will hold about ½ lb. of graphite. Smear the resulting mess on your boat as evenly as possible, preferably in two coats, then sand with 320 wet sandpaper. The result is a very smooth if not very attractive surface.

Over a number of years I have noticed that boats seem to go faster in light airs when they have been newly painted. Possibly this apparent speed difference is merely the result of the proud skipper sailing a little better than usual in his shiny vehicle. I'm inclined to think, however, that the high oil content of new paint may have something to do with this effect. Coach Logg of the Rutgers crew tells me that oiling the bottom of a shell just before a race helps the speed. On old rubbed finish certainly looks and feels smoother than a newly painted one, but until someone shows me that it goes as fast I'm going to go on painting my boat bottom just before major regattas.

Wave-making Resistance

Wave making, the second element in hull resistance, begins to be of importance at speeds of about .8 ($\sqrt{L}$) and assumes rapidly increasing values until, by a speed of 2 ($\sqrt{L}$) (approximately 8 knots for the 16-footer) it accounts for all but about 20 per cent of the total resistance.

As any hull moves through the water, it sets up a wave of translation. At a speed equal to 1.25 ($\sqrt{L}$), the boat reaches the speed of its wave translation and the hull appears to rest in a hollow between its bow and stern waves. The speed of a wave system is proportional to the length of the wave between its crests. Therefore, *any further increase in the speed of the boat means that the hull will have to exceed the speed of the wave it has produced by climbing up the face of its own bow wave.* Since boats don't sail uphill very well, much power will be needed to increase speed even slightly beyond 1.25 ($\sqrt{L}$).

Now the speed that a boat can attain before the length of the wave pattern reaches the length of the hull will vary considerably with the fineness of the hull as expressed by the length-displacement

ratio $\dfrac{D}{\left(\dfrac{L}{100}\right)^3}$ in which L is waterline length and D is displacement in long tons. The heavy hull of the ocean racer, with a displacement ratio of about 350 by this formula, has a fairly low maximum speed; whereas the rowing shell, measuring about 35, has a very high maximum speed. For practical purposes few sailboats other than the decked canoe have a ratio by this formula of much under 80. For example, the International 14, with a hull and equipment weight of about 275 lb. and a crew weight of 350 lb., works out at 101. The difference in resistance due to added weight, *i.e.*, increased displacement, is thus very great. For example, a 25-ft. hull with a displacement ratio of 40 would have just half the wave-making resistance at a speed of 6.25 knots as a hull of the same length with a displacement ratio of 160. Obviously Uffa Fox's dictum that weight belongs only in steam rollers has some merit. In addition Robert Bavier, in his articles on the planing sailboat (*Faster Sailing*, 1955), points out that few boats with a length-displacement value of over 120 plane very readily. While weight is not the only factor which influences planing, it is a very important one.

Lateral Resistance

To understand the forces affecting a boat while sailing consider a 14-ft. boat sailing to windward at 4½ knots in a 12-knot breeze. The crew is sitting on the rail to keep the heel down to zero. By calculating the probable weight, and position, we find that the boat is subject to a leeway-producing force of approximately 50 lb. Of this force the rudder absorbs a certain amount, probably about 5 lb., in the form of weather helm. Calculation shows that a weather helm of about 4 to 5 degrees gives the best relationship between lift and drag on the rudder blade. We are left with a centerboard which must resist almost all of the remaining leeway-producing force.

Centerboards

The centerboard acts as a true airfoil; like any true airfoil the centerboard produces lift and drag. Therefore a certain amount of airfoil data may be used in determining the effective shape and size of a centerboard, and for comparative purposes we may use the lift and drag formulas of wing sections to find the relative efficiency of centerboards.

Four factors govern the efficiency of a centerboard. These are the section, the size, the shape, and the angle of incidence. The best section seems to be one closely approximating the N.A.C.A. 0006.

This airfoil is 6 per cent as thick as it is wide (1 in. thick for a 17-in.-wide board). It has a relatively blunt leading edge with a radius of approximately 0.40 per cent of the chord and the maximum thickness about 30 per cent back from the leading edge. The trailing edge is long and very thin. Don't underestimate the importance of a knifelike trailing edge. Available data indicates that an airfoil of this shape will have significantly less drag for a given amount of lift than a flat plate. The exact shape of section need not conform with micrometer accuracy to N.A.C.A. standards. Any shape of these proportions which is smooth and free of ripples seems to do quite nicely. Remember to keep the center of maximum thickness well forward, however. Experiments I have tried with so-called "laminar flow" sections, which have their maximum thickness well back, have not worked out well on existing boats.

Leading and trailing edges of boards and rudders seem vitally important. There is much argument over the proper shape for a leading edge. Many experts advise razor-sharp surfaces. I feel that however effective these seagoing sabers may be for seaweed chopping, they are not a good idea for efficiency at normal boat speeds. Sharp leading edges stall much more easily than rounded ones, sinces the sharp edge tends to break the water away from the surface while the rounded one makes it cling (observe the behavior of water on the spoon under the tap). Since at the start of a race and after every tack a boat moves very slowly until she gathers way, the board can easily stall and cause much increased drag. A round leading edge discourages this. Once the boat is up to speed, the sharp edge may have a slight advantage, but I have never been able to find any perceptible difference in experiments with the two types. With rudders in centerboarders, since they are often used rather abruptly, I favor an even rounder leading edge than on the board.

Trailing edges are less complicated. They should be as sharp as you can make them. In really hot groups, such as the Interclub Frostbite Dinghy fleet at Larchmont, the trailing edges of both board and rudder on the best boats are so sharp that they can often be broken off with the fingers. Such fine surfaces are obviously a nuisance to maintain, but they pay off in race results. The necessity of a sharp trailing edge may be seen if you slant first a round-edged then a square-edged board under a water tap. You will see that the water tends to follow the rounded edge and stick to it, whereas it breaks cleanly away from the sharp edge.

The N.A.C.A. 0006 shows a lift coefficient of 0 at 0 degrees angle of attack and a maximum lift of about .8 at 10 degrees angle of attack. Using these coefficients in the formula $L = \frac{1}{2}\delta v^2 sc_2$, where $L =$ lift, $\delta =$ the mass density of water, $V =$ speed in feet per second, $S =$ area in square feet, and $C =$ the coefficient of lift, one may determine the angle of leeway which the hull must make for the centerboard to prevent further drift. It is essential to recognize that the board does not begin to work at all until the whole boat moves bodily to leeward.

If class rules allow any latitude in the size and shape of the board, consider the advantages of the very long, thin configuration. At an angle of incidence of 8 degrees a board of an aspect ratio (length/width) of 1 has only half the lift of a board having an aspect ratio of 4. I have tried an experimental board of an aspect ratio of 7 with considerable success. The average dagger board or high-performance centerboard has an aspect ratio of 4 or under. The added efficiency of a high aspect ratio board or rudder may allow you to cut down on the surface area of these high skin-resistance items quite markedly.

In 14's an experimental board two-thirds the standard area has shown a theoretical efficiency 25 per cent better than the standard board, an improvement which tests in light to moderate airs seem to bear out.

The other major key to increased centerboard lift seems to rest on controlling the fourth efficiency factor, the angle of incidence. Boatmen of 100 years ago knew this and shaped their centerboard trunks accordingly. If the forward end of the trunk is made wide and the after end narrow, the board will operate at a positive angle of incidence, thus eating out to windward. Since many class rules will not allow this simple and effective road to efficiency and since the large amount of turbulence set up by the wide trunk may prove detrimental, other ways of accomplishing the same objective may be necessary.

The board can be made to angle to windward by placing two small blocks, one on either side of the board, about two thirds of the way aft from the leading edge and arranged so that they will be just inside the bottom of the trunk when the board is full down. These blocks should fill the entire width of the trunk so that the board has the least possible amount of play at this point. This system causes the blocked part of the board to stay in the middle of the trunk as the water pressure comes against it while the free forward part of the board flops over against the windward side of the trunk. The effectiveness of this block idea will be enhanced if one shaves off the upper after corner of the board in the trunk until it is as thin in section as possible. This system of producing a jibing board works best on relatively narrow boards in wide centerboard trunks (see *Fig. 1*).

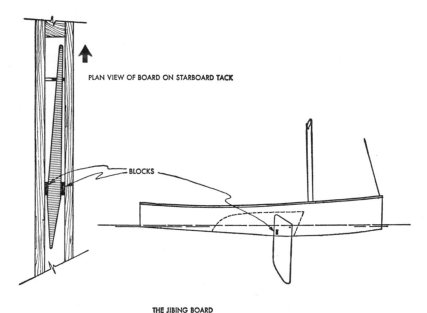

PLAN VIEW OF BOARD ON STARBOARD TACK

BLOCKS

THE JIBING BOARD

Fig. 1

It is also possible to control incidence by adjusting the angle to which the board is lowered. The swept-back board will twist to produce a negative angle of attack which increases leeway as it reduces the board's lift. The cure is to lower the board until the leading edge is straight up and down, or, if you want a favorable twist at the lower end, to rake the board forward of vertical. The effect of this twisting is far from negligible. *Many boats which just "don't go to windward" are suffering from boards which twist in the slot or are warped to a negative angle of incidence.* Nothing can be more detrimental. The replacement of a broken board with a warped one in a 14 National Championship dropped one boat from a 3–4 in the first two races to an 18–22 in the subsequent two.

On boats such as Lightnings and Comets which prohibit the use of gaskets, the centerboard slot should be made as narrow as possible to reduce the resistance of this opening in the hull. Boats using the more efficient wooden boards generally have rubber gaskets, which keep the water from surging in and out of the trunk. The best sort of gasket seems to be the rubber-impregnated fabric variety. Straight rubber perishes very easily. When putting on gaskets, stretch the rubber as tightly as possible fore and aft before fastening down. Opinion varies on whether the lips of the gaskets should meet each other or overlap. I've tried both without noticing a significant difference.

Rudders

Much of what I have said about boards applies also to rudders. I have a suspicion that a rudder with a long narrow blade of very low area may prove more efficient than the present low aspect ratio types. The most efficient section for rudders is probably the same as that suggested for centerboards. Considerations of strength make ¾ in. about the minimum for thickness of both boards and rudders if they are to be made of wood. Thinner ones seem to have a poorer lift-drag ratio, anyway.

Rudders have for many years been made in a shape that is difficult to make, lacking in strength at the neck, and lacking in area at the bottom where area is needed most. Lack of low rudder area can be quite exciting in a high, short, following sea; jibes under such conditions are especially stimulating. A better rudder with the same wetted surface area and of less weight may be made by extending the full blade width into the head without narrowing the neck and carrying greater area further aft and down by cutting the bottom off flat without rounding the corners. Remember also that the further aft the center of rudder area, the less rudder angle and resistance is needed for a given turn.

WEIGHT

By now the reader should be convinced that weight and fast boats don't mix. The only kind of weight which is helpful is that which is in the form of ballast. The more weight in ballast and the less in the boat and rig, the better. The rule makers often limit the sailor's natural desire to lighten things by placing a minimum on the weight of the boat. In most classes this measurement is of the stripped hull without board, rudder, rig, etc.

Generally one can find quite a few pounds' worth of movables and removables which can be taken out to bring an overweight hull down to trim. I once had an old International 14 from which I removed almost 50 lb. to bring her to weight. Hulls which are already down to weight can often be improved by moving as much of the weight as possible from the ends and replacing it amidships. Weight in the ends of a boat tends to make her pitch badly in a sea. It's no accident that winning crews seem to be sitting on each other's laps much of the time. A hull which has been purposely brought down to below weight can be brought up to the right figure (in some classes) with lead correctors placed amidships.

In most racing classes all the top boats will have hulls which weigh within a few pounds of one another. This is not true of their equipment, however. A table showing the weight of the equipment which went into two International 14's last year follows:

	A	B	
Mast	24 lb.	16 lb.	
Boom	10 "	8 "	(hollow)
Rudder	4½ "	2 "	(hollow rudder head)
Tiller	2 "	1½ "	(spruce rather than oak)
Centerboard	10 "	6 "	(better tapered)
C.B. hoisting rig	3 "	½ "	(simpler)
Sails	15 "	15	
	68½	49	

Other items such as life preservers, battens, etc., are fairly similar. You will note that the difference is just shy of 20 lb., a substantial figure, especially if the saving is translated into crew weight. Incidentally, both these boats sailed through a six-month season with no breakdowns of any sort, indicating that lighter gear does not necessarily constitute a hazard.

Most sail enthusiasts agree that weight in masts is not a good idea, but fairly few go to any lengths to save weight in rudders or centerboards. The argument is generally that these items, being below the center of gravity, need not be lightened. Heavy centerboards are held to be a virtue as an aid to stability. An examination of the way a centerboarder is sailed will show the fallacy of this reasoning. At the maximum angle of heel of 5 degrees, which is the most a winning centerboarder assumes, the center of gravity of a 50-lb. board moves to windward something less than six inches. The same weight in the form of a husky crew can be moved to windward by over three feet. Where would you like your weight?

Canadian International 14 sailors still retain weighted boards for certain wind conditions. They find that in a short, steep, lake chop the weight of a heavy board down low seems to pendulum the boat through, forcing the bow up and over as it slams into a wave. Under just such conditions last summer in the Canadian championships, I finally managed to pull away from Eric Olsen after I had let about 60 lb. of water into the boat through the bailers. With the extra weight low down the boat seemed to drive through the sea just a bit better. A heavy board for heavy weather would be a more seamanlike way of accomplishing the same objective.

MASTS

For many years wood has been the traditional small boat mast material. In recent years aluminum and various combinations of wood and aluminum have become popular. The aluminum sticks seem to offer many advantages. First, their wall cross sections are generally only about 75 per cent as thick as wood, a difference that spells less windage and less disturbance of the flow of wind to the sail. Second, they are generally cheaper than wooden sticks of the same weight. Third and most important, aluminum, unlike spruce, is not temperamental. Two years ago I built a beautiful spruce mast for my 14. After sailing for four or five months, this absolutely straight stick took a decided hook of about three inches which I was quite unable to remove. A year later for reasons best known to itself, the hook started to disappear. Now the mast is straight again. But for how long? Experiences of this sort have turned me and many others to aluminum.

Aluminum, however, at least in the smaller-sized sections, has not been available in the 20- to 25-ft. lengths needed for most small boats. The joints which have had to be used are heavy and often cause a sharp bend in the mast, especially when reaching and running. Another difficulty has been the impossibility of tapering the mast, especially toward the head. The latter problem was met on many International 14's by using aluminum up to the jibstay and a tapered wooden upper mast. Unfortunately the joint still caused problems, although this method of masting gave the lightest stick with the least windage. The ideal mast would seem to be an aluminum section tapered at the head (now available from England).

Another material for masting which has come into use lately is Fiberglas. So far I have seen no masts for small boats built solely of glass, but many wooden masts are reinforced with glass cloth. I tried Fiberglassing the 9-ft. wooden head of my International 14 mast this year, only to find that the shrinking of the epoxy split the after wall of the stick along the inside of the slot. The mast in question had only a ³⁄₁₆ in. wall thickness, which was probably too light to support the pressures of the drying epoxy. I have used glass cloth on thicker sections with great success. Perhaps the greatest drawback of glass is the difficulty of forming any exact estimate of the strength provided and of the considerable weight which is added. On the masthead previously mentioned, the Fiberglas added a third to the weight of the bare wood.

A pear-shaped section seems to be best for small boat masts. Captain J. H. Illingworth, R.N., in his excellent book *Offshore* (1949), has a comparison of oval and pear sections which shows the pear to be substantially more efficient for windward work.

Staying

The staying of masts offers the engineer-sailor a chance to work out some substantial improvements on existing practice. The essential factor in staying is the attainment of consistent strength throughout the rig. There is no point to having a mast which will stand 4,000 lb. of compression if it is to supported by an ⅛ in. shroud which will break at 2,200 lb. (A study of Skene's *Elements of Yacht Design* will give the amateur a useful knowledge of elementary stress analysis.) In general the object of rigging is to hold the mast up and relatively straight while at the same time imparting as little additional load as possible. The accompanying diagrams show five common types of small boat rig (see *Fig. 2*). The No. 1 rig is the type commonly found on Snipes, Jet 14's and Penguins. This rig does not seem suitable to rig over 115 sq. ft. of sail, as the mast must be made very heavy in order to stand without additional support. For smaller sail areas, however, this rig offers both simplicity and very low windage. Mast No. 2 is rigged in a way very popular with Canadian 14 sailors. Under the enormous sail plans carried (about 175 sq. ft. of actual sail), these masts bend fantastically—but the boats go like smoke. Here the lower mast finds support from the diamond shrouds but the 8½-ft. upper mast is left to fend for itself.

One top Canadian skipper, Bud Whittaker, went through four of these in 1956, so the strength is a bit doubtful. Lately many of these rigs have grown a second set of diamonds which support the upper mast. The No. 2 rig, however, can be very light, some as light as 16 lb. for a 24-ft. stick. The diamonds, with their short spreaders, add greatly to the compression.

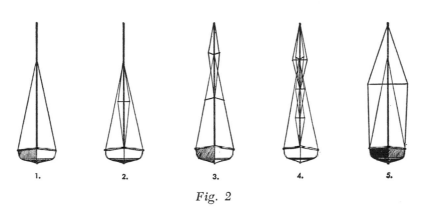

Fig. 2

The No. 3 rig has become increasingly popular. The mast gains support at the mid-point from a spreader which thrusts against the shroud. This system adds no compression to the mast and is thus better than the use of diamonds. The upper part of the mast is supported by a V jumper. This rig seems the best possible if a big genoa prevents wide spreaders.

The No. 4 rig shows a plan similar to that of the Thistles, Highlanders, and older 14's. The two faults of this rig are its very high windage and its high compression of the mast. These masts bend alarmingly and frequently break at a point near the middle spreader. The extra weight and cost of the maze of rigging must also be considered. One of these masts for an International 14 weighs 8 lb. more than the mast shown in No. 3. It has 80 per cent more windage than No. 3. The No. 2 has 40 per cent more windage than No. 3 due to the thick mast section which is essential to the unsupported topmast.

The rig shown in No. 5 is used by both Comets and Stars with excellent results. The long spreader keeps compression loads so low that the Comets may safely use $\frac{1}{16}$ in. shrouds. Unfortunately this rig is not adaptable to boats with genoas.

Flexible Spars

In recent years the problem of what the British call the "bendy" mast has come to the fore. This is a mast which may be bent by the use of the kicking strap, or the mainsheet to flatten the main in heavy weather. The usual rigging plan is similar to No. 2 or No. 5 above. If you cast your mind back twenty years or so, you will remember that the Stars went through a great dither of "bendyism"after the German *Pimm* managed to win four out of five races in the 1937 International Championships. Those of you who have seen late model Stars will have noticed that the masts bend very little. Star sailors now agree with *Pimm's* skipper who believed that the bending was largely coincidental. In the last two years I have tried everything from an extreme "bendy" to a fairly stiff stick on my 14 without proving anything conclusive, since few bendy sticks bend to the same degree two days running. The sailmaker may need a sixth sense in designing the main. In spite of (or because of?) this a sailmaker tells me that he thinks the bendies are better. The extreme bendy masts often throw a hard spot into the main just ahead of the battens. The best of the Canadian 14 sailors go extremely well with such a rig, however—one wonders whether because of or in spite of. Neither the stiff nor the bending mast is very straight in a breeze. Those ruler-straight masts that the writers on racing always insist on, seem out of the question on a boat like a 14 unless one is ready to pay heavily in weight and windage. Fine points of theoretical efficiency seem wasted in a blow when the mainsail luffs wildly. In moderate weather even the bending rigs stay fairly straight. Apparently you pays your money and you takes your choice. . . . You may find yourself paying your money more frequently on "bendies," as they break more easily.

In recent years the many experts on the subject of speed in sailboats have held widely divergent opinions on whether the mast should be free to float at the partners or tightly constrained by wedges. Many time Snipe champion Ted Wells and Jack Knights, Olympic alternate of the last games, argue that the mast will stay much straighter laterally if it is allowed to lie in the rigging, supported only at the step. Although this is true, the amount of lateral bend which partners will put upon the mast is far less than the forward bend which the thrust of the gooseneck puts on the unrestrained mast. A partner which restricts forward but not lateral movement may be a satisfactory solution. The mast supported by the step may be considered a pin-ended column, while the one supported at both step and partner is fixed-ended. Standard engineering tables tell us that the fixed-end column has double the strength of the pin end. A mast partner which restrains forward movement at least prevents the tight kicking strap from turning the mast into a gigantic bow with the boom as the arrow. I am convinced that eliminating this bow and arrow effect results in a tighter jibstay and therefore better windward ability. Even in quite light weather I find that a force of about 50 lb. on the kicking strap results in markedly better pointing ability due to the tighter jibstay.

The question of loose versus tight rigging has caused much learned discussion among the pundits. Ted Wells goes as far as to say exactly how loose the shrouds should be on a Snipe, while Eric Olsen of the American Olympic team likes to be able to play a tune on his rigging. The loose-shroud school feels that the mast will probably be straighter and that the boat will go faster on a run when the slack shrouds allow the masthead to go forward. They also mutter darkly about how tight rigging "kills" a boat in some strange way. Tight-wire proponents contend that the tight shrouds have a backstay effect which tightens the jibstay upwind. The jib luff certainly stands a lot better on a beam reach when the shrouds are tight. Boats that plane readily seem to go best with tight rigging, while the heavier Snipes and Lightnings seem happier with more floppy rigs.

Weight and Windage

For many years sailors have realized that saving weight aloft is of primary importance in a racing boat. In trying to save that last ounce, you will find that paring down the walls of your stick to paper thinness saves very little weight—spruce only weighs 27 lb. per cu. ft., while steel weighs 500 lb. per cu. ft., so even a small saving on steel rigging can be significant.

In the supreme weight consciousness of the last 30 years, many designers seem to have forgotten the importance of windage. Windage becomes especially important in the small centerboarder which is sailed at very nearly zero angle of heel most of the time. At such slight angles of heel the moment arm of weights aloft is quite small. The center of gravity of the rig is rarely as far outboard as the leeward rail. Windage, however, operates with a very great moment arm. In an International 14 the center of wind resistance is better than 11 ft. up. This offers the same heeling moment as equal weight held on the end of your boom when you are broad off. Over 3 lb. of weight must be added to the rig in order to get the heeling action of 1 lb. of windage. In short, if you have a choice between getting rid of weight and getting rid of windage on the small centerboarder, you had best consider letting the weight remain in order to reduce the windage. Fortunately you can usually reduce both at once.

A halyard lock reduces the compression on the mast by half the pull of the halyard. Most such locks are rather involved, and require pulls from precise angles. The one shown in the accompanying sketch (see *Fig. 3*) has no moving parts and requires only that the

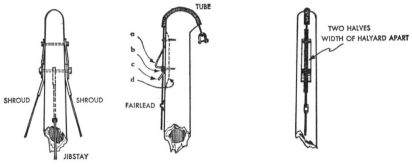

Fig. 3

pull be straight (controlled by a fair-lead). It is suitable for internal halyards. It operates by having a ball, swaged onto the halyard, slide up the ramp "a" formed by twin pieces of metal. As the ball clears the top of the ramp, it falls into the valley "b" with an audible click; the halyard end may then be released. To lower, the sail is hoisted another inch until the ball drops over the end of the second ramp "c." The ball can then slide back through a small tunnel "d" under the halyard lock. The only difficulty with this fitting has been that enthusiastic hoisting may override both ramps at once. A bit of tape on the lower end of the halyard helps to tell when you are getting close.

A tang to attach rigging to the mast seems useless in any boat of under Star size. If an eye-type swaged fitting is used on the wire, the bolt may be passed directly through the eye. Bending loads may be relieved by placing a 4-in. strap of light stainless outside the swaging and bolting it to the mast higher up (see *Fig.* 3). By drilling a hole in the foreside of the mast as shown, the same bolt can hold the jibstay and the shrouds, thus saving weight. Jibstays, incidentally, take little strain on the average racing boat since the luff of the jib is set so tightly. Wire $\frac{1}{16}$ in. wide seems more than adequate for anything up to a Star.

Much weight and no little cost can be saved by eliminating turn-buckles. If plenty of holes are available in shroud chain plates, all tightening can be done with the jibstay. Diamonds and jumpers can be tensioned by adjustable spreader ends made by inserting a bolt into an aluminum spreader tube with a nut against the spreader end.

BOOMS

As in masts a prime controversy exists concerning the bending or straight approach in booms. The bending boom is supposed to take the fullness out of the foot of the sail in blowing weather. Unless your sailmaker has a long, close acquaintance with your particular boom, however, you may find that your boom bends too much for the sail, causing a ruinous hard line from mid-foot to luff. Like bending masts, the bending booms are wonderful when they work well. However, they are expensive to buy, difficult to build, and break rather readily, making life exciting in a breeze. A fairly stiff boom tends to transmit more strain to the jibstay and more bend to the mast, which will flatten the sail a lot quicker than bending the boom.

The advent of the kicking strap or boom vang has changed the shape of booms a great deal. Since an effective kicking strap on even a 14 will have several hundred pounds of pressure on it at times, the boom must be very strong at the point of attachment of the kicker. Generally the boom has its maximum dimension here, tapering toward each end. A rather narrow, deep boom with its extra sail area for off-wind work will pay. The weight of the boom does not usually fall under the rules. Therefore weight saved here may be very helpful—particularly as the boom's weight can have a considerable heeling moment when on a reach.

HIKING DEVICES

All small, high-performance boats depend on effective hiking to maintain proper sailing lines and permit planing, as well as for sur-vival. The effective hiking aids include: muscle, toe straps, hiking handles ("ladies' aid" to Bermudans), hiking boards, the flying trapeze, and now the second hull.

Muscle in crews is a wonderful commodity. If you know any hydrocephalic weight lifter whose muscle does not lie entirely between the ears, you are obviously all set and may omit this section entirely. Unfortunately most of us seem stuck with mere mortals for crews and cannot rely on sheer muscle as an effective hiking measure. Effective hiking depends on moving the center of gravity of the body as far as possible from the center line of the boat in a horizontal direction. This means that the weight must be kept low. Every inch of heel or every inch the crew moves upward moves the center of weight closer to the center of the boat. At 90 degrees' heel, weight on the rail has no righting effect whatsoever. The main must be eased quickly in a knockdown so that crew weight does not lose its effectiveness. On small boats such as Fireflies or 14's an ability to come in from the rail quickly often overrides the value of extreme hiking. Capsizes to windward seem humorous only to your competitors. Lying along the boot top in a Star boat sprawl is thus best eliminated on the small boat. One very effective hiking position entails hooking an inboard toe under the thwart while placing the outboard foot (with nonskid shoe) on the topsides as a brace. This position has the advantage of being relatively comfortable and getting one leg (15 to 20 lb.) right out of the boat.

Toe straps, fore and aft or athwartships, make life much easier for the crew. The thwartships rig usually entails an awkward twist of the ankle, is frequently in the way when tacking or jibing, and restricts fore-and-aft movement of the crew. All these problems may be escaped by the use of fore-and-aft straps. These are usually rigged from the forward end of the centerboard trunk to a slot on the thwart about 6 to 8 in. outboard of the trunk and then back to either the after end of the trunk or to the keelson right aft. Putting the straps right down in the bilge may result in a less tiring leg angle. If you use this bilge mounting, arrange some rig to hold the straps about 3 in. up so that you can get your toes under them easily. A light piece of shock cord works well for this. I find that having the straps lower and farther outboard, so that the rail comes under the back of the knees, gives better hiking power. With such a rig the thighs lie along the topsides while the trunk can be out parallel to the water. Your weight assumes the most effective possible position in this way and windage is reduced. Since the strong stomach muscles take some of the strain, the legs will last longer.

The ladies' aid, or hiking handle, usually consists of a short lever which extends about 18 in. up from the rail, providing support for the crew. It works best in puffy weather since it allows the crew to come back into the boat rapidly. It also serves as a substitute jib sheet winch if you wrap the sheet around it a few times and sway back. The best hiking bars are hinged at or below the rail and flop inboard along the thwart when not in use. A short aluminum tube with a fitting which engages a track on the rail, kept from going too far outboard by a wire leading to the center line, is often used. The folding kind of lever can be made from ax handles very cheaply. Hiking handles are the only legal hiking aid in many classes which have rules prohibiting hiking apparatus from extending outboard of the rail.

Undoubtedly the most comfortable and effective piece of hiking gear is *the sliding seat or hiking board.* This is a board which extends across the boat on a slide, arranged so that it will protrude several feet to windward. Decked canoes have used this rig for years and it has recently appeared on the English Hornet Class. The size of the board, together with the fact that it takes up much of the useful space in the cockpit, does not encourage its wide acceptance.

A much lighter and simpler piece of hiking gear has recently made its appearance, *the trapeze.* A trapeze requires only a wire from the hounds, an agile crew member, and a strong belt. The Flying Dutchman and 5-0-5 already use the trapeze, and I hope that other two-man classes will soon adopt it, thus ending the hunt for mastadon-like crew members. While the trapeze looks rather athletic to the uninitiated, it is a positive dream of comfort compared to effective hiking of the older sort. It actually provides opportunity for the girls and other lightweights to get to the weather mark with the heavy-weights. One caution: be sure to keep your feet well apart with the after knee slightly bent when planing. If you don't you'll have difficulty coming back in when the wind lightens and will look ever so funny whizzing around the jibstay when the boat gets stopped by a sea.

If, at the end of this lengthy account, the reader feels he has got but a ha'pennyworth of practicality for an intolerable deal of theory, let him remember one thing: *knowing what to do will give you a boat which is as fast as any, but only the knowledge of the why's will allow you to make that next step to the boat that is faster than any.*

Aim to try to improve the good and eliminate the useless. If you take care of the ounces and seconds, the pounds and the minutes will take care of themselves.

5. Crewing

By WILLIAM ROBINSON, Montreal,
with a Postscript by Mrs. Donald R. McVittie, Seattle

Somebody once described the ideal crew as "strong as a gorilla, light as a cat, and with every tooth a marline spike." In planing hulls it seems equally important that the ideal crew should be able to alter his weight as the race progresses. Whatever his attributes, he should never duck an incoming wave—it is imperative to the skipper's morale that he keep his cigarettes dry (these same cigarettes might prove very useful during the spinnaker run in finding the wind on a calm day).

By all odds the most important prerequisite for a crew is that he have an irrepressible, optimistic, and competitive spirit. The skipper should not have to reiterate that a race is not over until *his boat* has crossed the finish line. The smaller the boat, the more contagious the mood of those aboard. The satisfaction that comes from knowing that you tried your darnedest may be all you salvage from a bad day. This will do more to ensure that such days occur infrequently than anything else you may learn. The practice of trying to bully your competition, however, lacks sophistication and usually veils insecurity.

In any boat the crew must complement the skipper. He must know when the skipper should be encouraged and the circumstances under which he should be restrained from making bad decisions. All this must be done with tact and discretion, since under no circumstances must antagonism arise between the helmsman and the crew. This is the responsibility of the crew.

The ideal crew should have just as much enthusiasm about the boat on shore as he has for it during a race. While major repairs are the owner's responsibility, it is up to the crew to see that the boat is spotlessly clean inside and out and that a check is made of standing and running rigging as well as whippings, lashings, sheets, etc. He should fix anything that can be fixed from the skipper's tool box. While most skippers will at least check the final prerace rigging, the best crews should be familiar enough with the skipper's ways to be able to rig the boat just as he would. The skipper can then, if necessary, devote all his energy to any unexpected problems which may arise in prerace planning. As to the postrace celebrating, the crew should not start until the boat is back on the trailer, even though the skipper may find it essential to work on a small libation. In a 14-ft. International hull the ideal crew is about six feet tall; the combined weight of skipper and crew, between 325 and 375 lb. This length gives the crew lots of leverage while hiking as well as the necessary reach for clearing canvas and setting spinnakers. All planing hulls go fastest when held absolutely flat.

NORMAL OPERATION OF THE BOAT

When I was discussing this chapter with my skipper, we both agreed that a good crew should have a thorough knowledge of the racing rules. We also agreed that he should have a general knowledge of racing tactics. He should also observe and be able to recognize instantly what the competitors are planning, in order that their designs may be thwarted if possible. My advice is: do some thinking yourself and don't badger your skipper with details and idle speculation. Some skippers, however, might not agree with me and would rather be informed of every detail. Therefore, *know your skipper.*

Whenever boats converge, overtake, or are being overtaken, the crew should know all maneuvers that can take place and be prepared to carry out his duties without any instructions from the skipper. Some examples of this are as follows:

1. Hard on the Wind

   a) Close crossing—the boat must be kept absolutely flat so as to get maximum speed. Yet the crew must always be prepared for the last second tack if required.

   b) Lee bow—after the tack, the boat must be hiked flatter than flat. If this is not done, the skipper cannot work to weather so as to put the competitor in his back draft.

   c) Port tack bearing away—the jib must be eased as the skipper bears off. As soon as the starboard tack boat has crossed, the jib is hardened in and the boat hiked flat so that the skipper can take advantage of the draft created by the passing boat.

2. Off the Wind

   a) Passing to leeward—this maneuver is usually the combination of skipper, crew, and wave. The job of the crew is to make sure that the boat is flat when the right wave comes along so that you surge through the lee of the weather boat.

   b) Passing or defending to weather—the board must be continuously lowered and the sails kept full. By full, I mean that the sails are sheeted to the speed of the luff. If the sheeting is done too fast or too slowly the attack or defense is ruined. This, of course, is standard in any boat but in a planing hull speed increases rapidly so that it becomes necessary to trim the jib when each plane starts; then ease it when you come off the plane or surge.

During the weather leg the crew should report on the position of the other boats and any maneuvering that might have an effect on his boat. When on port tack it is a good idea to count the boats underneath you. If you lose one, report it to the skipper and make sure he takes a look if you cannot see under the jib yourself. If you fail to do this, be prepared to abandon ship, for it usually means that you are about to be cut in half.

A crew worth his salt will be able to recognize the boats of the favored competitors, as well as those who may have local knowledge, and keep his skipper informed of their movements. Be prepared to turn in your Bilge Boys' Union Badge if you let your skipper go out to sea when the local boys are working the shore. He should also be able to report as to whether the boats ahead or on the other tack are getting lifted or headed.

During the leeward legs, when he isn't wiping water out of his eyes, the crew should be looking only at the canvas or for marks. In a planing hull, as every crew knows, the following are about the only words heard during a race: "Up board . . . Down board . . . In jib . . . Out jib . . . Pull the Guy . . . Ease the sheet—for . . . don't let that spinnaker collapse!" This section deals in a general way with the four primary responsibilities of the crew, which are handling the centerboard, trimming the hull, setting and sheeting headsails, and keeping the boat dry. In order to give yourself more time for a smoke (!), try carrying out the following operations before you get barked at.

Handling the Centerboard

Centerboard tackles are of an endless variety and each has its idiosyncrasies. The only thing they all have in common is that they get fouled at the least propitious moments. Try to learn the peculiarities of your tackle before you get to the leeward mark.

The exact position of the board will eventually be determined by the skipper but, on reaching a mark, other matters may be more pressing. The crew can safely raise or lower the board as follows:

1. *Bucking*—the board is always near vertical.

2. *Reaching*—approximately 45 degrees (increase degrees for close reach; decrease degrees for broad reach). The board should always be as high as possible without drifting to leeward. Also, the faster you go, the less board you need.

3. *Running*—all the way up. At times it will be found that a small amount of board gives stability and prevents rocking.

4. Jibe or panic stations—board up.

Trimming the Hull

Weight distribution in the boat, like the position of the board, depends upon the strength of the wind as well as the point of sailing. The skipper with his hand on the helm is usually unable to move rapidly and thus the first and all minor corrections of trim are the responsibility of the crew.

The following is a general outline only and varies with the skipper's weight, wave conditions, boat design, etc. It may also vary considerably with the skipper's current theories. The following suggestions should serve as a point of departure.

1. *Bucking.*

   a) Very heavy wind—boat hiked flat with weight as far forward as waves permit. The ideal fore-and-aft trim varies from hull to hull with the periodicity of the waves and with the total weight in the boat. For example, boats with very buoyant sections at the bow or stem must be ballasted so that these ends do not bury into the seas, as this will only cause excessive "hobbyhorsing." In general, increasing the distance between skipper and crew will slow the oscillations of the hull and vice versa. This factor must be adjusted to the character of the seas encountered.

   b) Moderate wind—boat hiked flat with bow in about 2 in. (14-ft. International)

   c) Very light wind—enough heel to give the sails some shape, and bow in about 2 in. (14-ft. International)

2. *Reaching.*

   a) Very heavy wind—boat hiked flat with weight aft so that boat planes with bow free.

   b) Moderate wind—boat hiked flat with weight amidships so that the boat heels just enough to give the sails some shape.

   c) Very light wind—again the weight is forward and to leeward so that the boat heels just enough to give the sails some shape.

3. *Running*—the weight is distributed as in reaching. However, in very light airs you do not want any heel, as this will make spinnaker handling extremely difficult. The crew should also be far enough forward so that the transom is just out of water. The problem of weight distribution in the boat is similar to bucking in heavy winds.

Setting and Trimming Headsails

It is here that the crew comes into his own. While to the novice handling the sails seems to be the most challenging and exciting aspect of the crew's job, the veterans are those who put the most effort into the seemingly less dramatic functions which have already been discussed. In close competition every detail counts, and the little things which are often neglected spell the difference.

No sheet should ever be cleated in a dinghy.

When reaching, the jib sheet should be held in the hand—which eliminates smoking on this leg of the course. To ease tired hands, one turn around a snubbing winch is permitted in a blow. *Never cleat the jib.* (An exception arises when bucking in light and moderate breezes; then the hand muscles get tired and the jib eases out undetected.) The wind varies just as much off the wind as it does on. Also the apparent wind direction goes forward as your speed increases. As a result of these variables, the crew is always *easing* the jib out or *slowly* pulling it in. A good indicator is small pieces of yarn stuck to the jib where the miter joins the luff. Don't forget it is not illegal to use feet or arms to get the best flow in very light airs.

There are two circumstances when the boat is hard on the wind that the jib may be very slightly eased to advantage. One is in very heavy or very light winds when increased speed is necessary to drive through wave conditions. The other is in moderate airs when it is necessary to sail through waves kicked up by power boats.

Now for spinnakers! One thing of which you can be absolutely certain is that the moment you take your eyes off the spinnaker it will collapse. *Don't take your eyes from the spinnaker.* The following points (the first three from the instructions drawn up by Hard, the sailmaker) should help keep the spinnaker full and hence keep the skipper's blood pressure down.

1. On a dead run the spinnaker pole should be worked back to windward as far as possible so that you expose as much of the spinnaker as possible to the windward side of the boat. Dropping the pole in very light air and raising the pole in heavier as the spinnaker spreads out will give you maximum efficiency. Also the spinnaker halyard can be released slightly as the wind increases.

2. Setting is probably most difficult when there is not enough wind to fill out the spinnaker. In this case, the most important thing is just to expose a flat, stable surface of cloth to pick up any slight breeze that may occur. To do this, the spinnaker pole should be on the lowest setting on the mast and dropped below the horizontal so that there is a very slight tension on the luff. The head of the spinnaker should also be raised as close to the halyard block as it can go. If any fresh air comes in that will fill out the spinnaker, the pole should be immediately raised and the halyard eased off in accordance with the velocity.

3. The leech of a spinnaker while reaching should be treated

similarly to the leech of a jib. There is air flowing off the leech; and if the leech is too close to the main, it will backwind the main severely, rendering it useless. Therefore, the leech of the spinnaker should be kept between 3 and 4 ft. away from the leeward side of the main in order to cut interference to a minimum. Three steps will help keep the leech away from the main: lead the sheet all the way to the stern, drop off the halyard, and raise the pole as mentioned above.

4. One extra word of advice—*keep the clews level.*

ABILITY, ANTICIPATION, AND TECHNIQUE

One skipper's pet peeve about crews other than his regular is that *at critical moments he finds them fiddling with bits and pieces,* looking at blondes on that new Chris Craft, or just plain dreaming. Sound criticism. If a boat is to be a winner, the crew as well as the skipper must be in a winning frame of mind. Don't forget that optimism generates winners.

Before leaving the dock, the crew should check that the spinnaker pole, paddle, bailer, sponge, and life jackets are aboard and properly stowed. He should also ensure that his pockets, or the boat, contain "valuables" such as pliers, rope, marlin, shackles, knife, etc., for breakdown repairs. One or two aircraft bolts with lock nuts may also come in handy.

On the way to the starting line, a good crew automatically checks the front end of the boat. He makes sure that the spinnaker halyard is free, that the sheet and guy are properly reeved, and that the jib clips are properly fastened. He then checks the standing rigging to see if all the cotter pins are in place, jumpers and spreaders taped, etc.

Before the actual start of a race there is rarely much conversation, and what there is usually centers on the best place to start. While the skipper is maneuvering in close quarters, the crew should spend his (spare) time watching for wind shifts and the hoisting of signals on the committee boat. This is also the time for the crew to memorize the numbers and boats of the favored competitors. If the crew is expected to do the timing, the easiest way is to give the skipper 15-second intervals with a count down of the last 10 seconds. Do this quietly, just in case the boat alongside has fouled up his timing.

Beating

In order to explain the fine, as well as general, points of crewing, let's take a fast winning trip around a Swedish course. Since a boat has to tack at least once to reach the weather mark, the following are the points, in order of importance, which come up during the tacking maneuver:

1. Make sure the sheets are free before the maneuver starts—skipper not sitting on same.

2. Hold the jib until it just backs—if you hold it too long, you are sure to get bawled out.

3. Go with the boat—avoid excessive rolling during the tacking maneuver caused by shifting weight too rapidly.

4. Do not sheet the jib too flat too soon—this is delicate and only comes with experience. In normal weather try to leave 1 or 2 in. of sheet which can be sheeted in once the boat is full and bye. In heavy weather the jib must be sheeted flat as soon as possible. It is almost impossible to sheet in that extra inch or so once the tack is completed in a real blow.

5. In very light to light winds, the skipper usually makes the final decision as to how flat he wants the jib. In this case, the safe position for the crew is too full rather than too flat. The crew's movements also slow down as the wind velocity decreases. In extremely light airs, baby the jib around with your hands rather than rock the boat by tugging at the jib sheets.

A word of advice—if you have to look under the jib on this leg of the course, do so by hiking the boat flat, not by climbing inboard.

Rounding

Believe it or not, you eventually reach the weather mark. In the next 10 seconds all you have to do is get the board up, ease sheets, and adjust your weight to wind and wave conditions for the reach to the next mark. Since the boat has to be flat until the maneuver starts, by hiking a little further out and looking under the jib you can determine whether you will be tacking or merely easing sheets. When easing sheets, keep the jib continuously full—do not let it luff by easing too fast.

Once again, remember to go with the boat and avoid excessive rocking.

Reaching—Light to Moderate Airs

Most skippers like to sit comfortably on the weather rail and let the crew fend for himself. When this is the case, it is up to the skipper to keep the boat flat and also to do a fair amount of the fore-and-aft trimming. From his position on the board box or in the lee bilge, the crew is expected to trim the jib perfectly, hold the sheet in his hand, and not get decapitated by the kicking strap.

Testing the jib is best done by *slowly* easing it out until slight flutters appear just above the intersection of the miter and the forestay. These flutters are then taken out by sheeting. Only experience will tell how often this has to be repeated; however, since you are in the winning boat, the process is almost continual.

In very light airs the jib sheet is usually held in the hand, as the weight of the sheet will tend to make it collapse. When the wind increases, reaching leads are used since this will give a steadier sail. You also have to be prepared at a moment's notice to give the skipper a hand in keeping the boat flat.

Reaching—Planing

At this point the crew becomes more than ballast. Keeping the boat flat must be an instinctive reaction and the jib must occupy his undivided attention. When squalls hit, it is imperative to bear off and any tendency of the boat to heel will greatly hinder this procedure. It may even be necessary to anticipate the squall by an instant in order to prevent the boat from rounding up or broaching. If this happens, the plane is broken and before you get going again you will almost certainly find yourself in different company.

Planing hulls at least double their speed when on the plane; hence, the crew's movements have to be extremely rapid when rounding on to this leg of the course. It is imperative to get the board up and yourself aft and out in the least possible time. Since no time can be spent on detailed adjustment, the safe position for the board is too high, rather than not hoisted enough. The harder it blows, the less board is needed. In order for the hull to plane, the bow must be free, so move well aft.

The jib is the key in getting a boat planing. A 14-ft. International will plane with the jib filled and main luffing but not conversely. Besides having to change direction due to puffs, the skipper must sail each wave. He must also carry out tactical maneuvers, such as passing to weather or leeward. All this makes the tending of the jib a 100 per cent time-consuming job. On top of all these directional changes, the crew still has to test the trim of his jib exactly as he would under less windy conditions.

As if the above were not enough, the crew also has to sheet the jib to meet speed variations. The faster the boat goes, the more the apparent wind direction moves forward and the more the jib has to be sheeted in. Besides taking care of the puffs and lulls, the crew must remember to sheet the jib going down the waves and ease it off when climbing the other side.

Weight also has to be adjusted nearly as often as the jib is trimmed. With increased speed the weight is moved forward. In the lulls the crew moves in and aft. At all times the bow has to be just free and the boat flat. Another sure way to find yourself in different company is to let the boat heel to weather.

The key to speed is forward—aft—in—out.

Jibing

For a novice, jibing in a breeze of wind is usually the most terrifying experience he encounters in a small boat. If the following points are followed, they will take some of the danger out of the jibe but still leave all the thrill.

1. Board *must* be at least three-quarters of the way up. When jibing in heavy seas, it is an advantage to have the board completely housed. This prevents the boat from tending to trip over the centerboard but in so doing may allow the boat to skid to leeward. This of course is undesirable if a close rounding is necessary due to the proximity of other boats.

2. Crouch—do not sit—in the center of the boat.

3. In small boats flying jibes are routine. This means that the crew must have one hand on the boom and at the same time use the other to keep the jib drawing until the very last moment.

4. Jibe the main on the skipper's command or when the pressure is off the boom. Sometimes a considerable effort will be required to bring the boom amidships, but once the motion is started *duck*. You also lose your Bilge Boys' Union Badge if decapitated by the kicking strap.

5. Several wild rolls may occur during jibing and it is primarily the skipper's job to counteract them. However, it will not do any

good to tell him that while hanging on to your upturned boat. *Go with the boat.*

Spinnakers

Although there are dozens of fancy ways of stopping and stowing spinnakers in nets, turtles, bags, etc., my favorite method is just to throw it in the bow of the boat with the head on top. The sheet and guy are, of course, properly reeved and tied with slipknots within easy reach of the skipper. Nowadays the head of the spinnaker is always attached to the halyard, which snaps into a fitting at the stem. In most cases the skipper will do the hoisting. The crew's job is to see that it goes up without twists and fills as rapidly as possible. This is best accomplished by grasping the leeches of the sail and separating them as the sail is hoisted. The other method, tugging on the sheet and guy, is usually far slower. At the same time, if possible, the crew should be furling or stowing the jib.

If by any chance the sail goes up with a twist, grasp one leech and pull straight downward. This will usually clear the sail. Yanking on the sheet or guy is useless. When the spinnaker is clear and flying, the pole should then be attached.

When flying, a spinnaker should be continually tested for fullness by easing the sheet until a small area of backing occurs at the leading edge. Don't ever test for fullness by altering the position of the pole. If the sail should collapse, it may be filled again by rapidly taking in the sheet. If this does not succeed in filling the sail, it is probable that the pole is too far aft and it should be eased forward.

In general, the pole should always be at right angles to the direction of the wind. On planing and surfing runs, keeping the pole at right angles to the wind requires frequent and rapid changes of the pole position. For, it always seems to the crew, skippers will never learn that the shortest distance between two points is a straight line. When these conditions occur, one way to handle the spinnaker is to wrap the sheet and guy around each hand and steer the spinnaker in somewhat the way you would steer a car around a series of curves. This method has the added advantage that the lengths of the sheet and guy remain constant. On large bodies of water where the waves are regular, *easing the pole as you slant down the wave and pulling it back as you go up the other side should become automatic.*

From his position on the weather rail most of the crew's attention should be devoted to making the boat surf as the bow reaches the crest of the waves. It takes an experienced crew very little time to figure how far out he has to hike to get the boat absolutely flat for the start of the surf. Hence the actions of the crew on this leg of the course are easing the pole forward when he is hiking and back when he gets his weight slightly inboard for the sail up the next wave. A word of warning: it is impossible to surf if the boat has a weather heel on the top of the wave. This action of easing the pole forward as you hike out and bringing it back as you get slightly inboard requires plenty of practice but will pay large dividends when mastered. Since practically 100 per cent of the crew's attention is concentrated on the waves, the skipper should also keep an eye on the spinnaker whenever possible.

In medium weather both the sheet and guy are eased out so that the spinnaker flies well up in the air and the foot is well in front of the forestay. As the wind increases, the spinnaker is usually flattened; *i.e.,* the sheet and guy are sheeted until the foot of the spinnaker is almost against the forestay. If the boat starts to roll, it is imperative to flatten the spinnaker as soon as possible, for a spinnaker flying out in front will tend to increase the roll. Also, as stated earlier, a little board will help eliminate the roll.

Jibing a spinnaker is easy *if* the skipper stays dead downwind *and* the sheet and guy are fixed. The only danger arises when you are using a bungee topping lift and you forget to remove it first—many a fine "mouse" has been acquired through this oversight. All you have to do is face the mast and carry out the following instructions slowly:

1. Remove the topping lift if it is a bungee type.
2. Unfasten the pole at the mast.
3. Attach the free clew to the pole—the spinnaker is now attached to both ends of the pole.
4. Detach the old clew from the pole.
5. Attach the pole to the mast.
6. Attach the topping lift.

If the foregoing is carried out slowly, the spinnaker should not collapse. At other times it is often more advantageous to carry out the maneuver very fast, not caring if the spinnaker collapses. If the skipper stays dead downwind for a split second after the jibe, a hefty tug on the sheet will get the spinnaker flying again. When speed in jibing is necessary it usually means a luffing match is about to start. When it does, the pole is eased forward and the sheet sheeted to the speed of the luff.

Of course, the easiest way to take the spinnaker down is to let the halyard go and then let the skipper pick it up when it floats out from under the boat (not recommended for skippers with short arms). The main considerations when lowering a spinnaker are: Will it be required again? Is it free of the jib sheets? And is it being stowed on the same side from which it was hoisted?

In small boats the jib sheave and spinnaker sheave are side by side; consequently, the spinnaker is always hoisted from the same side and should, whenever possible, be lowered on that side. If this can be accomplished, then all you have to do is keep the spinnaker and pole free of the jib sheets. When stowing the pole make sure it is under the jib sheets; otherwise it is liable to fly out of the boat the next time you sheet the jib.

If you have jibed on the run, the problem becomes more complex. In light to medium weather, there is often time to take the spinnaker down on the same side from which it was hoisted and fasten the halyard to its fitting on the stem. In heavy weather or when time does not permit, just stow the spinnaker and unfasten the halyard. Once you are on the buck, the halyard will hang straight down in the lee of the main and may easily be retrieved and fastened to the foot of the mast.

When you are lowering a spinnaker that you expect to use again, it will pay dividends to take a shade extra time to make sure that it does not twist when being stowed in the boat. If luck is with you and it is being lowered on the "right" side, all you have to do is leave the head attached and run the halyard through its fitting on the stem. As long as the pole is under the jib sheets it is immaterial whether you take the time to detach it. When lowering on the "wrong" side, detach the halyard and throw it around the forestay. From there it can easily be retrieved and fastened to its fitting on the mast the next time you tack. Be careful of this maneuver in a blow, for the halyard may easily fly out and wrap around the forestay or shrouds of your competitor. When rehoisting don't forget the spinnaker has to come up from underneath the jib sheets.

No matter what is happening, the important thing is to get the board down to the bucking position just before you reach the lee-ward mark. You can still sail to weather with the spinnaker jammed if the board is down.

Given a competent skipper and the crew who has followed in-structions thus far, your boat should be well in the lead. The natural inclination is to try to maintain this position, which can usually be done unless something goes wrong and panic stations develop. If it is a line squall or thunderstorm, get the board part way up and be prepared to take off the main. From personal experience, I know that 14-ft. Internationals can safely be sailed in the direction of the finishing line under bare pole in winds over 60 m.p.h. If it is a break-down, immediately do the repairs that are necessary to getting the boat going in the direction of the next mark. Then tidy up the mess. Dumped boats and competent crews are not compatible.

POSTSCRIPT—CAN THE CREW COOK?
by Mrs. Donald R. McVittie, Seattle

From the above, it is obvious that the crew should be as familiar with rules and tactics as the helmsman. It is at this point that most skippers go into a corner and cry—the carefully trained crew, in-grate that he is, has gone and bought a boat of his own. The same well-trained crew is less likely to do this if that crew is a girl; if the girl is the skipper's wife, the crew problem is on its way to being permanently solved.

There is one aspect which the crew should know completely—the skipper. It is on this point particularly that a girl crew can make up for her lack in height and weight. Especially in a husband-wife team, there is achieved a total unity of thought which may at times approach extrasensory perception and which is worth more than an extra 60 or 80 lb. Although any permanent crew soon can sense what the skipper is about to do, tactically, few but the wife can sense that subtle transformation in the air that announces the guy is about to crack up; even fewer have the sense and courage to apply the proper therapeutic measures. And therein lies a warning: an ex-cellent crew for one helmsman may be no better than so much lead for another, at least until he or she adjusts all responses to the new skipper.

As an example, in the West Coast Championships at Newport Harbor in 1958, my lord and master, skipper and husband, crewed several races with the brand-new National 14 champion, George O'Day. Of course Don tried to pick his brains. But when we sailed together again, something was wrong. The boat didn't feel right, didn't have the right "go." I could sense it; Don knew it and as a result was tightening up. The situation was going from bad to worse. I mentally checked off all the possibilities and when I got as far as the centerboard, bells rang. There was the trouble—it was *all* the way down, but all. While other skippers of considerable note can make their boats move that way, our personal experience was to the contrary. I started with, "Let's raise the board."

"I want it down."

Silence. Two more boats went by. Time to grab the bull by the horns.

"Who the hell do you think you are, George O'Day?"

That brought action. The board came up an inch, the tension was broken, and we sailed from tenth back up to second.

Psychology aside, superior timing on the part of a light, lithe crew can more than offset the strength factor. A girl can anticipate by a fraction of a second the tacking manouver, both by the tactical situation and by the feel of the boat. With the proper release of the jib (and chapters have been written on this alone) from a cam cleat (a snubbing winch makes a clean, fast, efficient tack much more difficult), a well-timed shift of weight, and a truly fast—not too fast—take up on the jib, very little strength is required.

Many a skipper leaves his wife at home because "After all, she only weighs 115 pounds." Don't worry about her weight, just be sure she has *guts*. If the girl can hike and stay hiked, a good skipper can still get the boat to weather with the pack, even if its blowing 25 plus. Off the wind, then, there'll be shouting, because that light team will be off on the plane practically before the others have their boards up. And in addition there will always be those days when the flyweights will ghost past the gorillas!

6.

The NAYRU-IYRU Racing Rules

By STUART H. WALKER,
M. D.,
Annapolis

The racing rules adopted by the NAYRU in 1947 and subsequently revised by the IYRU in 1958 provide for the racing sailors of the world the new opportunity of racing under regulations specifically designed for the sport. These rules are not merely restrictions which reduce the risk of collision during yacht racing but are a framework within which the helmsman may (and should) plan and execute his tactics. Too often the rules are treated as mere restrictions, however, and insufficient advantage taken of them. Successful yacht racing demands the full exploitation of the rules to the purposes of the helmsman—and full exploitation demands full understanding.

Exploitation with understanding requires the extension of tactical plans sufficiently far into the future to include all possible actions and reactions of competitors. For instance, a yacht starting to windward may take maximum advantage of the rules by assuming (1) the starboard tack (2) slightly to leeward of the lay line to the windward mark. (3) If moving at sufficient speed to keep clear of and respond to the luffing of competitors farther to leeward, or overtaking to leeward (4) but slowly enough to permit variation in progress, (5) boats overtaken or overtaking to windward may be luffed above the windward mark or prevented from interfering with clear wind and (6) the line hit with the gun. When on the port tack before the wind and overtaking a competitor on the same tack, but unable to break through to leeward, (1) a jibe to starboard tack may provide the right-of-way advantage. This attack may force the overtaken yacht to jibe but if (2) at the time of this jibe the attacking yacht is sufficiently far advanced that her mast is forward of the competitor's helmsman, she may luff as she pleases, breaking through to leeward. Full exploitation of such situations requires complete and immediate recognition of the pertinent rules and of the probable favor which would be shown in case of doubt.

Although the new rules are very similar to the NAYRU rules which we have become accustomed to, there are several important differences. The new rules have been rearranged in what appears at first to be a more complicated form but they can be readily delineated into their former familar patterns. All of the eleven former NAYRU rules are included, and only three have been changed significantly. The only other additions are in the form of more precise specifications regarding general grounds for disqualifications and clarifications of fringe rules. Former NAYRU Rule 5 (now IYRU rule 33.7) has been changed chiefly by eliminating the protective clause preventing a right-of-way yacht from altering course when the other yacht is "unable to respond owing to her position." Former NAYRU Rule 11 (new IYRU Rule 33.6) has been changed chiefly by eliminating the clause "when sailing on a free leg of the course," so that a yacht no longer may bear off to prevent a close competitor from passing to leeward on a windward leg.

Perhaps the most significant change is in the former NAYRU Rule 9, which required that a yacht on the wrong side of the starting line at the time of the starting signal must keep clear of all yachts that were on the right side until she has started properly. Under new rule 32.4.b, loss of right of way occurs only if the yacht is recalled and returning or is working into position from the wrong side of the starting line, *i.e.*, not if she continues in the race without attempting to return. In addition, under the new rule, loss of right-of-way privileges persists only until the yacht has returned and cleared the line, not, as previously, until she has restarted correctly.

The new definitions of terms used in the rules (Part III of the IYRU rules) are essentially the same as the familiar definitions of the former NAYRU rules, with certain minor exceptions. The new term "close-hauled" is included and defined as follows: "A yacht is close-hauled when sailing by the wind as close as she can lie with advantage in working to windward" and this term is used in the tacking rule 33.3 to determine when the tack is completed. The specification that "A mark is reached when a yacht no longer has the choice as to the side on which she will pass or round it" (with a similar specification for reaching an obstruction) is included and this definition is utilized in the giving room at marks rule 34.1 to determine when the right of way of an inside overlap must be recognized. Obstructions to sea room are specifically listed as in the former NAYRU Rules and the list is unchanged except for the addition of "craft capsized."

SAILING RULES PERTAINING TO RIGHT OF WAY

31—Fair Sailing

A yacht shall attempt to win a race only by fair sailing and superior speed and skill. However, a yacht may be disqualified under this rule only in the case of a clear-cut violation of the above principles and only if no other rule applies.

32—Introduction to Right-of-Way

1. WHEN RULES OF PART IV APPLY—as between yachts intending to race, the rules of Part IV replace the Government right of way rules from the time a yacht intending to race begins to sail about in the vicinity of the starting line until she has left the vicinity of the course; but except as provided in rules 32.4(a) and 32.4(d) she cannot be disqualified for infringing a rule of Part IV unless the infringement occurs after her preparatory signal and before she cleared the finish line after finishing.

2. AVOIDING COLLISIONS: (a) the rules of Part IV are framed to avoid collision. The yacht which by rule has to keep clear must always do so, and may be disqualified as a consequence of a breach of any of these rules, whether or not a collision results.

(b) If a right of way yacht makes no attempt to avoid a collision which may result in serious damage (subject to rule 33.5(a)), she may be disqualified as well as the other yacht.

3. ALTERING COURSE BEFORE STARTING [former NAYRU Rule 7 essentially unchanged] Until the starting line has been crossed and cleared, a yacht **clear ahead** or a **leeward yacht** when altering her course affects another yacht, may alter course but only slowly, and a **leeward yacht** may **luff** only when the helmsman of the **windward yacht** (sighting abeam from his normal station) is aft of the mainmast of the **leeward yacht**. Rule 33.5(d) also applies. A **windward yacht** may never bear away so as to force any **leeward yacht** to alter course.

4. KEEPING CLEAR RULES OF LIMITED APPLICATION (a) Unless scheduled to start first, yachts shall keep clear of the starting line and of the first leg of the course.

(b) [former NAYRU Rule 9 changed] A yacht recalled and returning, or one working into position from the wrong side of the starting line after the starting signal has been made, shall keep out of the way of all competing yachts which are starting or have started correctly. As soon as she has returned and cleared the starting line or its extensions she shall regain her rights of way. When this rule applies it overrides all other rules.

(c) A yacht under way shall keep clear of a yacht which is anchored or aground. Of two anchored yachts, the one which anchored last shall keep clear, except that a yacht which is dragging shall keep clear of one that is not.

(d) A yacht that has cleared the finish line shall keep clear of it, and of all other yachts which have not finished.

5. HAILS—Although it is only in rules 35 and 26.4 that a hail is mentioned, other situations may arise in which, under rules 1 and 31, a hail should be given before making an alteration of course which may not be foreseen by the other yacht or yachts.

6. RETIREMENT AFTER INFRINGEMENT—If a yacht infringes any of these rules, or sailing instructions during a race she ought to retire immediately, but if she continues in the race, other competitors shall be bound to treat her as a competing yacht and observe the rules and sailing instructions accordingly.

These new NAYRU-IYRU Rules are considerably more specific in requiring adherence to the racing rules. It is stated specifically that any yacht which infringes a rule ought to retire immediately. Paragraphs 32.1 and 32.2 state that disqualification may result from a breach of the rules whether or not a collision occurs and may result if a right-of-way yacht is compelled to alter course to avoid a collision. Rules 32.5 and 32.6 spell out and put teeth into the old proprieties of requiring a hail or a withdrawal where the situation indicates such action.

Rule 32.4 clarifies the conditions of starting, finishing, starting prematurely and anchoring. A major change from former NAYRU Rule 9 has appeared in new rule 32.4 b, which as noted above now grants continued normal right-of-way status to a boat which continues on course despite being recalled because of a premature start. This provides greater opportunity to the premature starter who may slow down and/or luff up, still maintaining his normal rights as a leeward or starboard tack yacht. Only when the yacht bears away or tacks to return does she lose her normal rights, although thereafter she must keep carefully clear until she recrosses and clears the line or its extensions. She then reacquires her normal right-of-way relationships sooner than formerly and may more safely insinuate herself into a line of boats approaching the line.

Rule 32.3 accords additional privileges to a right-of-way yacht clear ahead or to leeward by permitting slow course alterations before the start as an exception to Rule 33.7. No normal course is established before the start, and the right-of-way yacht is granted freedom to take and adjust her course as she pleases so long as she does so slowly enough to accord other yachts ample room and opportunity to keep clear. In addition the leeward yacht acquires luffing rights *whenever* the helmsman of the windward yacht is aft of the mainmast of the leeward yacht, regardless of whether or not the overlap was established from astern. NAYRU Appeal 46 specifically states that it is the duty of a windward yacht to acquire (and/or maintain) sufficient headway to be able to respond reasonably to any luff that a yacht overtaking and establishing an overlap to leeward might be entitled to make. This means that a yacht close to the line, moving slowly to avoid a premature start, must give careful consideration to all yachts overtaking to leeward.

On the other hand, Rule 33.2 continues to apply before the start, as does Rule 33.7, modified by Rule 32.3, and the provisions of Rule 32.3 require only slow course alterations by a right-of-way yacht. Consequently a windward yacht is accorded certain protection. An overtaking yacht must, when establishing an overlap to leeward, provide ample room and opportunity for the windward yacht to keep clear, *i.e.*, room to luff after the overlap is established without colliding. An overtaking yacht may not come charging up beneath a competitor and run into his boom before he can trim it or force the windward yacht to sail a course higher than that of the overtaking yacht *until luffing rights are established.*

When yachts are converging it is important to recognize that an overlap is established early. A windward yacht, bearing off near the line to avoid a premature start, may suddenly grant an overlap and right-of-way privileges to one or more overtaking yachts. She may just as suddenly break the overlap by rounding up ahead of them. When clear ahead holding right of way she may only alter course slowly, and she must at all times keep clear of yachts to leeward; but when she grants an overlap and loses right of way, she also loses the right-of-way restrictions and may luff up suddenly to keep clear and break the overlap.

Two factors indicated in Rule 32 and in the NAYRU Appeals indicate the strictness with which the rules are expected to be applied. First, a yacht may be disqualified for an improper hail if the other yacht responds. Second, the commitment of a foul does not deprive a yacht of subsequent rights under the rules. A right-of-way yacht may be fouled by another yacht which consequently acquires a right of way that the fouled yacht may be unwilling to accept; *i.e.,* after failing to respond to a proper luff a windward yacht may demand room at a mark. Such subsequent rights must be granted whether or not it is presumed that the yacht is disqualified and should withdraw; the recourse is to protest.

33—Right of Way [rules that apply at all times]

1. ON OPPOSITE TACKS, FUNDAMENTAL RULE [former NAYRU Rule 1 unchanged] A **port tack** yacht shall keep clear of a **starboard tack** yacht.

When racing there are only two exceptions to this rule, *i.e.,* withdrawal of right-of-way privileges of a starboard tack yacht over the line early at the start or overlapped on the inside of a leeward mark. *In all other instances,* the starboard tack yacht has right-of-way and, in case of doubt, the starboard tack yacht will be presumed to have been right. NAYRU Appeal 32 ruled that a port tack yacht should be disqualified if the helmsman of a starboard tack yacht considered it necessary to bear away in order to avoid her. Any deviation from the normal course of a starboard tack yacht required by the presence of a port tack yacht is cause for disqualification of the latter. The burden of proof rests on the port tack yacht to prove that she would have cleared the Starboard tack yacht. When on the port tack, don't take chances!

2. **On the same tack,** fundamental rule [former NAYRU Rule 2 essentially unchanged]
(*a*) A **windward yacht** shall keep clear of a **leeward yacht.**
(*b*) An **overtaking yacht** shall keep clear and, when establishing an **overlap to leeward,** shall allow the **windward yacht** ample room and opportunity to fulfill her newly acquired obligation to keep clear of the **leeward yacht.**

The only exceptions to this rule are the same as the exceptions to Rule 33.1—withdrawal of right-of-way privileges of a leeward yacht over the line early at the start or overlapped on the inside at a leeward mark. However, there are major modifications attendant upon the acquisition of status as a leeward yacht—similar to the restrictions on right-of-way during tacking onto the starboard tack. A leeward yacht by definition is a yacht overlapped by or over-lapping a yacht to windward and an overlap exists when neither yacht is clear astern, *i.e.*, leeward yacht status is acquired when the bow of the leeward yacht is forward of an imaginary line pro-jected abeam from the aftermost point of the windward yacht's hull or spars and continues until the leeward yacht is clear ahead. When she is clear ahead she continues to have full right-of-way (the only exception being when she is over early at the start). Thus, the only significant determinant of right-of-way status as a leeward yacht is the presence of an overlap, and it is the sudden change from overtaking to leeward yacht status—from "keep clear" to "right of way"—that makes for the difficulty in utilizing this rule.

When establishing an overlap to leeward, an overtaking yacht shall allow the windward yacht *ample room* and *ample opportunity* to fulfill her suddenly acquired obligation to keep clear. The terms "ample room"and "ample opportunity" are crucial. As reported by Robert N. Bavier, Jr., in *The New Yacht Racing Rules,* the NAYRU committee on rules revision intended that the leeward yacht should be required to establish an overlap distinctly to leeward. In other words, sufficient room must be allowed for the windward yacht to head as high as she wishes, including luffing head to wind, without in the process having her stern swing into the leeward yacht; and, in no case, should the windward yacht be forced to sail above the course of the leeward yacht. This, then, is the definition of "ample room." "Ample opportunity" is a time factor requiring that the overlap not be established so rapidly that the windward yacht is unable to keep clear by luffing. The "ample room" clause pertains particularly when both yachts are sailing approximately the same course, preventing the leeward yacht from continuing on a course close aboard the windward yacht when establishing an overlap. For instance, before the start a more rapidly moving overtaking yacht may not sail so close to leeward alongside a slowly moving competitor nearer the line as to force the windward yacht to sail above the course of the leeward yacht—until the leeward yacht acquires luffing rights. The "ample opportunity" cause seems to pertain more particularly to the establishment of an overlap by the yacht converging to lee-ward. In contrast to the complete freedom of a starboard tack yacht to continue her course without regard to a port tack yacht, the leeward yacht must approach a converging windward yacht with discretion, providing adequate time for the windward yacht to keep clear after the establishment of the overlap. It must be recognized, however, that the overlap is established earlier and "ample opportunity" more readily available in direct proportion to the degree of divergence of the courses of the two yachts.

Despite the restriction on the activities of the leeward yacht favoring the windward yacht, the former is actually granted far-reaching right-of-way privileges under almost all circumstances. NAYRU Appeal 6 indicates that a leeward yacht may continue on its proper course regardless of the presence of a windward yacht— so long as ample room and opportunity have been granted to keep clear at the time of establishment of the overlap. NAYRU Appeal 36 states that "ample opportunity to keep clear" is not a continuing restriction; *i.e.*, once sufficient time has been granted for the windward yacht to take action to keep clear, the leeward yacht may continue on her proper course without respect to the windward yacht. And NAYRU Appeal 6 specifically states that, when there is doubt as to whether a yacht is sailing a proper course, she should be given the benefit of the doubt.

These interpretations refer to conditions subsequent to the establishment of the overlap; but it is reasonable to assume, as stated above, that in case of doubt as to the time and opportunity provided at the time of the establishment of the overlap the windward yacht would be favored.

A crucial test of these interpretations often occurs when a port tack yacht tacks immediately ahead of a starboard tack competitor about to round a mark to port. While tacking, the originally port tack yacht must keep clear but immediately acquires right-of-way privileges by virtue of being clear ahead if the starboard tack yacht can keep clear after the tack is completed. At this point the overtaking yacht may elect to establish an overlap to leeward so as to gain privileges while rounding the mark. The greater relative speed of the overtaking yacht makes it quite possible for such an overlap to be established so rapidly and so close aboard that "ample room and opportunity" are not granted and so that the windward yacht is unable either to continue on a course no higher than the leeward yacht, to luff, or to round the mark without colliding. Under these circumstances the leading yacht cannot be considered to have tacked too close and the yacht overtaking to leeward should be disqualified for violation of Rule 2.

3. **Tacking and Jibing** [former NAYRU Rule 6 essentially unchanged]
   (*a*) A yacht while **tacking** or **jibing** shall keep clear of a yacht **on a tack.**
   (*b*) When a yacht **tacks** or **jibes** into a position which will subsequently give her right-of-way, she must do so far enough away from a yacht **on a tack** so that the latter need not begin to alter her course to keep clear until the **tack** or **jibe** is completed and thereafter be able to keep clear.
   (*c*) A yacht which **tacks** or **jibes** thereby assumes the onus of proving that she has complied with this rule, and unless she discharges this onus of proof she must be disqualified.
   (*d*) A yacht may not **tack** so as to involve probability of collision with another yacht which, owing to her position, cannot keep out of the way.

4. **Tacking and Jibing Simultaneously**

   If two yachts are **tacking** or **jibing** at the same time, the one on the other's **port** side shall keep clear.

Rule 33.3 may almost be considered a fundamental rule as it refers to a third state in which yachts are neither on the same nor opposite tacks, *i.e.*, not "on a tack," but are in the process of tacking or jibing. It is the initiation of a particular right-of-way condition which is of concern when "on a tack," as indicated in Rules 33.2 and 34.1. It is the completion of the condition tacking or jibing, however, that is of concern in Rule 33.3, as right of way may be established suddenly when tacking or jibing ceases. A yacht tacking or jibing must do so far enough away from a yacht "on a tack" to enable the latter to hold her course *until the tack or jibe is completed and thereafter to keep clear.*

The definition of tacking states that a yacht is tacking from the moment she is beyond head to wind *until she bears away to a close-hauled course or to a course on which her mainsail fills.* A yacht is jibing from the moment when, with the wind aft, her main boom crosses her center line *until her mainsail fills* on the other tack. Jibing can be accomplished almost instantaneously, as it is not necessary for the yacht to alter course or for the boom to have reached a specified position but only for the mainsail to fill (which it does almost as soon as the boom crosses the center line). Therefore, when jibing, it is not *time* that a yacht needs but *room*—room to swing the boom, usually the full arc in a planing boat. For even if the jibe is completed when the mainsail fills, any boat hit by the jibed boom will be presumably a leeward (right-of-way) yacht. Tacking takes considerable time, however, and reduces the speed of the boat, often considerably, so that time as well as room must be allowed for its accomplishment. In addition, it must be recognized that when there is doubt it shall be presumed that a yacht tacked (or jibed) too close.

Tacking into a right-of-way position must be considered for two distinct situations: tacking to the starboard tack to cross a port tack yacht and tacking clear ahead or to leeward of an overtaking yacht. The only doubt likely to occur when tacking to cross (the proprieties recommend a warning hail) results from possible action of a port tack yacht in altering course before the tack is completed. Although the necessity of such a maneuver may be in doubt, such a doubt will be resolved in favor of the port tack yacht.

Tacking to clear ahead or to leeward, however, presents several additional complications. If the overtaking yacht can keep clear (*i.e.*, if, after the tacking yacht comes into position parallel to the overtaking yacht's course, a transom collision does not occur and/ or the overtaking yacht is able to pass without colliding to windward or leeward of the transom) it may be presumed that the tacking yacht has properly complied with Rule 33.3 (see NAYRU Appeal 50). If the overtaking yacht establishes an overlap to windward at the completion of the tack, she must continue to keep clear under Rule 33.2 and there can be no doubt if subsequent interference occurs. If, however, she establishes an overlap to leeward, she must do so according to the provisions of Rule 33.2 by granting "ample room and opportunity" for the windward yacht to keep clear. Suddenly, when another yacht, without right of way during the process of tacking, tacks ahead, the overtaking yacht must make a major alteration in course, not only to keep clear of a transom collision but to establish an overlap far enough to leeward for the leading yacht to keep clear by luffing head to wind if she desires.

This major alteration in course is all too rarely accepted as necessary and even more rarely accomplished in practice. The problem is particularly likely to occur when a train of yachts is laying the mark and another crosses and tacks into or just above the line. The overtaking yacht has no desire to bear off much below the lay line

to avoid the interloper and so establishes a close overlap to leeward. Subsequently, because of the reduced speed of the now windward yacht, the leeward yacht may run into her boom, or the windward yacht may swing her transom into the leeward yacht while
attempting to keep clear, or the windward yacht seeking to avoid
such a collision may be unable to luff up to give the leeward yacht
room to round the mark, And perhaps, neither able to tack without
colliding, they may converge upon a third yacht with starboard
tack right of way! Nowhere is the understanding of and compliance
with Rule 33.2 more important in avoiding a sequence of disasters
as here.

The other half of this problem is considered in NAYRU Appeal
51, which evaluates the problem of establishing an overlap to leeward by tacking to leeward of a converging yacht. The tacking yacht
is subject to Rule 33.2 in addition to 33.3 and in establishing such an
overlap to leeward must give the windward yacht "ample room
and opportunity" to keep clear, a requirement considerably more
extensive than that of Rule 33.3. In such situations it is probably
sensible for the windward yacht to make an immediate move to
keep clear, causing immediate minimal contact, if necessary, to
prove that she has not been granted ample room and opportunity as
this requirement "cannot be construed as a continuing one" (see
NAYRU Appeal 36).

Sequential complications may readily follow jibing, as this maneuver is so rapidly accomplished. When a yacht jibes to the starboard tack in order to gain right of way she may force a converging
port tack yacht to do likewise. The first yacht must jibe far enough
away so that after the jibe's completion the second yacht may jibe
to keep clear if this is the necessary maneuver. If the second yacht
is able to keep clear initially but subsequently jibes she must do so
far enough away to enable the first to keep clear. If she delays
further she may find that after the completion of her jibe the first
yacht has a sufficient overlap to acquire luffing rights. A sudden luff
immediately after the completion of her jibe may catch her completely unable to respond without contact (a favorite team racing
tactic). Thus, when on port confronted with a yacht jibing to starboard, jibe immediately and keep clear.

Rule 33.4 requires that when two yachts are tacking or jibing
simultaneously, the one on the other's port side shall keep clear.
The possibility of simultaneous tacking may be unrecognized but

should be considered in the resolution of protests involving Rule 33.3 (NAYRU Appeal 28), as interference readily results when a yacht tacks without knowledge of another's tacking.

33.5. Luffing after the Starting Line is Crossed. On Same Tack, Luffing [former NAYRU Rule 10 essentially unchanged]
(a) After a yacht has crossed and cleared the starting line she may luff a yacht **clear astern** or a **windward yacht** as she pleases and head to wind if she pleases to prevent the latter passing, until the helmsman of the **windward yacht** (when sighting abeam from his normal station and sailing no higher than the **leeward yacht**) comes abreast of the mainmast of the **leeward yacht**. Thereafter, or if he (when sighting abeam from his normal station) was forward of the mainmast of the **leeward yacht** when the **overlap** began, the **leeward yacht** may not sail above her **proper course** while the **overlap** continues to exist.
(b) For the purpose of this rule: an **overlap** does not begin or continue to exist unless the yachts are clearly within two overall lengths of the longer yacht; and an **overlap** which exists between two yachts when the leading yacht crosses the starting line, or when one or both of them completes a **tack or jibe,** shall be regarded as beginning at that time.
(c) When there is doubt, the **leeward yacht** may assume that she has the right to luff unless the helmsman of the **windward yacht** has hailed "Mast Abeam," or words to that effect. The **leeward yacht** must be governed by such hail, and, if she deems it improper her only remedy is to protest.
(d) The **windward yacht** shall not cause a **luff** to be curtailed because of her proximity to the **leeward yacht** unless an **obstruction to sea-room** in accordance with rule 34.1(a) restricts her ability to respond.
(e) A yacht shall not **luff** unless she has the right to **luff** all yachts which would be affected by her **luff**, in which case they shall all respond, even if an intervening yacht or yachts would not otherwise have the right to **luff**.

Rules 33.5 and 33.6 provide modifications of Rules 33.2 and 33.7, which apply only after the start: Rule 33.5 applies to a right-of-way yacht's altering course to windward, Rule 33.6 to its altering course to leeward. The first paragraph of Rule 33.5 states the substance of the rule and is comparable to Rule 32.2b, which pertains before the start; the final paragraphs are the same in both rules.
The following provisions of Rule 33.5 are different from Rule 32.2b: (1) Luffing by a right-of-way yacht after the start may be *as she pleases and head to wind if she pleases.* (2) There is a proper

course after the start and the leeward yacht may not sail above it if she does not have luffing rights or if she loses them. (3) Luffing rights are acquired only by the establishment of a leeward overlap in a specified manner.

Too little advantage is taken of the right to luff under Rule 33.5, although it is an extremely effective way of preventing the passing of a windward yacht. The windward yacht should be careful to establish an overlap to windward far enough away to allow for the luff of a leeward yacht. If luffing rights are not acquired or are lost after the start, the leeward yacht must adhere to the provisions of Rule 2 requiring cautious establishment of an overlap and adherence to a proper course.

To acquire luffing rights after the start, a leeward yacht's mast must be forward of the helmsman of a windward yacht, (1) at the time of the start, or (2) at the time the two yachts first come within two over-all lengths of each other, *i.e.,* when they are converging, or (3) at the time one or both complete a tack or jibe. If not acquired at the start, luffing rights may be acquired by an overtaking yacht by widening out to beyond two over-all lengths to leeward and then converging. Usually, however, luffing rights are utilized by a leading yacht as a defensive tactic and if accomplished swiftly may be extremely effective. A prolonged sail high of the course is rarely sensible if more than one competitor is close and effective only if the ultimate course of the luffing yacht is faster and shorter than the windward yacht's. Prolonged luffing may be successful if the windward yacht is carried to a position where both yachts must jibe to lay the mark, the leeward yacht then being dead ahead with clear wind.

The possible acquisition of luffing rights at the completion of a tack or jibe should be considered by both yachts concerned, as their immediate application may be disastrous to one and extremely helpful to the other. A tack into a safe leeward position may, after judicious luffing, place a competitor in a hopeless position which forces him to tack. Luffing rights may be suddenly acquired by the leeward of two yachts running before the wind in a succession of two quick jibes or by a yacht on the starboard jibe as she forces a port tack competitor to jibe to keep clear.

Rule 33.5 provides that when there is doubt and unless the helmsman of the windward yacht hails "Mast abeam," the leeward yacht may assume she has the right to luff and will certainly be favored if protested. The windward yacht must keep sufficiently clear so that even if the mast abeam position is reached the leeward yacht may bear off suddenly and rapidly to her proper course without colliding (NAYRU Appeal 20). The leeward yacht must thereafter assume her proper course and her only remedy is to protest if she deems a "mast abeam" hail to be improper. The determination of the mast abeam position at the initiation of and throughout the overlap is essential, as, if luffing rights are not initially acquired or are once lost, they may not be regained during the duration of that overlap.

There is no required distance from a mark at which Rule 34.1 becomes effective, and, as indicated in NAYRU Appeals 15 and 31, a leeward yacht with luffing rights may initiate or continue a luff as close to the mark as desired so long as she either finally allows room to round the mark if an overlap persists or goes to the wrong side of the mark with the windward yacht. A sudden luff just before the mark is reached may break an overlap and provide a considerable gain, but must cease in time to permit the windward yacht to bear away astern and round. Carrying a windward yacht to the wrong side of the mark is not permissible, however, unless luffing rights are established, the proper course being to the required side of the mark, and is only effective in team or match racing or when two yachts are separated from the remainder of the fleet. It is perfectly legal at the finish line and, if the windward yacht is leading but not mast abeam, should be attempted. If other yachts are not pressing, the windward yacht can be carried sufficiently far to enable the leeward to jibe, return, and finish ahead.

33.6—On Same Tack, Bearing Away [former NAYRU Rule 11 Changed]
A yacht shall not sail below her **proper course** when she is clearly within three of her overall lengths of a **leeward yacht** or of a yacht **clear astern** which is steering a course to pass to **leeward.**

This is a clear-cut restriction on the right-of-way privileges of a yacht clear ahead. Formerly, under NAYRU rules, when on a windward leg the yacht clear ahead or to windward, so long as she complied with Rule 2, might bear away to prevent an overtaking yacht from passing to leeward. Under the new rules there is no such exception.

If the yachts are within three over-all lengths of each other, the yacht clear ahead must adhere to a proper course if she detects a yacht clear astern steering a course to pass to leeward. This means that if a leading yacht on any leg of the course wishes to sail to leeward of the proper course she should immediately assume such a course upon rounding the preceding mark. Although NAYRU Appeal 6 indicates that when there is doubt a yacht will be presumed to be sailing a normal course and a normal course to complete the leg as quickly as possible may vary considerably from the straight line, additional and deliberate bearing away beyond the course initially sailed to interfere with an overtaking yacht is *expressly forbidden by the terms of Rule 33.6 and the proper course definition.*

> **33.7—Misleading or Balking** [former NAYRU Rule 5 changed]
> (*a*) When by any of the above clauses one yacht has to keep out of the way of another, the latter (subject to rule 33.5) shall not alter course so as to prevent her doing so.
> (*b*) Although the right-of-way yacht is not bound to hold her course, she shall not so alter it as to mislead or balk the other, in the act of keeping out of the way.
> (*c*) A yacht is not misleading or balking another if she alters course by **luffing** or **bearing away** to conform to a change in the strength or direction of the wind.

This rule is again a modification of the two fundamental rules. Former NAYRU Rule 5 in effect deprived the right-of-way yacht of the freedom of a variable course by requiring that she adhere to a proper course (at all times not specifically excepted) when near another yacht. Under this new NAYRU-IYRU rule the restriction on alteration of course by a right-of-way yacht applies only to alterations which may prevent a non-right-of-way yacht from keeping out of the way or which may balk or mislead her. This restriction was and still is, of course, modified by the interpretation of proper course expressed in NAYRU Appeal 6, which indicates that a right-of-way yacht may vary from the direct course to the mark or a close-hauled course to adjust to variations of wind, waves, or current and which states that when there is doubt the course will be considered proper. There are, in addition, the specific Rules 34.1, 32.2b. and 33.5, which grant the right-of-way yacht additional privileges to alter course under certain circumstances which override Rule 33.7.

The lack of restriction on the course of a non-right-of-way yacht much be considered as a distinct advantage, however. This is particularly true of a port tack yacht sailing to windward which may slow down or bear off to pass astern of a crossing starboard tack yacht when she wishes to continue her course, or luff up, slow down, or bear off to clear a starboard tack yacht and round a mark to be left to starboard. A starboard tack yacht wishing to continue her course without forcing a port tack yacht to tack is unable to make any course alteration to achieve this end and must hold her course when approaching a mark to be left to starboard, unable to adjust the moment of tacking relative to the crossing of a port tack yacht without overstanding. Rule 33.7 specifically relates to altering course, however, and does not restrict alterations in speed which can partially compensate for the defects mentioned above. In addition, paragraph (e) and the definitions of luffing and bearing away give specific privileges to a right-of-way yacht which may alter her course to conform to a change in wind strength or direction without "balking or misleading."

Additional privileges in altering course are granted to a right-of-way yacht before the start by Rule 33.2b, but even these privileges do not permit the complete freedom allowed a non-right-of-way yacht at this time—so long as she keeps clear. Rule 33.6 further restricts a right-of-way yacht, preventing her from bearing away to interfere with an overtaking yacht attempting to pass to leeward. In combination with Rule 33.7 this means, essentially, that a right-of-way yacht, when in close proximity to a competitor, may alter course only by luffing, while the non-right-of-way yacht may assume any course she desires and alter her course as often as she desires so long as she keeps clear.

This rule no longer includes the restriction on an alteration of course by a right-of-way yacht when the other yacht is "unable to respond owing to her position." This greatly increases the demands upon a non-right-of-way yacht to avoid sailing into positions in which she will be unable to respond. Former NAYRU Rule 5 gave some protection to an overtaking yacht intervening between two leading yachts. As implied in NAYRU Appeals 18 and 44, if the two leading yachts are so close together that the overtaking yacht in establishing an overlap to leeward on the windward yacht gives insufficient room to the windward yacht to keep clear or is in danger of fouling the leeward yacht, or both, she may be disqualified. Formerly, if the distance apart of the leading yachts was deemed sufficient, the overtaking yacht might intervene, be granted right of way on the windward yacht by establishing an overlap, and be protected from luffing by the leeward yacht as "unable to respond owing to her position." Such protection is available no longer under

Rule 33.7, although Rule 33.5 prevents the leeward yacht from luffing unless she has luffing rights on all yachts which might be affected. The situation becomes more complex when the two leading yachts are on opposite tacks (as they may be on a run) for in this situation the intervening yacht may be required to keep clear of both a leeward yacht and a starboard tack yacht. Although she is protected no longer by Rule 33.7, she is protected by Rule 34.1, which requires the leeward yacht to give her room to pass the starboard tack yacht considered as an obstruction. (Although in this instance the obstruction may pass instead of being passed!)

34—Giving Room at Marks or Obstructions to Sea-Room.
[former NAYRU Rule 3 essentially unchanged]

1. (*a*) If two yachts **overlap**
   (i) on the same **tack**
   when one of them **reaches a mark** which they are about to pass or round on the required side (unless rule 34.2 applies), or an **obstruction to sea-room** which they are about to pass on the same side, or
   (ii) on opposite **tacks**
   when with the wind aft they are about to pass a **mark** on the required side (except at the start) or an **obstruction to sea-room** on the same side,
   the outside yacht shall give the inside yacht room to pass or round it.
   (*b*) But if they do not **overlap,**
   the yacht **clear astern** shall anticipate the passing or rounding maneuver and shall keep clear when the **yacht clear ahead:—**
   (i) reaches the **mark** or **obstruction to sea-room, or**
   (ii) alters her course in the act of rounding it, or
   (iii) is too close to give room.
   (*c*) An outside **leeward yacht**, having the right to **luff**, may take an inside **windward yacht** the wrong side of a **mark, provided** she also passes the wrong side of and sails past the **mark.**
   (*d*) A yacht **clear ahead** shall be under no obligation to give room before an **overlap** is established. The onus will lie upon the inside yacht to prove that the **overlap** was established in proper time.
   (*e*) A yacht **clear ahead** may **tack** round a **mark** or **obstruction to sea-room** only when she can do so and clear the yacht **astern**, just as she would be required to do if the **mark** or **obstruction to sea-room** were not there. (See rule 33.3.)
   [2. See below.]
   3. Rule 34 makes exception to the provisions of rule 33 only so far as to require the outside yacht, although otherwise holding right-of-way under the latter rule, to allow the inside yacht room to pass or round the

mark or **obstruction** when her **overlap** has been made in proper time. In all other respects rule 33 remains in full force.

Rule 34.3 is a fringe rule which overrides the two fundamental rules under the particular conditions of passing marks and obstructions. It is essential to recognize two modifications of the rule (in addition to being overridden by Rule 34.2: (1) It does not override Rule 33.3 which controls the actions of yachts when tacking and does not override Rule 33.1 except when yachts are passing on the required side of a mark terminating a downwind leg of the course, and (2) the establishment of the Overlap must be so accomplished that the leading yacht has ample room and opportunity (as in Rule 33.2) to provide the room for both yachts to round simultaneously.

No yacht can claim the right to tack under this rule whether approaching, rounding, or leaving the vicinity of the mark. Former NAYRU Rule 3 permitted a yacht to utilize the right-of-way privileges authorized in this rule when tacking around a mark from a reach to a reach. The new rule provides no such exception to the general limitation on tacking around a mark. A starboard tack yacht may maintain her proper course without regard to port tack yachts who are in the process of rounding if the mark terminates an upwind leg of the course—a beat or a close reach. This particularly refers to rounding a mark to starboard, as boats actually rounding will be on the port tack and must keep clear of converging yachts on the starboard tack by slowing down, luffing, or bearing away. A weather mark to be left to port is rounded on the starboard tack by all yachts so that no confusion should exist at such a mark. On the other hand when rounding to starboard, the port tack yacht is given temporary right of way as starboard tack yachts must tack to round and in so doing are subject to Rule 33.3, *i.e.*, while tacking they must keep clear of and not interfere with the proper course of port tack yachts.

When Rule 34.1 does apply, the-right-of way privileges granted to a yacht with an inside overlap must be properly acquired. The second section of the rule specifies that if the inside yacht does not have an overlap at the time the leading yacht no longer has the choice as to the side on which she will pass or round the mark (definition of "reaching the mark"), she must keep clear. This refers particularly to doubtful situations in which the following yacht is moving more slowly than the leading yacht, *i.e.*, when being passed to windward and blanketed, having just completed a tack to leeward of the leader, having come off a plane, having trouble getting the spinnaker down, etc. Under these circumstances if the overlap previously established is lost prior to the time that the leading yacht reaches the mark, no room may be claimed. The latter part of the second section, requiring that the following yacht keep clear if the overlap is established too close to enable the leading yacht to give the required room, refers particularly to situations where the following yacht is moving more rapidly than the leading yacht, *i.e.*, blanketing the leading yacht at the termination of a downwind leg, planing when the leading yacht is not, sailing on a higher course, jibing into a better wind angle, receiving a stronger puff in a variable wind, etc. Under these circumstances if the overlap is not acquired until too late to enable the leading yacht to give the required room, no room may be claimed and the following yacht must keep clear.

In case of doubt, the rule clearly states that it will be presumed that the inside overlap was improperly established. In boats planing at 12 to 14 knots, such doubts and favoring of the leading yacht must be fully recognized well in advance.

Rule 34.1 applies to yachts about to pass a mark or obstruction regardless of the degree of convergence of their courses and, on downwind legs, regardless of the tack they are sailing. The greater the difference between the courses of the two yachts, the sooner will the inside yacht acquire an overlap, the later will the leading yacht reach the mark, and the more readily will the inside yacht acquire the right to claim room to pass or round. A yacht sailing to leeward of the fleet and making a gradual turn to increase speed (higher on the wind) must clearly recognize that she is granting an inside overlap well in advance of passing the mark and that, unless she can increase speed sufficiently to be clear ahead when she is no longer able to choose the side on which she will round the mark, she must give room. On the other hand, a yacht clear ahead which is staying close to the line directly to the mark or which has sailed above it to keep her wind clear, may make a normal rounding as widely as necessary without regard to the following yacht, *i.e.*, may bear off sufficiently long before reaching the mark so as to permit a normal rounding, as long as she reaches the mark or alters her course in the act of rounding before the following yacht establishes an overlap.

Although there was nothing in former NAYRU Rule 3 which

referred to being "in the act of rounding," NAYRU Appeal 33 indicates that when a leading yacht has made a material change in course to round, having been clear ahead when abreast the mark, a following yacht may not demand room even though she subsequently acquires an overlap due to the leading yacht's course alteration.

NAYRU Appeal 53 states that there is no fixed distance from the mark at which Rule 3 (and presumably Rule 34.1) begins to operate. Indeed, it is well affirmed in NAYRU Appeals 31 and 53, and now in paragraph *c* of Rule 34.1, that a leeward yacht having luffing rights (but only with luffing rights) may luff an inside overlapping windward yacht as close to the mark as she pleases so long as she finally gives the required room or goes to the wrong side of and passes the mark with the windward yacht. The same reasoning applies after rounding as indicated by NAYRU Appeal 12, which states that an inside windward yacht must assume a proper course with reasonable promptness after rounding, *i.e.*, must not presume that Rule 3 (or 34.1) gives her continuing rights after the mark is passed.

34.2 [former NAYRU Rule 8 essentially unchanged] But on approaching the starting line to start, a **leeward yacht** shall be under no obligation to give room to any **windward yacht** on the same **tack** to pass to **leeward** of a **mark** of the starting line which is surrounded by navigable water; but after the starting signal is made a **leeward yacht** shall not deprive a **windward yacht** of room at such **mark** either:—
  (*a*) by heading above her **proper course** for the first **mark** in the course if the wind be free, or
  (*b*) by **luffing** above a **close-hauled** course if on the wind.

Rule 34.2., as indicated in the text of Rule 34.1, is a specific exception to Rule 34.1 under the circumstances of the start and in relation to the windward starting mark. Rule 34.1 continues to apply near the leeward starting mark and applies at the windward starting mark if it is not surrounded by navigable water.

Before the start there is no specified proper course and the provisions of Rules 33.2 and 32.3b permit right-of-way yachts to make alterations in course which may force windward yachts above the lay line to the windward starting mark when approaching to start to windward. A safe starting course is, therefore, somewhat to leeward of the lay line, providing room to respond to the luffing of yachts farther to leeward without being forced to windward of the lay line. Once to windward of the lay line a yacht has no right-of-way privileges which will permit returning to pass the starting mark on the required side. Even after the start signal, leeward yachts may hold a course to freeze them out though not above the first mark or not above close-hauled. Barging, however, is perfectly legal if it does not result in interference with leeward yachts, *i.e.*, if a hole can be found in the succession of yachts approaching the mark along the lay line.

The problem of the responsibility of an intervening yacht in a mass start at the windward end of the starting line is considered in NAYRU Appeal 37. Although not subject to disqualification if an innocent victim caught between a leeward yacht luffing and a windward yacht refusing to respond, the intervening yacht must not use her "leeward side as a refuge" by not attempting to force her luff. Disqualification should depend upon at least the following factors: Was she barging? Did she hail the windward yacht in time? Did she force her luff? Did she stand to lose or gain by the windward yacht's failure to luff? Had she properly acquired her intervening status?

At the instant of the start signal under the circumstances of Rule 34.2, the leeward yacht is suddenly required to assume a proper course close-hauled or not above the first mark. NAYRU Appeal 47 specifies that she is not obligated to take any action until the actual signal and thereafter must be granted the necessary time to fulfill her new obligation. On a reaching or running start a leeward yacht, reaching along the line must be allowed an appreciable interval to bear off to her proper course, an interval during which the windward yacht cannot demand room to pass to leeward of the start mark. Where there is doubt, the leeward yacht will probably be favored.

35—Close-hauled, Approaching an Obstruction to Sea-Room or a Mark
[former NAYRU Rule 4 essentially unchanged]
1. (*a*) If two yachts are standing **close-hauled** on the same **tack** towards an **obstruction to sea-room** which requires the yacht **to leeward** to alter her course to clear it, and if she is unable to **tack** without colliding with the yacht **to windward,** she may, when safe pilotage requires her to take action, hail the yacht **to windward** for room to **tack.** After such hail the yacht **to windward** shall at once allow the yacht **to leeward** room to **tack.**
(*b*) A yacht **clear ahead,** which according to rule 33.3 cannot **tack,** has the same rights under this rule as a yacht **to leeward.**
(*c*) If, however, the **obstruction** is a **mark** or a right-of-way yacht on the opposite **tack,** the yacht **to leeward** may not hail for room to

tack if the yacht **to windward** can fetch the **obstruction.**

2. A yacht so claiming room shall not hail and **tack** simultaneously, but shall be bound to **tack** as soon as she has room to do so.

3. In cases of doubt as to whether the yacht **to leeward** has the right to hail for room to **tack** except when rule 35.1(c) applies, the yacht **to windward** shall respond and should protest if she thinks fit, when the onus of proof that the hail was justified will lie with the yacht **to leeward.**

4. If a yacht **to leeward** reaches a position where in order to escape peril she has no alternative but to hail the yacht to **windward** for room to **tack** to clear a **mark** or a right-of-way yacht on the opposite tack, which the yacht to windward can fetch, she may do so, but shall retire from the race immediately thereafter.

5. If the yacht **to leeward** elects to clear the **obstruction** by **bearing away,** she shall allow the yacht **to windward** room to do the same, if she so desires.

Rule 35 is a further modification of the fundamental rules covering situations in which it is necessary for a yacht to tack in order to clear an obstruction. If such tacking interferes with the course of a right-of-way yacht it can be accomplished only under the specified circumstances of Rule 35. If the leeward yacht cannot fetch the obstruction without tacking and cannot tack without colliding with the windward yacht, she may hail for room to do.

However, if the obstruction is a mark of the course or a right-of-way yacht on the opposite tack, the leeward yacht may not hail for room to tack if the windward yacht can fetch the obstruction. The NAYRU definition of an obstruction includes craft at anchor, possibly a committee boat or a mark boat. It is essential for the utilization of Rule 35 that the instructions specify and the helmsmen understand whether objects bounding the course are to be considered marks or obstructions. For example, though a pier is normally an obstruction, if a pier is a mark bounding the starting line, a leeward yacht may not hail for room to tack to clear it unless the windward yacht is also unable to fetch it. If a committee wishes to permit a pier or vessel bounding the starting line to rank as an obstruction the instructions should so specify.

NAYRU Appeal 9 states that when Rule 3 (or 34.1) is in effect it overrides Rule 4 (or 35, *i.e.,* a yacht may not invoke Rule 35 to tack to clear an obstructing right-of-way yacht if in so dong she tacks around the mark. She must instead comply with Rule 3 (or 34.1), her rights being determined by the presence or absence of a proper overlap and with Rules 1 (33.1) and 6 (33.3). It seems probable, therefore, that the only occasion for utilizing Rule 35 at a mark would be when the mark is an obstruction so large that both yachts must tack to clear. According to NAYRU Appeal 8 a breakwater (or similar object) may be a mark if so specified in the racing instructions.

The other doubtful situation in the utilization of the rule occurs when it is used by a leeward port tack yacht to tack to leeward of a converging starboard tack yacht. Under these circumstances the windward port tack yacht when hailed may be in doubt as to whether she can clear the starboard tack yacht. If she can clear, she may so advice the leeward port tack yacht and hold her course. However, if she later finds it necessary to tack to clear the starboard tack yacht, or, of course, if she interferes with the starboard tack yacht, she is disqualified. Usually in small boats under these circumstances, it will be better for the windward yacht, if she has an overlap, to invoke Rule 34.1 requiring the leeward yacht to bear off and give her room to pass astern of the starboard tack yacht. If the windward yacht does call for room under Rule 34.1, this presumably overrides rule 35 (at least in former NAYRU specifications) and the leeward yacht must bear off instead of tacking. In any case if the leeward yacht elects to bear off to pass astern she must comply with Rule 34.1 by giving room to the overlapping windward yacht (paragraph 5).

CONCLUSIONS

These rules and their interpretations as expressed in the NAYRU Appeals represent a simple and understandable, yet complete and extremely effective basis for yacht racing. The more completely they are understood, the more they must be respected as providing a fair distribution of privilege and opportunity to yachts racing under all foreseeable circumstances. However, as the rules admit to circumstances of doubt and possible misinterpretation, it is evident that they must be carefully studied and carefully applied with forethought rather than hindsight.

Often the precise cause of a particular instance of interference can be determined only by a protest meeting. Often either one or both parties is ignorant of the cause or of the applicable rules and each tries to discover which rule most favors his position in retrospect. It is obviously essential that protest committees be composed of members who are thoroughly familiar with the rules and their interpretations and who are capable of obtaining the facts from the occasionally prejudiced participants. An attitude considering protesting to be unsporting is all too prevalent; in order to insure full understanding and compliance protests are essential. Whenever possible, protest meetings should be conducted publicly to provide greater insight for all competitors and encourage protest committees to more thorough understanding and expression of rule interpretations.

As demonstrated in an article by George E Hills, "Burden of Proof," in *Yachting*, November 1951, and indicated by the NAYRU Appeals, in the consideration of a protest the burden of proof should be on a non-right-of-way yacht to prove by a fair preponderance of the evidence that she did not infringe a rule. When more competitors recognize this simple precept, there will be fewer protests, more appropriate decisions, and better racing for all. Strict rules, severe penalties, and self-enforcement are the traditions of yachting which set the sport apart and make it the satisfying intellectual pursuit that it was designed to be. While it is permissible and desirable to take every advantage and every opportunity that does not violate the rules, precise adherence to them by all is essential to the sport. With the class measurement rules they provide the fair basis that makes all boats and all helmsmen, novices and experts, equal.

We must recognize that we race to gain the respect of our competitors and so come to respect ourselves. How better can we achieve this than by racing with full understanding of the rules, giving and taking in strict compliance with them?

PART II

The Techniques in Light to Moderate Air

Preface

These are the conditions of displacement sailing where boat speed is limited regardless of available thrust. In light air, when the aerodynamic force is inadequate to produce maximum displacement speed, individual boat speeds will vary widely throughout a fleet. Success in light air racing is therefore attained chiefly by finding the areas of maximum wind strength, developing maximum thrust through the best cut and best set sails, and by reducing drag factors to the minimum. Tactics and boat management are of minor significance. The start, the distance, and the course sailed are relatively meaningless except in terms of the acquisition of additional power from areas of increased wind strength. Preparation of the boat and a little luck are essential.

In moderate winds, however, boat speeds throughout a fleet readily reach an approximately equal maximum, little affected by variations in wind strength, developed thrust, or drag. The distance and course sailed now become of major significance. Reducing the distance sailed to windward by tacking with the shifts of a northwesterly or increasing boat speed through an improved sailing angle to leeward on a reach are essential. As boat speeds vary little when boats are separated in the middle of a leg, the tactical exploitation of the crucial moments at the start, when rounding marks, and at the finish by avoiding harmful interference and creating favorable interference is extremely important. Getting clear wind at the start or an inside overlap at the leeward mark may determine the outcome of the race.

The ability to learn through study and experience, to remember, and to apply what is learned—the skipper himself—is the determining factor in these conditions.

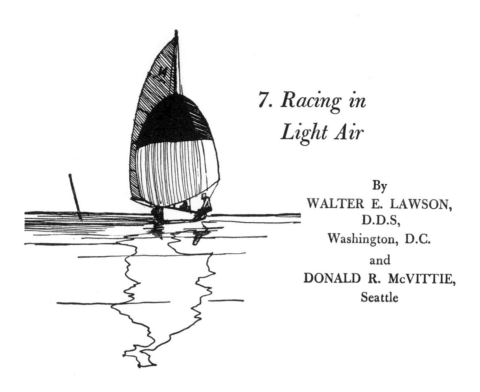

7. *Racing in Light Air*

By
WALTER E. LAWSON,
D.D.S,
Washington, D.C.
and
DONALD R. McVITTIE,
Seattle

The outcome of racing in light air is determined chiefly by boat speed and strategy. Maximum-displacement hull speed cannot be reached in light air and therefore boat speeds throughout a fleet may be highly variable. As boat speed is dependent upon the thrust produced by the sails in the presence of varying profile and induced drag, attention to drag factors in tuning and the utilization of properly set and trimmed sails may result in major increases in boat speed. Helmsmanship should be concerned with sail adjustments to acquire the maximum thrust and with the strategy of finding the areas of maximum wind strength and favorable current. Tactics are of minimal significance except in the negative sense of benefit derived from avoidance of interference.

As boat speed is directly related to the amount of forward resistance produced at varying speeds and as wave-making resistance is insignificant at speeds much below the maximum, profile drag becomes all-important in light air racing. The factors discussed in chapter 4 ("Hull and Rigging") which relate to underwater drag and to wind resistance should receive particular attention. Careful smoothing and reduction of wetted surfaces below and rig resistance above will be of greater value in light air than at any other time. Reduction in total boat weight, including crew weight, is never more significant than downwind in light air. (Remember how the Juniors sail through the fleets off the wind?) Extra gear should be left ashore and the boat must be kept dry.

PRODUCTION OF MAXIMUM BOAT SPEED

The long flat run and broad transom of a planing hull tend to increase drag at low speeds. Therefore, the normal crew and skipper positions for stronger winds will need to be changed usually by moving forward. A slight difference in fore-and-aft trim in strong wind may not effect the boat noticeably but in light air may be critical. Constant attention to this balance is important. Some skippers are guided by the "feel," others use a bubble level, while most watch the eddies and disturbances created aft of the rudder. I know one skipper who placed a Lucite panel in his transom and a black band on the water line of his rudder in order to observe the relation of the water surface to this band and thereby maintain his proper trim.

The angle of heel in strong winds is assumed best if near zero or flat. In most boats this reduces wetted surface and the turning effects of asymmetric shapes and thus is best in light airs also. However, in a hull with slack or gently rounded bilges a slight degree of heel may be desirable if other adjustments are made to keep a neutral helm. The sails will assume a better shape when their weight is directed to leeward and the aerodynamic slope of the swept-forward main will be improved.

The position of the centerboard must be altered in light air to achieve perfect balance. On a reach or run in heavy wind and sea a board completely up can be fatal, but in light air a completely housed board will decrease wetted surface and improve speed. Retracting the rudder (when legal) is equally desirable.

Upwind the board should be full down to achieve the maximum lift effect and the optimal balance of side forces. In light air the apparent wind is further forward for any angle of inclination resulting in forward movement of the center of effort. This must be balanced by forward movement of the center of lateral resistance to achieve the desired balance and pointing ability. At the same time, with decreased total aerodynamic force there is a relative increase in side force. As maximum speed upwind for any wind strength is achieved at the point when lateral resistance is sufficient to balance side force at a leeway angle of approximately 5 degrees, the increased side force should be balanced by a fully lowered board.

Sail shape is extremely important in light air when the last ounce of thrust most be coaxed from each zephyr. When boat speed is low compared to wind speed, *i.e.*, with the initiation of motion from a newly arrived puff, a flat sail section is most effective. However, as soon as the boat is under way, even in very light air, boat speed becomes relatively high compared with wind speed and a full sail section produces maximum thrust. This variation in effective section may account for the sometimes paradoxical advantages of flat sails in extremely light air when the wind periodically disappears altogether. Generally, light air sails should be the best available, of maximum dimensions, with plenty of draft.

If the same sail is used that is effective in heavy air, adjustments should be made to increase its draft. The vang should be used to shape the sail and steady the boom, but frequent tension adjustments may be necessary. A vang tuned to high "C" and a bent boom will usually stop a boat dead in a drifter and prevent the delicate sheet adjustments and feel so necessary in variable winds. The increased velocity gradient in light air demands a loose vang to permit additional twist and proper inclination to the apparent wind at all levels.

With a very flexible mast, adjustments may be necessary to prevent fore-and-aft bend which will flatten the sail excessively. Taking up on the upper jumper stays and moving the main sheet traveler attachment toward the center line will facilitate this. As mainsails are sewn with various foot and luff rope tensions and curvatures, adjustment of halyard and outhaul tension will change the amount and position of draft. The degree of adjustment of these factors can be judged only by trial and error but is extremely important in light air.

In addition to a stiff mast and a stiff boom to prevent flattening with mainsheet tension, effective adjusting devices for luff and foot tension should be available. A downhaul on the luff which can be eased under way will increase mainsail draft and move it forward. This technique is better than easing the halyard, which lowers the sail and thus reduces its exposure to the stronger wind aloft. An adjustable outhaul on the boom leading to a cleat at its inboard end is particularly important in light air, not only to increase draft when the sail is operated at the stall downwind, but to provide draft adjustments for varying wind strengths. As noted in the chapter on sails a variety of zippers and pouches are being built in to mainsails to provide additional fullness which can be removed when the wind strength increases. Where full-length battens are used these can be forced further into their pockets under increased tension to increase draft.

One of the most effective techniques for increasing the arch of either mainsail or jib sections is the use of adjustable sheet leads. Usually with adjustable travelers the mainsheet is led from the mid-line in light air to prevent pulling down to excess when sheeting in for windward work. This can be greatly improved by the use of a mid-boom mainsheet rig with a mid-boat track. Even Dragons are now using this arrangement, which permits moving the mainsheet lead to windward of the mid-line, pulling the boom fully amidships without flattening the sail. A very full sail may be retained in this manner at an optimal angle of inclination.

Inboard jib sheet leads or adjustments to move the leads further inboard carry out the same function as the mainsheet leads described above. In the International 14-ft. Class leads 6 in. or more inside the usual rail leads seem desirable in very light air to provide a full jib section at a high angle of inclination. Although the optimal angle of inclination of the airfoil is lower in light air, by moving the airfoils more inboard the pointing of the hull can be almost as high as in moderate air. Downhaul adjustments on the jib tack provide draft alterations for varying wind strengths. I once had a jib on my Thistle which worked extremely well in both very light and heavy air when its draft was adjusted by such a tack downhaul. For reaching, the jib sheets should be lightweight and often the clew itself should be held up by hand to prevent sagging and flattening of the arch aloft.

HANDLING THE BOAT IN LIGHT AIR

It is particularly important in light air that all the working parts of the boat should function smoothly. Jerking on sheets, centerboard pennants, and outhauls knocks wind from the sails, frays the temper, and slows the boat. It is essential to have a mainsheet rig from which one or more parts (mechanical advantage) may be dropped in light air, so that trimming may be accomplished easily. Nothing is more frustrating than trying to ease the mainsheet 6 or 8 in. only to have three parts of ⅜-in. line drop into the water, with the boom remaining where it was or even coming inboard. This can be remedied by using blocks of adequate size, light sheets, and no more than two parts.

Even the most experienced sailor can't tell the wind direction by his chin whiskers when there is doubt that the wind is moving at all. I recommend the use of a masthead flag of very light fabric. My flag is made of a piece of silk scarf from the dime store, held on a wire frame, with two-thirds of its length free to flutter. This flag responds to the faintest breeze. Its flutters give a rough indication of wind velocity and give me faith in its action. Metal or plastic wind vanes or a feather have no life, and I never know whether to trust them or not. I also use feather telltales on the shrouds as a second check on wind direction; if I am in doubt as to which to believe, I take a vote with smoke. Of all these wind indicators, cigarette smoke is the best and most accurate; it is also the most difficult to use, since the temptation is to put the butt in your mouth and smoke it rather than to hold it in your hand and look at it.

When sailing in light air at least two-thirds of the skipper's thoughts should be devoted to the weather. He must be constantly alert for any indication of a change in the wind direction or velocity —cat's paws on the water, smoke on the shore, behavior of boats in his class or in other classes, and the motion of the clouds. He must constantly form and re-form short-term local weather forecasts for the area between himself and the next mark, then test these theories against observed facts. Light winds are propelled by weak forces and are usually thermal in nature. The appearance of a small cloud can change the whole local weather pattern (see Ian Proctor's *Sailing, Wind and Current*). Light winds are neither steady nor even. In order to sail the fastest course between marks it is often necessary to take large detours to stay in the wind streaks and avoid the holes.

When reaching in light air, it is best to put the crew to leeward and the skipper to weather. When running, put the crew to weather and the skipper to leeward. The skipper and crew should sit as far as possible athwartships. This increases the transverse moment of inertia of the boat and reduces the tendency to roll. With the crew and skipper close together fore and aft, the boat has light ends and will tend to go over waves and wakes rather than through them.

With weight split athwartships the boat will roll and slat less when the water skiers go by.

Once both skipper and crew are in the right place, they must sit still. Any motion will be imparted to the sails, and will shake the wind out of them.

While looking for wind with an eye and a half, the skipper should keep the other half eye on the trim of the sail. I ask my wife, who crews for me, to devote her full attention to the trim of the jib and to let me know when any major changes take place, so that I may trim the main accordingly. I watch the main, too, of course, but she keeps me from getting absent-minded. Since both wind speed and boat speed vary constantly in conditions of light air, sail trim also is constantly changing. Many times I have sailed by boats with a faint breeze from the port quarter, while they were trimmed on the starboard tack, wondering where all my wind was coming from.

SAILING TECHNIQUE IN LIGHT AIR

In light air, it will take longer than usual to reach starting position particularly if that position is downwind. Position should be taken near the line, uptide, with a close reach for the line to insure being on time. In light air it is more important than ever to have your wind clear when starting (or soon thereafter). I believe in keeping a boat moving at all times and not pinching her too high in light air. Try to pick the end of the line(or a location along the line) which will be uncrowded or which will be nearest to the wind or to the expected wind. Usually the wind will be stronger at one end, and if so the line should be crossed as close as possible to this end on the tack which will carry you toward the stronger wind. When the wind is very light the boat which has the most wind moves the fastest and wins regardless of any deviation from the shortest course. Even direction shifts are of little importance if when you sail into the desired header you have less wind than the boats which continued on the wrong tack into a lift. If the wind is stronger to starboard of the starting line, it may be desirable to start on the port tack reaching down the line with maximum way or waiting for a hole to slip between the starboard boats. Even if it is necessary to pass astern of the entire fleet, a tack toward a stronger breeze will be a winner if the other boats continue to sail away from the wind or stop dead when they have to tack. If the wind is stronger beyond the port end of the line, the starboard tack is favored; but here as with any light air start it is essential to keep clear wind. If an ideal start can be made, moving at maximum speed, right with the gun, at the leeward end, with wind clear, lee bowing the fleet, then it should be done. But it is a gamble. A slight miscalculation can lead to having to luff to slow down and being overrun by a dense blanket of Dacron to windward or being caught second-best with another boat doing the lee bowing. It may be safer to start further up the line; where there is no danger of being blanketed and no one will be close on the lee bow. If the wind strength is much the same at both ends, then the usual desirability of choosing the end of the line farthest to windward should be accepted.

If the start is crowded everywhere, an attempt should be made to work out a clear area by alternately luffing the boats to windward and bearing off to leeward. Once the gun fires, all considerations should be forgotton except to get clear wind in the direction of the greatest wind strength. Tack immediately if lee bowed, bearing off behind most of the fleet if necessary to get to the wind to starboard. Or bear off to leeward on a close reach if necessary to get into free wind to port if this is the desired direction. Tremendous differences in boat speeds appear in a crowded light air start, and the boat which gets clear first may build up an insurmountable lead in a matter of minutes.

When to tack on a shift is always a difficult decision and depends on an ability to distinguish between an honest shift and an increase in velocity which often appears as a shift. Tacking should be as smooth as possible and the sails not trimmed too tightly after a tack until good headway has been regained. Rudder movement should be smooth and such as not to kill headway. Moving your weight slightly forward and never aft during the tack will prevent a transom drag at the time there is less drive to the hull. Your boat will point just as high and move faster if you ease your boom out to allow a gentle curve to the leech and a mild quiver of backwind at the luff (assuming amidships or windward traveler lead). Check to insure that your crew keeps the jib properly eased to provide adequate draft at all times.

If the wind lifts while on the wind in light, variable air, permitting the boat to point higher, it is inadvisable to head up suddenly. Heading up will merely kill hard-earned headway. Also, if the shift is temporary or only a velocity increase, sudden heading up will lead to a bad luff, a subsequent falling off, and a bad loss of headway. The result is usually a decided slip to leeward. Instead of pointing up rapidly in a lift, ease your sheets. This increases drive or headway on the same course and may move you into better wind. If the new wind persists after this advantage has been utilized, slowly trim your sheets and slowly point up to the new course. If the wind now heads, you at least fall off with good headway.

Avoid tacking often in light air. Momentum and inertia are directly proportional to weight; and as tacking always slows the boat, tacking should be avoided in proportion to boat weight. A 450-lb. Thistle will coast a long way once it has been started by a puff but will be readily overtaken by a 225-lb. International 14 if both must tack. Keep to the side of the course from which the strongest wind is expected but don't tack after every puff which appears on the water surface to windward. The puff will probably be gone by the time you arrive anyway. Plan your strategy and stick with it on one major tack; don't be misled into constant changes in plan to follow a competitor's good fortune. Stay to the side of the fleet to avoid interference and to be in position to receive the new wind first.

When reaching in light air, boat speed will vary constantly so that constant jib, mainsheet, and helm adjustments are essential. For this reason light weight and reduced purchased sheets and well-oiled blocks are essential. Maximum speed with an overlapping jib is achieved with the wind forward of the beam, so try to sail in this manner as much of the time as possible, particularly while attempting to pass through a wind shadow or bad blanket. This extra speed for a short time can help in starting, finishing, and establishing or escaping overlaps at marks.

Keep to the side of the course on the reach. Avoid at all costs being "in the middle." The wind interference produced by other boats so disturbs the air, in light conditions particularly, that the boats taking the straight course to the mark sail continuously in disturbed air as their competitors sail past on both sides. The decision as to which side is favored is always a difficult one, however.

In summertime light air sailing the chief wind source is usually from thermal winds. If the day is hot and sunny look for the sea breeze (if sailing in coastal waters) and keep to the side of the course from which this is expected. In the absence of a known sea breeze in such conditions stay close to the shore. Small thermal columns rising off the heated land will produce a suction wind, but the effect of such winds may be felt only a few hundred feet from shore. If the day is cool and overcast in a stationary weather front, don't expect a sea breeze or any thermal effect, but look for the eventual effect of the prevailing wind aloft—and stay to the indicated side of the course. The implication of these factors is that the windward side is usually preferable.

However, boat speed is enhanced by keeping the boat pointed high on the wind, particularly in light air. The latter part of any reaching or downwind leg should be taken higher on the wind than the nearby competitors to insure maximum gain at the finish or when rounding. At all times avoid getting any further to windward than is necessary to keep clear wind and to be closer to the expected new wind than your competitors. Always work to leeward in the puffs, bearing off to stay in the wind longer, still moving at good speed. This permits riding upwind to maintain speed in the lulls without getting too far off the direct route. If there is little difference in wind strength on each side, stay to leeward to maintain maximum speed at all times. Sail far enough to leeward to keep clear wind, taking the slow bearing-away portion of the leg initially to save maximum speed for the crucial period at the end. If the wind shows signs of strengthening, make your gain by sailing to windward initially, bearing away in the stronger wind later. In general, the more steady the wind the more desirable it is to stay to leeward of the fleet.

On the run, the side of the course is still the most important consideration. Take the side with the strongest expected wind, but if in doubt go to leeward. It is particularly important in light air downwind to avoid the center of the course, particularly near the finish where the wind is usually greatly disturbed. Keep to leeward so that at all crucial points you can be higher on the wind than your competitors. Approach the mark wide to leeward, if possible, coming up higher and higher, faster and faster, as you round in a smooth easy swing without losing way. I've often picked up several boats at a time in this manner, coming from abeam but well to leeward 100 ft. from the mark and rounding wide to maintain speed and sail through them to leeward.

Avoid sailing dead before the wind in light air as this is the slowest possible point of sailing, often reducing the apparent wind to near zero. In these conditions, tacking downwind can be extremely effective. The optimal angle varies with the particular boat but should usually be no higher than is necessary to keep the headsail full. Jibing usually increases rather than decreases speed if it can be done without rocking the boat excessively. It is usually best to take two or three long legs rather than many shorter ones, however, as this keeps the boat out of the disturbed air in the center of the course. Avoid crossing close in front of other boats, as you may become trapped in their wind shadow. Maintain the tack until the line or mark can be laid at the optimal angle on the opposite tack (preferably starboard). At all times avoid the close proximity of other boats.

The standard disaster which has befallen all of us occurs when, after having worked out a beautiful lead on a run, we sail into a hole. While we sit and slat, the fleet, almost hull down behind us, picks up a new puff and comes sliding down on it.

With light-displacement boats, the puff generally arrives just about the same time that the whole fleet arrives. This situation cannot always be avoided, but steps can be taken which will minimize your loss and leave you in a position to regain the lead. If you fall into a hole and boats astern start coming down on a fresh wind, round up quite sharply to insure being on the weather side of the fleet when it arrives. In this manner, you will be in a position to use the wind when it finally gets to you. What wind you get will not be cut up by the sails of the rest of the fleet as they pass. This may require quite a long luff out to weather of the straight-line course to the next mark but is better than sitting still while boats pass on both sides. If you step in a hole close to a mark of the course, position at the mark takes precedence over other considerations, and you should head for the side of the fleet which will be on the inside at the mark. In either case, head for one side of the fleet or the other, don't stay in the middle.

The spinnaker will be discussed at length in other chapters but in general is not an effective sail in very light air. The less wind there is, the smaller the spinnaker should be until the jib becomes more effective in drifting situations. The airflow disturbance and the trapping of dead air in the many folds of a collapsed spinnaker is far more detrimental than the lack of area in a jib which is free of major folds. Use sails which will hold their shape, trim the boat to help them retain that shape, and avoid sudden movements which will disturb the limited air flow around them. If the pole is limited by a small J measurement, as in the International 14, it is usually better to tack downwind higher on the wind to keep the jib drawing to leeward.

In light air racing, then, reduce drag and provide the maximum power through full sails properly hoisted and trimmed, keep to the side of the course where the wind is expected to be the strongest, and avoid other boats.

8. Starting in Moderate Air

By GEORGE D. O'DAY,
Boston

Starting a boat in a large fleet is like playing Russian roulette with five bullets instead of one. One mistake and the finish is very quick! After the last race of the 1959 Buzzard's Bay Bowl, I was strongly reprimanded for my horrible start by a friend who claimed I was lucky to have come out on top. Actually this particular start was planned down to the last second; my friend did not realize that my start enabled me to control 90 per cent of the fleet! No one could tack until I tacked first. I was the only boat able to tack immediately toward a heading shift and this advantage put my boat second, 100 yd. from the line, ahead of the twenty-one earlier starters. Only one boat was ahead; he made the perfect start to win the race, but I won the series by taking advantage of a poor line, early boats, bargers, and local knowledge.

The value of a start is thus determined by a boat's position at the first mark, not by its position when the gun goes. Starting takes planning and technique, and these two essentials will be considered chiefly for a start to windward. Special starting situations will be considered separately at the end of the chapter.

PLANNING

Plans based upon observations and information obtainable well in advance of the start are the major key to success in all racing. Not only the start but each leg of the course should be planned in advance to insure that major strategic concepts are adhered to and that temporary tactical expedients are prevented from interfering with basic essentials. The boat, its sails, and equipment must be adjusted for the weather conditions evident before the start. The circular must be checked—and rechecked—and the starting signals thoroughly understood (particularly in home waters, where familiarity breeds contempt and mistakes). The fleet itself should be checked and, if a later race in a series, the score carefully evaluated to determine which boats must be watched. Obviously the best-laid plans often go awry and must be adjusted to the circumstances of the moment (of which more later), but the plan is basic. Plan the ideal start and then adjust your plan only if necessary.

Position On the Line

The optimum starting location should be determined, chiefly in regard to the utilization of the first leg. Decide first which side of the windward leg is favored. Is the wind stronger to one side? Is there a windward shore off which a lift may be expected? Is there a current, and if so will the shallow or the deep water be advantageous? It may be essential to start at the end of the line which will permit the most rapid access to the favored side of the windward leg.

However, the line itself may be so established in relation to the wind direction that starting at one end immediately places the boat ahead of all other starters. Look at the flag on the committee boat and mentally draw a line perpendicular to its direction. If this line extends ahead of the starting line, the committee boat end is further upwind and has the advantage; if it angles behind the starting line, the buoy end has the advantage. No line is ever perfect; there is always an advantage to one end or the other. But do not let this immediate advantage sway you completely; other factors, particularly the plan for the windward leg, may be far more significant.

Is the wind shifty? Has the favored end varied while under observation? If so, two necessities must be accepted. One is to insure that you will be on the lifted tack immediately after starting and the second is to place yourself in position from which you will be able to tack without interference to adapt to the wind shifts as they appear. If the leeward or port end is favored temporarily as the gun goes off, starting at this end will be of little value unless you are on or can immediately assume the lifted port tack. If you are first across the line on starboard at the leeward end, you may lead the fleet for three minutes but, if unable to tack, will find yourself at the bottom of the heap as the port tack boats sail into a beautiful header on the next shift far to windward of you. In such conditions, it may be far better to start in the middle or even at the windward end to be certain of being the first to assume the port tack.

In addition, it will be of no value to be at the perfect location on the line if you have no wind. Unless you are reasonably certain that you can obtain clear wind when the gun goes, it may be better to start in a less congested area and forego the ideal start. It is amazing how many give lip service to this doctrine but how few are able to resist the temptation.

In planning, then, decide where you want to be after the gun, how you can get there in the presence of an unfair line, a shifting wind, and many other boats, and pick your starting location accordingly.

Timing

Next determine how you will get to the selected position on the line when the gun goes. Essentially this means to determine how long it takes to proceed a given distance in the expected conditions. The average small sailboat will make approximately 4 to 5 knots when close-hauled in moderate winds, a maximum speed for windward work. This means that she will travel about 70 to 80 ft. per 10 seconds. Determine the distance traveled in 10 seconds at top windward speed in your own sailboat; this figure is of real value and should be remembered. Almost all adjustments will be downward. More or less wind, interference from other boats, waves, luffing, getting started after tacking or slowing, etc., will all decrease the speed and distance traveled per unit time. *Plan to approach the line with at least twice the time necessary to cover the remaining distance available until you are sufficiently close to judge time and distance accurately. Then, in terms of a known maximum distance per 10 seconds, sheet in and sail the final seconds at top speed to hit the line with the gun with full way on.* In a fleet of any size, it is impossible to sail away, tack, and return to the line all under a planned full speed (especially in a planing boat, whose speed is so variable on the reach away from the line) with any hope of being on time.

Right of Way

Particularly in large fleets, it is essential to approach the line with right of way over neighboring boats—or at least to calculate carefully the risks inherent in lack of right of way. Under almost all circumstances, therefore, it is best to start on starboard tack if the line can be laid on starboard (and sometimes even if it can't). Port tack is justified if the line can be laid only on port (and then still watch out for the lone boat on starboard running along the line or dipping down from above the line) or if the leeward end is heavily favored. In the latter case, particularly if the leeward end advantage is consequent to a temporary shift which necessitates immediate assumption of the port tack, approach the leeward end on a port tack reach, prepared to reach along to leeward of the starboard tack boats until a sufficient hole appears and shoot through —to clear wind and the lifted tack. This may actually be less dangerous than attempting to tack onto port from the midst of a starboard tack fleet. Avoid such a port tack start at all costs if many others are attempting the same maneuver, however, as only one or two boats will ever make it and the interference of the others will seriously impair your mobility.

Seek to be to leeward when starting on starboard. Avoid barging, which spells almost certain danger in large fleets, and avoid the weather end of the line if many others are barging. Even if the rules are carried to the proper disqualification of the instigators, everyone usually loses in the resultant jam when a large number of bargers blanket the leeward boats and attempt to find room in the final seconds. Particularly if there is any possibility of a wind shift which with a lift may suddenly place you in a barging position or with a header may leave you hopelessly blanketed, avoid the immediate vicinity of the windward mark. The only exception is that if you plan to be (and retain sufficient mobility to be) late you may successfully start from the barging position. If you are certain that a header is developing, this is an excellent solution—but who can be sure?

If you are starting further down the line to avoid the windward end jam or because the leeward end is actually favored, utilize your leeward rights by constantly luffing boats to windward and avoiding close relationship with boats further to leeward. The most devastating interference is produced by the boat on your lee bow, which must be avoided like the plague. When luffing down the line don't look ahead and to leeward all the time; concentrate on the boats behind and to weather. Give them a little shove up every so often while awaiting the gun. Keep your bow just a little ahead to be certain that your wind remains clear; if you are moving too fast, luff up. Unless you are certain that the windward boat is over the line, and if you are no longer able to see the windward end, keep your bow at least even and your wind clear.

It is rarely safe in a large fleet to start from above the line with the expectation of finding a hole. If the hole does not materialize in the line of boats running toward the leeward end, *keep out*— luff up and wait until it does. Avoid judging a leeward end start too close, particularly if the committee boat or a mark boat with a long anchor line is located at this end. Once in the coffin corner, it may be impossible to get out; although luffing up, without losing leeward and starboard right-of-way status, should be attempted until a large hole which can be tacked into appears. If the leeward end mark is only a small flag buoy, fouling the mark or starting prematurely may be avoided by dipping below the mark, jibing, and returning on a port tack reach to find a hole. A protected corner may be found occasionally, above the lay line to the stern of the windward end committee boat, which can be dipped into from above the line. A boat may cross the starboard tack fleet and tack to port without interference above the lay line of the boats starting normally if the white flag on the committee boat is sufficiently far from the stern.

The fewer the starters, the less significant the right-of-way factors become; but in large fleets adherence to the principles of right-of-way maintenance is essential. *Start on starboard, close on the lee bow of the boat to windward, staying well clear of the backwind of boats further to leeward. In series racing it doesn't pay to take chances; when in doubt—particularly when on port and in doubt —don't!*

Approaching

Establish carefully the position of the starting line in terms of recognizing when you are on it or over it in the midst of a dense cloud of Dacron. It will rarely be possible to see, let alone judge, your position from the observation of both ends of the line at once. If land is visible beyond the ends, establish a range between each end mark and a point on shore beyond that end which extends the actual line. This can be most accurately determined by sailing beyond the end of the line aligning both ends and establishing the range mark for the opposite end. A sight in one direction only then will indicate accurately when you are on the line.

The length of the final approach should be determined by the strength and steadiness of the wind, the size of the fleet, and the speed and acceleration of the boat. Fast boats which accelerate quickly require shorter, and therefore are capable of more accurate, approaches. The larger the fleet, the longer the desirable approach, as other boats prevent precise timing of tacking and demand more available time for final adjustments. Most important, the stronger and steadier the wind, the longer the approach which can be judged accurately; and the lighter and more variable the wind, the shorter the distance which should be sailed from the line and the less the time and distance which can be judged accurately. In very light air the final turn may be made within 50 ft. of the line with only 30 seconds to go, while in a breeze it may be better to be 100 yd. away with 90 seconds to go. Usually 1 minute is a good compromise for the final approach with a distance remaining which can be sailed in 30 seconds at full speed—approximately 200 to 250 ft. in a fast boat in a good breeze.

It is essential to establish, with range marks on the shore and judgment of distance from the desired position on the line, the location of the desired initial approach position so that it can be returned to precisely. Once this position and the time to be used for the final approach are established, a method for arriving at the approach position on time can be worked out. Usually the boat can be luffed along on a reach, slowly approaching the approach position, allowing plenty of extra time, and tacked or luffed into position at the right time. The boat may be luffed at the position or the position may be overstood with a time allowance for returning in order to commence the approach at the proper time.

TECHNIQUE

The early phase of the final approach should be concerned with maintaining an approximate speed which will bring the boat to the line on time and an approximate course which will bring the boat to the desired point on the line, meanwhile keeping as clear wind as possible. The final phase must be considered separately, as it consists of a spontaneous crystallization of all prior planning into a precisely timed dash for a particular opening on the line (see *Fig. 1*).

It is essential to allow both time and distance for adjustment to unforeseeable factors, particularly interference by other boats, in the early phase of the approach. Twice the needed time for the final approach should be made available by starting from the planned approach position sufficiently in advance. It is equally important to allow space for adjustment to interference. If you intend to start

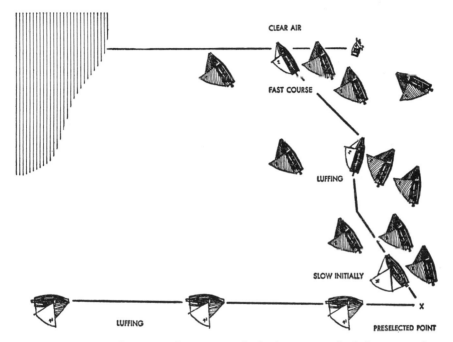

Fig. 1. Starting technique indicating method of timing and of obtaining clear air, free of backwind at moment of start.

at the windward end, plan for variation from the lay line. If you are likely to be luffed, stay a little below the lay line; if the wind is very strong and excessive leeway is expected while luffing along on the approach, stay a little above the lay line. Similarly, if the leeward end is favored, settle for an approach in both time and space which allows a little leeway; aim to be a little late and a little high of the end of the line.

Avoid lee bow contacts at all costs. As you approach the line from below or run down it to the leeward end, either bear off below boats to leeward or luff up and hold back. In general, if at a distance from the line with plenty of time or particularly if late bear off across the stern of a leeward boat with enough way to carry through and come out on her lee bow. If close to the line or particularly if early, luff and push up the boat(s) to windward to provide some breathing distance from the boats to leeward.

Maintain sufficient speed to break through boats to leeward and to get ahead of windward cover. Try to maintain a relationship with other boats on the approach which provides clear wind to weather as well as freedom from lee bow backwinding, usually by keeping close aboard, but bow ahead, of the boat immediately to windward. This position provides freedom to bear off to pick up speed when necessary, if late, without fouling leeward boats and freedom to slow down by luffing. It also provides opportunity to keep clear of boats luffing from further to leeward and effectively controls all boats further to windward. Most important, if this position can be maintained until the gun goes, your wind will be clear, free of backwind, with boats to windward controlled by your own backwind.

If the initial approach line is assumed slightly below the lay line to the weather mark, luffing space will be available without reaching a barging position, but other boats further to windward may be forced above the lay line and brushed off on the mark. Such fine tactics are rarely successful except in moderate air. In heavy air a slow approach while luffing is associated with extensive leeway. In extreme conditions the boat may slip as far laterally as ahead on the approach, an occurrence which must be allowed for in planning and in conducting the approach. In general, in heavy air it is best to commence the approach from well back to permit a faster approach speed, less leeway, and more accurate course control.

The competition, the speed of their boats, and their normal starting tactics are all necessary items to consider on the approach. Over the years, I have been able to put a number of competitors' methods into the file. There are those who 99 per cent of the time will barge; there are others who almost always get to the line early and stall; and there are those who try to jam a start by demanding right of way on bargers, then get there too early. Perhaps 10 per cent of the competition knows how to start, but they usually get shot down by the miscalculating bungling of the multitude. Remember the usual tendencies of the neighboring boats and plan in advance to adjust to them.

The final phase of the approach is entirely dependent upon the circumstances of the initial phase: how close you are to the planned

Planing in Hamilton Harbor, Bermuda

T. J. Wadson, Bermuda

Reaching plane — note lift of hull

Sam Chambliss, Annapolis

George Cornell design on the Severn River

Awaiting the start in Round Bay

Reaching plane – note boat kept bolt upright

Sam Chambliss, Annapolis

Sam Chambliss, Annapolis

Reaching plane — note flat wake

Bermuda News Bureau

Spinnaker run – note level clews, horizontal pole

M. E. Warren, Annapolis

Reaching in Round Bay

Charles Bourke design — note adjustable jib fairleads, hiking straps, centerboard hoist

Uffa Fox design — note boom vang with winch in thwart

Harold J. Flecknoe, Silver Spring

Capsize in the Potomac — righting
technique

Righted — lack of buoyancy will prevent
self rescue

Harold J. Flecknoe, Silver Spring

Before the squall on the Severn

M. E. Warren, Anna

timing, how far you have deviated from the planned course to the ideal position on the line, how clear you have kept your wind, and how neighboring boats have arranged their starts. Ideally you should be exactly a 10 second distance from the desired position on the line with 10 seconds to go, so that you can trim sheets and hit the line precisely with the gun under full way. This is rarely possible; but the more accurately you have been able to sail the initial phase, the more readily this ideal final phase can be achieved. If clear wind is available, only a timing adjustment of the final phase should be necessary so that a full-speed run is attempted as soon as the second hand reaches a point indicating a time remaining equal to that needed for the distance remaining.

At this point, within 10 to 30 seconds of the gun, the precise ideal location on the line should no longer be sought; but the location nearest to that planned location which can be reached without pinching and with clear wind should be aimed for. *It is essential to cross the line under full way with clear wind; missing the ideal location by a few feet or even 100 ft. is of little consequence by comparison.*

If you lack clear wind or other boats are in position to interfere with your wind when you reach the line, disregard all intentions of achieving either an accurately timed or positioned start (except to avoid being over prematurely) and seek clear wind. You will be close enough to the ideal consequent to the initial phase of the approach; now concentrate on the other boats only. If there is clear space to leeward, bear off into it, run down the line, and find the clear wind (without approaching boats further to leeward too closely). If space is clear to windward, luff up into it, breaking away from any boats on your lee bow, holding back until they are well away. If boats are close on both sides and blanketing ahead and to windward, luff up and let them go by until you are on someone else's lee bow with wind clear again. If your initial approach has been fairly accurate, you will find that the boats ahead and to windward are early and will either have to bear off across your bow, giving you an ideal hole above them, or will be forced to luff up with you. In the latter case you will be in control, able to bear off first, gather way first, and break clear on their lee bows.

The accuracy of the decision to trim in or bear off to full way in the final seconds is usually the determining factor in the success of the start in a large fleet. Many boats will be in a position to get a good start in the final seconds but only a few will make it. Those who sheet in too soon will be over early, those who delay too long will be blanketed or backwinded by those who sheet in on time. It is all or nothing, and a second either way at this point will mean the loss of minutes and dozens of yards later if you fail to gain clear wind, and an even greater loss if you are over early.

Check your range to determine the exact position of the line, wait until the precise moment, then trim in, bear off, and go for it! Don't let any boat to windward get her bow ahead of yours unless you are certain she will be over early.

If you have timed the final dash properly you will be moving when the gun goes, probably faster than boats to leeward, and, if positioned properly, far enough above them to be free of their backwind, and will soon be well ahead. If you have your bow even with or a little ahead of boats to weather, they will be in your backwind and will fall back rapidly, and again you will be clear ahead soon. *Once the gun goes (if you are not over early), put every ounce of effort into driving the boat at maximum speed.* These are the moments that count, this is the sprint which will determine the final outcome of the race. Three-quarters of the fleet is now floundering in someone else's backwind or blanket zone. Those boats which are moving well will acquire insurmountable leads in a few minutes.

Trim the sails to perfection, hike as hard as you can to keep the boat bolt upright, and bear off a little more than usual for maximum speed. A common fault is to pinch up and try to fight back the boats to windward. If they are really capable of breaking through your backwind zone, pinching and slowing your boat will not stop them. Meanwhile the boats to leeward will be romping off to leave you in their backwind. Remember that every boat in the fleet, except the single one farthest to leeward, is in someone else's backwind, that this backwind becomes increasingly damaging the farther the leeward boats move ahead, and that everyone is fighting the same problem. Your approach was designed to avoid lee bow contacts; now make use of the slightly greater room to leeward that you have acquired, by bearing away slightly to reach maximum speed. And keep working with every bit of skill and effort until you are truly free of all interference.

Another common mistake is to sheet in too tightly with this maximum effort. In the disturbed air which is bound to be present in a large fleet, you cannot point as high and you need the maximum drive you can get. Ease both main and jib a bit and drive her.

If you lose or cannot acquire clear wind with the gun, look for the first opportunity to get it. Often boats farther to windward will tack to clear their wind, leaving you free to tack, but remember a lee bow position reverses itself when both boats tack; wait until sufficiently far beyond to tack free of backwind. If the cloud of boats to windward is dense and no holes appear, bear away farther to leeward, if a clear area appears in that direction, or luff up or ease sheets to let the windward boat go by until you can tack safely. Don't just flounder along without wind. It is better to give up ten boats initially than twenty later.

Now is the time to remember the original basis for the starting plan. Why did you start as you did in the first place? On which tack and on which side of the course did you intend to sail the early part of the windward leg? Do not be misled too far by the necessity of getting clear wind; particularly, don't allow yourself to tack too far from the desired side of the course. Get clear wind and no more; tack back to the desired tack and direction as soon as possible. If the port tack is favored and/or the starboard side of the course advantageous, be the first to get on port; but avoid shooting off too far on port if the fleet is sailing in a starboard tack lift, or the port side of the course is out of the tide or blessed with more wind, or the course is a one-leg beat on starboard. It is sometimes better to take your medicine in someone's backwind while the rest of the fleet scrambles for clear air in the wrong direction!

SPECIAL STARTING SITUATIONS

Windward-End Starts

A start at the windward end of the line is indicated when the starboard side of the windward leg is favored due to an offshore shift, reduced adverse current, etc.; when it is heavily favored due to the relationship of the line to the wind direction; or when in a shifting wind the starboard tack has been lifted. As this is the end at which most boats usually start, regardless of conditions, clear wind is difficult to acquire and the start must be precisely timed to avoid floundering in the ruck. The safest solution is to aim for a location slightly to leeward of the windward end and to hit the line here under full way, lee bowing the boats to windward. If the port tack is sought, the safest solution is to barge slightly and come in late. If above the lay line when near the mark, be careful not to press your luck; stay above the mob, waiting and luffing, until a definite hole appears, then bear off and shoot into it.

If you cannot resist the temptation to seek the ideal start at the flag with the gun, don't expect to accomplish it with full way on timed from considerably back of the line (except in small fleets). Run or reach away from the line with two minutes or less remaining and jibe in the midst of the approaching fleet with about one minute to go, right on the lay line, about 200 ft. from the windward mark. (Jibing is quicker, takes less space, and can be more accurately controlled than tacking in congested areas.) Luff along the lay line, holding back to avoid being early at all costs. Be careful not to get above the lay line or your final dash will be ruined by a leeward boat's squeezing you out at the mark (unless the breeze is very strong, with resultant excessive leeway). Let the bargers rush past your bow, unable to restrain themselves in the final seconds, to be forced over early or foul someone to leeward. If you are within a boat's length of the mark before the gun goes, boats clear ahead must either be over or luffing up or bearing away across your bow at an angle to the course. This means that there should be a hole; if there isn't, someone isn't legal, so start screaming along with the rest of them to "get up or get out." When you have but 2 seconds and 8 ft. to go, sheet in, bear off, and go. If you were able to stay on the lay line, you should have the perfect start. If your intention is to tack to port, don't delay, gather full way, clear the committee boat, and go, before a faster boat or one moving faster but starting later works out to windward and prevents you from tacking.

Leeward-End Start

This start is frequently used because so many committees feel that moving the leeward end upwind prevents windward-end barging and gives a fairer start to all. Although initially more boats may appear to have clear wind, inasmuch as backwind is the major interference factor in all starts and backwind is increased by turning the fleet more into a line, each on the other's lee bow, more interference is actually produced. Only one boat at the extreme leeward end gets away in clear air; the rest, suffering in progressively increasing amounts of backwind, rapidly fall astern or attempt an extremely dangerous port tack from a slow position across the path of the entire fleet. Although a heavily favored windward end is bad, the boats to leeward can get away in relatively clear air if they are on the line, while a heavily favored leeward end helps no one but the single boat on the end. For these reasons it may be advisable to avoid the leeward end, to start to windward, and so be in position to take an early port tack out of the massive backwind zone. A port tack across the bows of the fleet at the leeward end should never be possible in a good fleet; but a hole will always appear in the line of starboard tackers, if you have the restraint to wait for it. If you can achieve a breakthrough, you will have a tremendous advantage over the mass behind, which will be barely moving in the disturbed air and afraid to tack in the presence of other boats behind and to windward.

If the leeward mark is not a large boat with an anchor line which may trap you in the coffin corner, a perfect starboard tack start at the flag with the gun may be worth attempting. Start your approach close to the leeward end, perhaps 100 ft. away with 30 seconds remaining, usually by tacking or jibing just ahead of and beneath the fleet running down the line. Be sure that your turn brings you out precisely on the lay line to the mark. If you maintain sufficient speed, you should be able to scare away any boats from passing to windward, as they will fear to reach the mark too soon. If you are really on the lay line, you should not have to worry about boats passing to leeward, as, if you are already close to the mark, they will not be able to pass to leeward and still come up to lay the mark. If you can retain sufficient speed to hold back the boats to weather, but can proceed slowly enough to avoid reaching the mark too soon, you should be able to fend off all attackers, sheet in for the final rush, a few seconds before the gun, a few feet from the mark, and be away to clear wind, alone and uncatchable.

Other variations in windward starting techniques are discussed in the chapters on racing rules, current conditions, light air racing, and starting in heavy air.

Reaching Starts

As in starting to windward, a reaching start should be planned to facilitate getting to the advantageous side of the course, if possible, from the favored end of the line, with right of way and precise timing. The favored side of the course is often determined by the advantage of being inside at the next mark. This is particularly important if the leg is a short one. If the reach is longer, the advantage of starting to leeward with less backwind and a higher sailing angle should be recognized. If the reach is close, however, it is essential to start to windward to be prepared for the possibility of the leg's becoming a beat and to obtain the best planing angle if the wind is of sufficient strength.

Secondary to these considerations is the evaluation of the advantages of a start at the end of the line which is closest to the mark. Unless the distance is greatly reduced, consideration of the favored side of the course should rule. If the windward end is farther ahead, the leeward-end start may be less desirable because of blanketing; while if the leeward end is farther forward, it is almost certain to be the better end to start.

Right of way is usually acquired by approaching the line from farther to leeward than neighboring boats. If the first leg is a dead reach or broader, the boat may be luffed up the line on starboard tack with complete control over boats to windward and no danger of being forced over early.

As the approach line to the desired position on the line may be varied without loss of right of way, the major consideration is timing. It is usually desirable to make a few practice runs at full speed from the initial approach position on a full and by course to the desired starting point and to allow about time and a half for the actual run. It is essential to hit the line on a reaching start under full way, as a boat moving faster may break completely through to leeward and cripple you in her backwind for the duration of the leg. Therefore, hold back to a ten-second, full-speed distance until ten seconds remain, then sheet in and drive her at top speed to be certain that you hit the line full out. It may be nerve-racking to hold back as other boats luff past; but if you are moving and they are not, by virtue of being too close too soon, you will shoot right past when the gun goes. Keep on neighboring boats' lee bows; pass to leeward and keep to leeward.

Running Starts

Starts on a run are similar to reaching starts in that the desired side of the course should be given primary consideration. If the wind is light or the current strong stay close to the line, as it takes a long time to cover distance on a light air run. Tacking downwind may or may not be indicated for the first leg but is almost always indicated for the start. The approach, to insure right of way and speed, should be on a starboard tack broad reach. Slowing can be by luffing, or bearing away without loss of right of way. Maintain the reaching angle until the gun actually goes, if possible, to continue maximum speed as you actually cross the line, shooting through neighboring interference. It is not necessary to assume a normal course for the purposes of allowing room at the windward mark until the gun goes, and the NAYRU Appeals recognize that the boat must have time to achieve this new requirement. Therefore a windward boat may be forced above the windward starting mark if the leeward boat arrives close to the mark with the gun and cannot readily give sufficient room thereafter. Do not set the spinnaker until after the gun.

Premature Starts

Be particularly careful not to be over the line early in a favorable current, on a reaching start, particularly in planing conditions, or in light air, as the return will be considerably slower and the total loss magnified considerably. In many circumstances the risks of being over early must be accepted and calculated with the other starting considerations. When the line is laid to favor the leeward end, the entire fleet works itself farther and farther down and across the line in the final seconds. The boat which holds back, uncertain as to the exact location of the line, only ends up blanketed, backwinded, and hopelessly beaten. If the ends of the line are no longer visible in the mass of Dacron, the only criterion must be the bow of the boat to weather. To avoid being in the hopeless leeward position, you must push on to keep your bow even or slightly ahead (but close aboard) to keep the windward boat in the hopeless windward position—unless you can see the range and know that the windward boat is over. If the entire fleet pushes over and the committee, unable to distinguish individual numbers, accepts it, your only remedy is to go along and keep at least your jib luff in clear air. Be more daring in large fleets, as a start without clear wind may be fatal; and more cautious in small fleets, as a premature start will be more harmful than a minor and temporary interference with clear wind.

If you have any suspicion that you may have started early, listen carefully for the signal so indicating and luff immediately when you detect that it means you. Luffing will prevent the boat from continuing away from the line but will permit retention of right of way over neighboring boats which will undoubtedly be swarming along behind. Look about with the boat slowed and, as soon as you see an opening, tack—or better, jibe—into it, slipping back along a parallel course to avoid any interference with boats coming across properly.

Under several circumstances the difficulties of returning a premature start may be reduced, and the advantages of a precisely timed crossing may justify the risk. A wind-clear start at the leeward end may be impossible if even a few seconds' delay are permitted. The advantages of getting away with clear wind in this position are so great as to justify attempting to hit the flag with the gun, but only if the leeward mark is a flag which can be ducked below or reached around above if you are early. A jibe and a port tack reach to a hole after such a premature start may still produce a better start than two-thirds of the fleet. At the windward end, breaking through a line of bargers requires precise timing but if successful may give a commanding lead (particularly if the port tack is favored). This start is justified because if premature it may be ameliorated by a quick turn around the mark or committee boat to a late but still ideally positioned start (again better than two-thirds of the fleet). Starting from above the line is successful only if the leeward end is favored and the boats spread out along the line, but under these circumstances may be very effective if a hole appears. If a hole does not appear, luffing up and waiting (be cautious!) until one does may still provide a start better than most.

SUMMARY

Plan your start to facilitate the strategy of the first leg, considering the inequality of the line relative to the wind, the possibility of benefit from a wind shift, the need to acquire clear wind, and the need to maintain right of way. Plan to approach the desired position on the line from a predetermined initial approach position with about twice the needed time remaining. Try to stay on course as closely as possible, moving slowly, until a point is reached within a short distance of the line at a time when the remaining distance can just be traversed in the remaining time, then sheet in, bear off, and go for it. Keep close on the lee bow of the nearest boat to windward, avoiding boats to leeward as far as possible. After the gun, drive her as fast as possible to obtain or consolidate your clear wind and assume the planned strategy of the first leg.

9. Finishing

By HOWARD GAPP, Newport Harbor

Most sailboat racing is done in series, final standings being determined by a totaling of finishing positions relative to other boats. It is disturbing to recognize that faster boats, boats which are ahead throughout most of a given race, and boats which could readily win match races with their competitors are often behind at the finish line and in the final standings

Sailing races are won and lost at the finish line—an artificial end point injected into what is supposed to be a contest of speed. Fast boats often win, and boat speed is the major factor in staying ahead throughout most of any race; but there are certain crucial positions, the start, the turning marks, and the finish, imposed by the race committee, which determine the final positions. Thus a race between sailboats is not a mere contest of speed, but a series of sprints from one crucial point to another, the outcome of which is more often determined by the management of the boat at these crucial locations than by its speed.

Where boat speed varies greatly, it becomes the most important factor. Immediately after the start the speed of different competitors varies widely, as some are in the lead with clear wind and water and some are behind with severe backwind or blanketing. Some boats may start on time in the right position to retain and obtain the best of clear wind and water. Others may start late at the wrong end of the line with obstructed wind and the necessity of sailing in disturbed wind and water all the way up the weather leg. The effect of wind and water disturbance is less significant on the windward leg, where boats can spread widely apart. Yet the initial effects of such disturbance at and for the first few minutes after the crucial crowded start are often the determining factors in the positions at the first mark.

Once the first mark is reached, particularly if there are no subsequent windward legs, the boats must sail closer together, along almost identical courses on the reaches and runs, the speed of each determined largely by the relative position and capabilities of their nearest competitors. Regardless of how fast or well sailed the boat is, it is profoundly effected by backwinding and wake from a boat ahead, luffing from a boat to leeward, blanketing from a boat to windward, and constant feints to pass from the boats behind. Poorer boats may find their positions fixed by these factors after rounding the weather mark, never to change; better boats will find a way to break clear of such interference and then to sail sufficiently faster so as to change position. However, even the latter will be slowed for at least a short period of time, forced to deviate from the ideal course, and pressured into temporary tactical expedients rather than adhering to ultimate strategic plans. And this entire pattern is dependent upon the technique and position in which the boat rounded the crucial weather mark. When at last the better boat does work clear to attempt a pace equal to that of the leaders, the initial offwind leg is over, another turning mark, another crucial point appears, and the entire sequence is resumed.

The chapters in the first portion of this book on the elements of sailboat racing provide the information needed to prepare a boat, enter it, and legally and safely sail it in a race in any weather or sea condition. These chapters are concerned with strategic factors which aid in sailing the boat around the course in the shortest possible time and with tuning it to sail at the maximum possible speed. Such considerations are developed without regard to the presence of other boats. In actual practice the technique of "making the boat go" and sailing it over the shortest possible route may have only limited application to a short period in the middle of a leg. The presence of other boats and the avoidance of their interference, particularly at the crucial points, may preclude adherence to strategic plans and prevent production of maximum boat speed. The damaging effects of the proximity of other boats cannot be underestimated and every effort should be made at all times to avoid such interference. *But as interference must be accepted at the start, at the turning marks, and at the finish, a technique must be developed to make it possible to take maximum advantage of these crucial moments, to capitalize upon the slowing of the competitors, and to emerge each time with clear wind and water in the strategically desirable position.* Starting technique is discussed in two special chapters, and rounding of marks is discussed in relation to the completion of a particular type of course in appropriate chapters. In this chapter on finishing, the most crucial moment of all will be considered.

NAYRU-IYRU RULES WHICH APPLY AT THE FINISH

Rule 13. Finishing

Check the race committee's instructions to see whether bow or mast finishes are to be used. When finishing upwind, in light wind especially, your position will sometimes be such that it is possible to luff up sharply toward the line and allow momentum to carry you over, thus saving precious seconds. Obviously it is possible to luff up earlier if bow finishes are called for than if mast finishes are required.

Once the bow or mast is across the line a boat has finished. Thereafter it does not matter if she goes into irons and drifts back across the line or capsizes or goes straight home. However, note that for purposes of disqualification, the rules apply from the yacht's preparatory signal until she has finished and cleared the line. For instance, if you do finish by luffing, then go into irons and drift back across the line without clearing it (*i.e.*, if not all parts of the boat have crossed the line), you remain subject to the racing rules, and right-of-way boats could cause disqualification.

Similarly a boat may finish as her bow crosses the line but if any part of her hits the mark (her boom, for instance) she is subject to disqualification. I lost the West Coast Championship one year in just this manner when my boom touched the mark after my bow was well over the line but my transom was not yet clear of it.

A yacht finishes when any part of her hull or equipment crosses the finishing line from the direction of the last mark. This rule is clear enough except that in two special cases it is unworkable: (a) when the finish line and the last mark lie in the same straight line, (b) when the last mark is obscured by fog or haze.

Limit for Finishing

Do not forget to read the race committee's instructions to determine whether there is a special time limit for the race. One boat finishing within the prescribed time limit makes the race valid for all other competitiors in the race. If you have reason to believe that one boat has finished, you should finish as well even though you finish after the time limit.

Shortening Course

Rule 11 states that the race committee may shorten a race while it is in progress because of unfavorable wind, weather, or tide. Former NAYRU Rule 32 dealing with committee signal S (the shorten-course signal) will probably usually be described in the instructions and means when displayed: (a) at the start of the race, "sail the short course prescribed in the instructions"; (b) near or at the finish, "finish the race with this round at the prescribed finish line"; (c) elsewhere, "finish between the nearby mark and the committee boat." If conditions are such that you suspect the course may be shortened, be on the lookout for the committee boat near a mark other than the expected finish mark, with the S flag flying. Your tactics in rounding the mark will be quite different if you are rounding it as a mark of the course (where preservation of your overlap would be the important thing) or as a finish line mark (where keeping your bow ahead is essential).

FINISHING STRATEGY

The four major strategic factors to be considered at the finish are: (1) *the wind direction and the possibility of shifts,* (2) *the nearest point on the finish line,* (3) *the tide, and* (4) *the disturbance of the wind at the line.* Tactical considerations of interference at the final crucial point often outweigh all strategic factors, however.

When finishing upwind, if shifts are expected, keep to leeward, sailing toward expected headers, attempting to be as close as possible to the new lay line after the shift. If the expected lay line is reached before the present lay line tack, continue along the expected lay line so as to be in position to take maximum advantage of the expected shift. When finishing downwind, assume the side of the course which will produce the fastest course terminally. Keeping to leeward of the leg on a broad reach or run permits a fast finish high on the wind and the possibility of overtaking a competitor to windward. If a heading wind shift is expected, keep to windward at first so that bearing off to a freer course will provide more speed at the finish. Be particularly careful to keep to leeward if a lifting shift is expected. Don't allow yourself to be luffed or tempted to luff on a planing reach, as once you are too far to windward you will be unable to plane at the finish and unable properly to comply with "up in the lulls, down in the squalls."

The most favorable point to cross the line at the finish, *i.e.*, the end requiring the shortest sailing distance, should be determined if possible at the time of the start. Note the tide so that allowances can be made for any change which will occur by the time of the finish. The nearest point when finishing upwind will be the downwind end of the line, while the nearest point when finishing downwind will depend upon the angle of the line across the course. Differences in tidal current and wind strength and direction along the line may alter the location of optimal crossing, however.

Assuming that the optimal crossing point on the finish line has been chosen, due allowance should be made for the probability that the wind in the vicinity of the finish line will be less reliable in strength and direction than in open areas. It has usually been chopped up and deflected by boats of other classes, spectator boats, and by the committee boat itself. Often one has the feeling near the finish line that the boat just won't go properly. The lighter the wind and the more boats there are in the vicinity of the line, the more the wind disturbance and the more one should overstand the ideal crossing point to allow for the effect of this chopped-up wind. Unless wind or tide variations or covering a competitor dictate otherwise, one should keep clear of the middle of the area most likely to contain chopped-up air.

Finishing on the starboard tack may be most effective under some circumstances, but do not neglect the port tack as it may make possible a finish clear of the area of chopped-up wind. (Many boats finish on the starboard tack by habit.)

No matter how far behind you may be, always finish a race. In the 1957 Mallory eliminations I was crewing for Neil Allen. We were the last boat at the windward mark due to a series of bizarre happenings. About 25 yd. from the mark the wind failed and we began to drift away with the strong tide. All the other boats had rounded before the wind dropped. The water was too deep to drop an anchor and it was three hours before we were able to round. Of course Neil finished the race last but a point better than DNF. In the three race series this put him in second place. In other circumstances he might have been first.

In another race at Alamitos Bay, California, a heavy fog reduced visibility to a few yards. I sailed up onto the beach by mistake. When we realized that we were completely lost, my crew ran up to the highway and managed to discover where we were from a local gas station. It turned out that the jetty we were aiming for was not far away. All this took a great deal of time, so that when we had got the boat and rigging unscrambled from the rocks and sand and had found the jetty and sailed into the bay, we sailed straight to the dock and did not trouble to round the last two marks. Had we adhered to the principle that all races should be finished, we would have sailed round those last few marks and been second in the race! It turned out that the main body of the fleet had missed the jetty by an even greater distance than we and did not turn up until a good thirty minutes after we had reached the dock. We needlessly spoiled our chances in the series by becoming discouraged and not finishing.

There is further good reason to finish every race. Dropping out before the finish detracts from the achievement of those who win, suggests that the race is of not much importance, and discourages those who take the trouble to finish even though they do not place. In addition, one loses the opportunity of gaining the peculiar though very real satisfaction which is reserved in all great sports for those who are unsuccessful but refuse to give up.

Try to sail your own race between the start and the last turning mark, avoiding involvement in covering duels as far as possible and lightly considered changes in your original concept of the quickest course to follow. At the finish it is position that counts and not time, but before the finish it is usually time that counts and not position.

Covering duels early in the race are pointless, are exhausting physically and mentally, and tend to produce a state of mind in which the more important effects of tides, wind shifts, and plain sailing the boat fast are forgotten. There are too many unknowns to permit a decision as to which boat to try to beat. Each boat is sailing against the fleet in these early stages, not against any one competitor.

There are of course exceptions to this guiding rule: when tacking can be timed in order to cause the maximum nuisance to the nearest competitor without departing from the original plan, when alone with another boat ahead of the rest of the fleet, etc. It is advisable usually to stay roughly between the nearer boats and the next mark.

Between the last mark and the finish line, however, you can discard the concept of sailing against time and begin sailing against boats. Unless the distance to the line is great, the courses that the nearby boats will follow are usually fairly predictable. Tactical considerations to beat the greatest number of boats across the line should now be paramount, rather than basic strategy.

Perhaps there is good reason to treat the last race of a series as one would the finish in other races. Point scores should be known by heart and the courses followed by close competitors should be watched. It may pay to cover them even at the risk of losing other boats with less threatening point scores (a plan that should seldom if ever be followed earlier in the series).

FINISHING TACTICS—FINISHING TO WINDWARD

The major tactical factors to be considered when finishing upwind include: (*1*) *breaking clear at the start of the final leg*, (*2*) *the position and speed of the final tack, and* (*3*) *the possibility of successful interference with other boats.* Once clear of the interference at the tactically critical final turning mark, an optimal course should be undertaken on strategical considerations.

The decision to tack for the final approach must be carefully considered in advance, as either understanding or overstanding may make a critical difference. If the final leg is essentially a one-leg beat, any distance expended in continuing across the course prior to tacking for the line may be wasted. If in doubt, tack immediately, particularly if close competitors continue on without tacking in a misguided effort to cover. Even if you are unable to lay the mark initially, any wind shift will be beneficial. A header will put the leeward boat (first to tack) in the lead, and a lift will permit her to lay the line while boats to windward overstand. If the boat ahead tacks immediately it is probably better to continue on before tacking for clear wind, in hopes that the boat ahead will be unable to lay the line. If your boat points unusually well, gamble on an early tack; if she does better pointing on a freer course, carry on a little farther before making the final approach. If the final turning mark is rounded to port, the long tack will be on starboard so that boats to windward will have right of way over the leeward boats which have understood the line and must tack. *Make the final tack in free air, toward the nearest point on the line, allowing for wind shifts or tide changes, and drive her.*

Tack to cover competitors astern on the final leg, seeking to consolidate your present condition initially. But if it is possible to interfere with competitors who are gaining or to pass a boat ahead, concentrate on this. If following boats or boats to leeward are not within three over-all lengths, you may bear off, sprinting for the line at top speed and simultaneously getting between leeward competitors and the line. As the favored tack will be along the lay line most perpendicular to the line, try to force competitors to continue beyond this line. Tack immediately for the line when you reach the lay line yourself, encouraging competitors to sail a few lengths beyond to clear their wind.

The most common error in finishing upwind is overstanding the nearest point on the line. Avoid this at all costs; plan well ahead for the final approach tack. Don't waste those precious feet if there is another boat close. Finish on the tack which lays the line at the most perpendicular angle, if possible, as this provides the most rapid approach in the final crucial seconds. If then a competitor crosses close ahead, bear away for maximum speed, driving along the most perpendicular course to overtake the competitor, who must either tack or continue on an oblique approach (see *Fig. 1*).

Although a starboard tack finish may be advantageous occa-

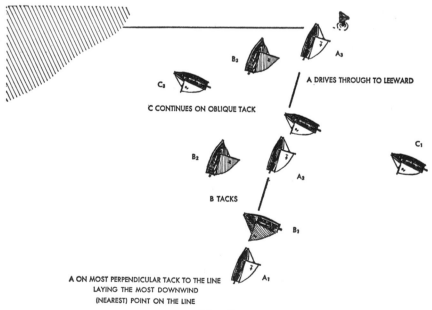

B₃

C₃

A₃

A DRIVES THROUGH TO LEEWARD

C CONTINUES ON OBLIQUE TACK

C₁

B₂

A₂

B TACKS

B₁

A ON MOST PERPENDICULAR TACK TO THE LINE
LAYING THE MOST DOWNWIND
(NEAREST) POINT ON THE LINE

A₁

Fig. 1

sionally, the above requirements to finish at the nearest point on the most perpendicular tack far outweigh such right-of-way considerations. Actually the port tack provides more freedom to bear off and is more likely to induce the competitor to cross ahead and tack rather than to tack on your lee bow. The extra distance of the crossing before tacking may permit the boat right on the ideal lay line to break through to leeward. When ahead, tack for the lee bow position if you are certain you can lay the line.

On the other hand, the lee bow position can be extremely dangerous if you are unable to lay the line or if a slight header is expected. Under these circumstances avoid the lee bow position at all costs or you may find yourself carried beyond the lay line at the mercy of the boat to windward. If on starboard prior to the final tack for the line you can catch a competitor on port and force him to tack into the lee bow position, you may successfully eliminate him. He should be carried to a point where when you tack your boat will be just in the clear-ahead position. It is evident that carrying another boat beyond the lay line is most effective when both boats are close to the mark. When both boats are distant from the mark, adequate overstanding may result in the loss of other boats. As the lee bow position reverses itself after both boats tack, on the final approach the leeward boat will remain at the windward boat's mercy until the leeward pulls clear ahead with room to tack.

A competitor may sometimes be persuaded to do stupid things and thereby to give you one last chance to cross the line ahead of him.

If you find yourself in the hopeless windward position beating toward the mark, you will probably notice that the skipper of the boat ahead is turning anxiously from time to time to see how you are moving as compared with him. If you can point higher momentarily each time he turns, you may perhaps persuade him that he is sailing too low. If he pinches hard enough and kills the speed of his own boat, you may have a chance to drive through to the line.

A similar deception may be attempted when a boat is about to cross your bow near the finish line and you know he will try to tack on your weather bow and put you in the hopeless leeward position. Just before he crosses your bow and up until the time he tacks, hold a course below the mark. If your competition is watchful, as he should be, he will be misled into thinking that you cannot lay the mark. He will then continue farther before tacking to insure laying the mark himself. When you both assume the correct course to the mark, you may find yourself in a safe leeward position!

FINISHING DOWNWIND

Essential factors for finishing downwind include: (1) *getting clear wind after the rounding of the preceding mark,* (2) *assuming the fastest course for the leg,* (3) *planning for top speed on the final approach, and* (4) *interfering with nearby competitors.* Getting clear wind on a downwind course usually means going either to windward or leeward of the mob unless you are clear ahead. Consider the need to have clear air astern or abeam along your apparent wind line. Avoid passing to leeward or ahead of boats on your apparent wind line by staying well to leeward or windward. Particularly if it is light, avoid the middle.

The fastest course should be assumed in terms of providing the maximum sprint at the finish where inches and seconds count.

It is usually noticeably better to *avoid the most direct course which will contain disturbed wind.* In light air, where the final leg is not a dead run but neither the jib nor the spinnaker will draw well on a direct course to the optimal finishing point, keeping to one side pays off even better. Running downwind on a course on which the spinnaker draws well will take you out of the disturbed air in many cases. Final jibe to the line should be made at a point where the jib or reaching spinnaker will subsequently draw well. This method works best in light winds when boats sailing the direct course are well below hull speed. Under these conditions slight increases in thrust cause relatively large increases in speed. Finishing on a broad reach will give you right of way over boats dead before the wind. In heavier breezes where planing is possible on a reaching course but not before the wind, the same tactics will be handsomely rewarded.

When there is enough wind to give hull speed directly before the wind or enough to permit planing on a run, tacking downwind should be avoided; then the shortest course is the fastest course. This wind velocity (which will be higher if there is a chop and lower if a calm sea prevails) is great enough that eddy currents due to other boats can be neglected, as they are blown quickly away. The problem then is to choose the shortest course which will allow maintenance of hull speed.

Combination courses saving the fastest for last may be useful.

Bear off to set the spinnaker at first on a light air reach and then come in to the finish fast, high on the wind with the jib. Or if forced to go high to get clear air initially, continue until optimal spinnaker angle is reached and bear away under the chute. If planing is only just possible in moderate air, save the planing angle for the end, bearing off initially. If the reach is too high for planing, work up initially and then bear off for the line. Usually in these circumstances variable wind strength and direction will encourage working up in the lulls and planing off in the puffs whenever they appear.

Consolidate your position by staying between the line and your nearest competitor astern but don't cross in front of him. Try to keep your wind clear just to the side of him. As long as you stay near the direct course to the mark he will be unable to pass to leeward. If he wants to work to windward, let him; keep to leeward for the final sprint high on the wind. If behind, attempt blanketing by staying in the apparent wind line of the boat ahead; observe his masthead fly. On a run this line is usually over the windward corner of his transom. When blanketing, sudden changes are likely to occur with the windward boat surging ahead while on the apparent wind line and the leeward boat surging ahead when her wind breaks free aft. The wind-blanketing effect is produced when close aboard but watch out for the sharp luff. Time the blanketing precisely so that you cross the line with the surge of the blanket and before the leeward boat surges ahead again or crosses astern to blanket you. In planing winds hang on to the leading boat's quarter until a real puff hits, then hike hard and roar past as the competitor wallows in the blanket. As soon as you are abreast bear off (not below the proper course) to get between him and the line and finish him off with a good dose of backwind.

In planing conditions particularly it may occasionally be possible to ride a wave or a puff through to leeward and then pass a boat ahead. This is rarely possible, however, unless the leading boat can be drawn sufficiently far to windward initially so that the overtaking boat may keep its wind clear throughout the passing. By constant threats to pass to windward, the leader may be drawn gradually farther and farther above the course so that, even if the original course is a dead reach, both boats will eventually be on a run for the final few feet, the leeward boat's wind clear astern as his bow moves ahead of the competitors to windward (see *Fig. 2*). A boat with a real propensity for luffing may eventually be carried so far up by threats to his windward quarter that both boats must jibe for the line, giving the overtaking boat clear wind on the opposite jibe!

It is often possible when yachts are finishing downwind on a port tack to run up to windward of a leading boat, jibe, and claim right of way. Jibing to starboard does not give immediate right of way, as the port tack boat does not have to begin to keep clear until the jibe is completed. In case of doubt you will be presumed to have jibed too close. Properly timed and executed, however, this tactic may force a competitor to jibe or luff up to cross astern and permit beating him to the line.

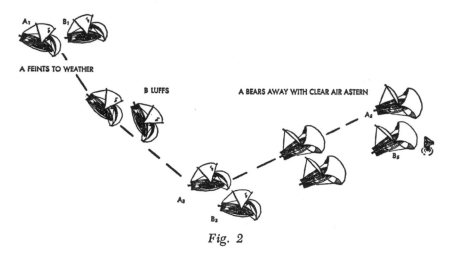

A FEINTS TO WEATHER

B LUFFS

A BEARS AWAY WITH CLEAR AIR ASTERN

Fig. 2

If you find yourself to leeward but have lost your luffing rights, it is often possible to jibe and then jibe again, to establish a new overlap. If you are forward of the mast abeam position at the completion of the second jibe you may then luff away.

The double jibe is usually a better way of breaking an existing overlap than moving away two lengths abeam from the longer yacht. Furthermore, in very light winds a couple of jibes may help propel the boat.

Luffing a boat above the finish mark is desirable if you are approaching the finish downwind and have luffing rights but your bow is not ahead, or you judge it will not be ahead, by the time the line is crossed.

You may luff another boat above the mark only if you go to the same side of it yourself or permit her finally to round properly.

Under these circumstances luff the other boat beyond the mark or until he calls "mast abeam," then jibe, harden up, and come back round the mark again. You should be closer to the mark and have the inside overlap.

Do not attempt this maneuver if there are other boats in the vicinity about to cross the line, as it takes too long to complete.

A susceptible helmsman ahead may be overtaken by constant threats to windward and to leeward. The overtaking boat controlling the maneuvers can make smooth gradual course alterations while the helmsman ahead, frantically noting the competitor in a different threatening position every time he looks astern, sharply swings and slows his boat from side to side; when close astern at last, wait for him to look, make a feint to windward which will force him into a quick luff, and as he looks ahead to direct his crew, shoot off to leeward under his stern.

ILLEGAL PROPULSION

Rule 25 states, "No yacht shall employ any means of propulsion other than the natural action of the wind on the sails." Close to the finish line, particularly in very light airs, there is a temptation, which must be resisted, to produce forward motion by illegal means: running aft suddenly; pulling in the main suddenly, then letting it go slowly; repeatedly jibing (fast pull in and slow let out); rocking the boat (the head of the mainsail produces a small component force forward as the mast moves in an arc to windward); sculling with the tiller, etc. However, anchoring when the wind drops to prevent being carried astern by the tide is legal and often essential.

MORE PHILOSOPHY

Between the finish line and the bar there is a further stretch of water which might also be considered part of "finishing" a race. It should certainly be considered somewhere, for it is here in the mental-let-down period just after the race that those who did not place are open to attacks of disappointment, disgust, frustration, jealousy, anger and so on. Probably everyone who races has had these feelings at times to such a degree that the whole day's sailing suddenly seems unattractive.

Seen in the right perspective, there is enough that is enjoyable in racing a sailboat, other than the joy of winning, to make it worth while, win or lose. A number of very sensible, helpful, and amusing things have been said about the general philosophy behind the racing and sailing of boats. The following references are heartily recommended: (a) "The Purpose of It All" in *Thoughts on Small Boat Racing* by C. Stanley Ogilvy; (b) "Letters to Michael Bratby" in Uffa Fox's *Sail and Power;* (c) *The Pleasures of Sailing* by Alfred Stanford; and (d) the famous "Poem" by Kenneth Grahame in *Wind in the Willows* concerning the joys of "just messing."

10. Beating in Moderate Air

By GEORGE WHITTAKER, Toronto

In moderate conditions the beat is the most important leg of the race; the first boat to the weather mark is usually the first at the finish. And beating is largely a matter of helmsmanship. Except for the adjustment of the side and turning forces which act upon the boat and the acquisition of sails which provide maximum power within this adjustment, there is little than can be done in advance of the windward leg. My experiences have emphasized the importance of technique and tactics, and these are the factors which I have emphasized in this chapter.

TUNING

I do not believe there is any specific rake of the mast which has proven best. I have had boats with rakes from 18 to 4 in. with no appreciable change in weather work. The same thing applies to the slackness of the shrouds. Boats with very loose stays have gone as well as boats with piano-tight stays. However, speaking from experience, the latter condition often leads to compression strains and broken spars and I would suggest not going to the extreme. Nonetheless, I firmly believe in a tight jibstay—and this is almost impossible without tightening the other stays too much. I feel that many small racing craft should be using much heavier wire for the stay than they are. The heavier the stay, apparently, the less the tendency to droop to leeward. The mast should be perfectly perpendicular on the dock. Unless you are experimenting with jib leads, both should be in identically the same position. Both points seem obvious but nevertheless are violated continuously.

A great deal has been written and argued about the relationship of the jib and the main and the slot effect. I believe that the foot of the jib should be slightly tighter than the leech to allow the latter to fall off in harmony with the main. The jib should be cut with a niggered leech, as opposed to the main which should be cut with a roached leech. Small girdle stays can be inserted in the seams just inside the jib leech, to help solve any fluttering problems.

A word about kicking straps: although they are essential, they do create terrific pressures. An A frame, with its apex against the forward surface of the spar at the gooseneck, does not solve the problem; it only redistributes the stress higher up. One solution is to move the after boom block for the mainsheet forward until it is at the point where a line from the top black band on the spar to the traveler bisects the boom. This tends to minimize the powerful forward thrust of the boom when the mainsheet is led from the end of the boom and the kicking strap pulled tight, and in addition it seems to help the common fold through the forward edge of the battens in the mainsail. Batten tips should be flexible but they should gradually stiffen to the outside edge of the sail. This tends to help the leech from fluttering and prevents an S curve to leeward.

The factors which are significant in balancing the turning forces acting upon the boat are presented in Table I. The lateral-resistance factors must provide a turning moment to leeward which does not quite balance the turning moment to windward of the aerodynamic forces acting upon the sails. The residual weather helm then constantly acts to take the boat to windward. Every time the helmsman's attention lapses, the boat gains to weather and the rudder surface itself provides constant lift in the proper direction.

In general, the farther forward the mast and the center of effort of the sail plan, the higher the pointing; and for any given sail plan the farther forward the center of lateral resistance, *i.e.*, the centerboard, the higher the pointing. Cat-rigged boats always point better than sloops, *i.e.*, iceboats, but if a jib is used it becomes the most important sail to windward and must be given adequate space to function. A long base to the foretriangle and a wide slot seem essential in modern International 14's (and are probably even more important when reaching). Eventually, however, higher pointing is associated with excessive weather helm, increased drag, and decreased thrust, so that a compromise must be reached by which maximum pointing is achieved without significant loss or drive. Drive actually aids pointing, as the greater the boat speed the greater the lift to windward from the fin surfaces.

Pointing is extremely important because at a deviation from a straight-line course of approximately 45 degrees, a one-degree increase in deviation increases the distance sailed by nearly 3 per cent or about 50 yd. in a mile! Thus, slight increases in pointing ability, transient luffing in puffs, the urge of a slight weather helm, occasional efforts to keep the boat upright by pinching, all cause significant cumulative reductions in the distance sailed.

Differences in pointing ability on different tacks are consequent to defective pointing ability on one tack and should be carefully investigated (see *Table II*).

CENTERBOARD AND RUDDER

The only function of the centerboard is to keep the boat from sliding to leeward; and it should be down only so far as it performs this function, regardless of what convention says.

Weather helms can be corrected sometimes by raising the board but this should be done only insofar as it does not create slippage to leeward. Remember: the faster you go, the less board you need. A small weather helm is desirable. The rudder, however, acts as a brake and any unnecessary or radical movements must be avoided.

OTHER AIDS

Plastic windows are a great help in both jib and main if possible. Telltales on the shrouds and spreaders should always be carried; and a masthead pennant is necessary, if only for eye appeal. Small threads on either side of luff of the jib are used by some who stand by their efficiency. I cannot judge this as I have never used them, but I feel they are wrongly considered a cure-all for finding the proper degree of pointing. They should constitute only one of many small factors which make a boat go fast upwind. Always watch the classes ahead, if any, to estimate what is in store.

CREWS

Although a crew is necessary to the proper sailing of most small boats, if the rules did not specify that one must be carried I would often rather do without! Any crew is useful for releasing the skipper's pent-up emotions and frustrations. Some are horrible burdens, others are godsends. Windward work for crews is often regarded as "hunky" labor, particularly in small, light, racing classes where their main function is keeping the boat flat. That function is all-important, but a crew who can also describe intelligently what is going on to leeward and behind is worth his salt. The need for accurate observing and reporting is frequently omitted from their training but should be stressed.

Proper coming about comes with experience and depends largely on the crew's efficiency. Letting the jib go at the right moment, keeping proper athwartships trim, hauling in quickly but not tightly, depending upon the wind strength, freeing off the weather sheet and getting to windward are all part of the procedure and demand coordination. If your boat is light, do not baby it in a come about —slam it around. Hiking techniques vary; but as long as the boat is flat, there is no room for criticism. Both crew and skipper should work in unison, going out and coming in together, and both should be as low as possible.

TRIM

Usually, assuming the absence of other boats, both main and jib should be in tight or possibly the jib eased about 1 in. The higher the wind, the tighter the jib sheet should be. The main traveller should be let out only in very extreme conditions and even then only if the jib leads are set out too. I doubt the benefit of ever letting out the traveller in moderate winds. Small boats are designed to be sailed upright and this requirement must be followed even at the expense of luffing a portion of your main. The crew's job is extremely important in this regard. The skipper should concentrate on the luff of the jib, always trying to point a little higher. He can overdo it, however, and a fine touch can be acquired only through experience.

START

The main thing is to have clear wind and as much undisturbed water as possible. Therefore it is often better to accept a seemingly less advantageous start in order to reap these benefits.

In large fleet starts often the end does not matter, but finding a hole in which to start is all-important. Holes always do appear. The start, in my opinion, includes 100 yd. beyond. It is imperative to keep your boat moving and if necessary to sail slightly freer in order to work out in front.

If your start is not good get your wind clear even if it entails a series of short tacks.

Always start on starboard tack. There are a few conditions in which an exception to this principle can be made, such as a sudden wind shift before the gun, an improperly set starting line, or a very small fleet.

SHIFTS

Observe the age-old maxim of tacking on a heading. This consideration is complicated by the fact that you never know whether such a heading will be prolonged. It is best to carry on for a few moments before deciding, then come about. If a heading alters your position adversely it is advisable to go about immediately, whereas if your position is benefited it is often best to tack when the opposition immediately behind tacks. If you are pointing higher than other boats on your own tack or less than 90 degrees to boats on the other tack, hold your course; if you are pointing lower than other boats on your own tack or more than 90 degrees to boats on the other tack, tack! Don't panic in a continually shifting breeze, as the breaks usually even out. When in doubt, don't tack. In a heavier breeze it is often better to take the shifts as they come to avoid frequent costly come abouts.

In puffy weather you can often see the puffs approaching. As one hits, you will be headed, then faired through the greater portion, and then headed again as the true wind returns. Take full advantage of these faired spells by pointing high enough to cause the jib to luff, but do not confuse them with a heading or a fairing.

When the wind fairs, there is very little to do except take advantage of it. If you are to leeward this is a great disadvantage. If a permanent fairing is foreseeable, it is best to tack toward the opposition and save as much as possible before it hits. As soon as it does, tack back. In shifty conditions apply the old rule of keeping between competitors and the wind—closer to the median wind direction. (see *Chapter 11.*)

WAVE CONDITIONS

If there is a lumpy sea or waves remaining after a strong breeze, the boat should be laid off ever so slightly to give added power to break through these waves.

Waves which have some height to them or with breaking crests should be "hobbyhorsed" over. As the crest approaches, head up until it is about at the forward third of the boat, then head off a bit into the trough, then head up again toward the next crest, and so on. These motions should not be erratic but smooth and rhythmic. As a result they avoid slamming while maintaining speed.

If the waves are not in line with the wind, a combination of the above techniques must be used.

TACTICS

The effects of backwinding and blanketing are so important that they must be constantly considered. The blanket zone extends farther aft than many people think, in a progressively narrowing cone from five to seven mast lengths from the windward boat and is more in line with the apparent wind than the true wind. Should you at any time think you are being adversely affected by either of these factors, don't stay around to find out but tack at once and clear your wind.

Broken water is not taken into consideration by most skippers. To windward it is significant even forward of the backwind zone but is often difficult to detect. It is effective anywhere inside the triangle formed by the bow and stern waves. It should be avoided at all costs, particularly when attempting to break through to leeward or to windward.

In racing today there is rarely any luffing of a windward boat from on the wind, although on the wind there are few of the disadvantages that are evident off the wind. In the latter case a real luffing match is apt to cause a great deal of lost ground. Except in team racing it is often wise to let the faster boat go. On the other hand, there is no better deterrent to an overtaking windward boat on a beat than a violent luff. If the luff is properly timed she has no alternative but to tack or go to leeward.

Another often attempted and seldom well executed tactic is the establishment of lee bow interference. A lee bow effect is achieved when one boat is placed in such a position relative to another that the backward flow of air deflected off its sails (backwind) disrupts the normal flow along the leeward side of the sails of the second boat resulting in a significant reduction in lift. The speed of the second boat will be markedly reduced and it will be forced to fall off to leeward, pointing in this new, artificial wind. The lee bow effect is evident within two to three mast lengths to windward and up to five mast lengths astern. Lee bowing may be accomplished by one of two converging boats tacking either dead ahead of or slightly ahead and to leeward of the other. Only the slightest lead is necessary; even a boat abeam or slightly ahead to windward (if close aboard) will be adversely affected. It is essential of course, that the leeward boat be able to pick up full way and be recovered from the tack before the windward boat drives through and blankets her.

Lee bowing is a devastating maneuver, but if achieved by tacking it must be done with perfect timing and precision. Once accomplished there is no defense; the windward boat will be forced either to tack or sag astern and drive off to leeward.

APPROACHING MARKS

Marks should always be approached on starboard tack unless the way is so clear that there is no possibility of entanglements.

The approach should be planned in advance so that the proper maneuvers can be made. For example, if you are on starboard to leeward and ahead but cannot lay the mark, take your port tack hitch early; do not wait until you reach the lay line to the mark. To slightly overstand a mark is better than to understand it. If on your approach you see that you cannot lay the mark, don't pinch. It is better to accept the error in judgment and to keep your boat moving at maximum speed. However, when it is unavoidable, a mark must be head reached around. In this case keep your boat upright or heeling to windward, wait until the mark is abeam, and then pivot around it as hard as you can, keeping your boat over to windward.

Weather finishes are always tricky and can be disastrous if the line is at the wrong angle. It is best to aim at the buoy end, assuming that you take this mark on the same side as the leeward mark, and then adjust your thinking as you get closer and can accurately judge the angle of the line. If in the lead, stay directly between the second boat and the buoy end of the line or the nearest end when the angle becomes apparent.

CONCLUSION

You cannot regularly beat experience in any sport. The more racing you can do the better you'll be. In this chapter I have gathered up what I (and probably many others) have learned through experience. I hope that my version may cause some dormant idea to come to life or at least some controversy to start.

Table I

Factors Improving Pointing Ability

1. *Hull*
   a) Fine lines, particularly forward of the mast.
   b) Deep sections, probably V'd or hollow, forward of the mast.
2. *Jib*
   a) Straight, leading edge, *i.e.*, tight jibstay (*critical*), consequent to:
      (1) proper mast staying to prevent lateral bowing;
      (2) adequate vang tension;
      (3) prevention of excessive forward bowing of mast;
      (4) moderate mast rake.
   b) Flat jib with fulness forward—the stronger the breeze, the tighter the sheet trim.
   c) Properly led sheets—sail should luff first at junction of upper and middle thirds.
   d) Adequate slot opening between jib and mainsail (the stronger the wind, the wider the slot necessary):
      (1) head of jib should be hoisted no higher and no closer to mainsail than remainder of leech;
      (2) leech of overlapping jib should be hollow (concave—no roach);
      (3) jib sheet leads should be set at an angle of 10 to 20 degrees with the center line or inboard as far as possible without excessive backwinding of the mainsail—the lesser the angle, the higher the resultant pointing;
      (4) mast should bend smoothly to weather between deck and hounds.
3. *Mainsail*
   a) Draft consistent with the wind strength adjusted by battens, luff and foot rope tension, vang tension, zipper pockets, etc.
   b) Proper trim of main boom (*critical*) in both lateral and vertical plane:
      (1) boom pulled adequately inboard toward center line without adversely affecting draft;
      (2) light air requires fuller sail curve forward (less pull down boom—main traveler slide pulled to weather; heavy air requires slide eased to leeward);
      (3) the further the boom is trimmed inboard, the higher the pointing—but (if excessive) the greater the side force and the less the resultant boat speed.

c) Leech tension reduced with increasing wind strength—chiefly through a boom which bends to leeward at the after end in increasing wind, *i.e.,* with a mid-boom mainsheet.

4. *Mast*
   a) Proper fore-and-aft positioning to achieve balanced helm:
      (1) the lighter the air, the farther forward the mast;
      (2) the greater the importance of reaching ability, the farther aft the mast.
   b) Reduced windage and weight aloft (side force and heeling reduced).

5. *Centerboard*
   a) Proper positioning of centerboard and pin (*critical*) to permit a balanced helm on the wind in a light breeze with the board full down—5-degree weather helm optimal—adjust centerboard pin to mast, not vice versa.
   b) The board carried full down or angled forward of vertical and the board section and centerboard slot so arranged that the board pivots to windward (*critical*).

Table II

Factors Which Account for Varied Windward Ability on Different Tacks

1. Asymmetric jib sheet leads.
2. Asymmetric mainsheet leads (not from center line).
3. Asymmetric lateral mast bending and different slot openings due to imperfections of mast material, improper staying, mast not located on center line, varied shifting of mast if free at deck level.
4. Asymmetric boom bending due to imperfections of material, asymmetrical mainsheet or vang attachments, etc., with resultant variations in sail shape.
5. Asymmetric centerboard shape or angling due to warping, asymmetric shape of board or centerboard slot, improper pin positioning or wedge positioning (*critical*).
6. Asymmetric trim due to variation in crew positioning and hiking on different tacks.

11. Beating in Varying Northwesters

By
STUART H. WALKER, M.D.,
Annapolis

I remember George Moffatt's starting about 5 minutes late in a light northwest wind at the 1956 Buzzard's Bay Bowl Regatta and, subsequent to several tacks which seemed to be in the wrong direction, arriving at the windward mark fourth in a 35-foot fleet! Since then (and for a long time before) I've been trying to analyze the northwest wind to determine by what rules it operates and by what principles a boat must be sailed to take advantage of its characteristic shiftiness. For when a varying northwest wind blows, the determining factors in any race will be the time and the location of the tacking on the windward leg.

CHARACTERISTICS OF THE NORTHWESTERLY

"Northwesterly" is used herein as a generic term referring to land breezes characterized by vertical instability and a pronounced variation in direction. They may appear in any given area as winds from directions other than the northwest, but on the Atlantic Coast of North America are characteristically from this direction. They are common winds because they regularly appear from the west when the cold air of a high-pressure zone (following a low-pressure front) brings in clearing skies, colder temperatures, and a rising barometer. Because the cold air is moving over warmer land, there is a constant tendency for the lower layers to rise and the upper layers to fall, *i.e.*, vertical instability. This permits the more rapidly moving upper layers to appear recurrently on the surface, resulting in "puffiness," with wind moving in a wide variety of directions within a short period of time at any one location.

These winds behave as if they were composed of many separate pieces large enough to involve an entire racing fleet simultaneously but each with an individual strength and direction. They usually become more stable farther offshore and at night, as the vertical instability is decreased by the cooler water or cooler land and are conversely subject to maximal puffiness and variability close to shore in the heat of the day. Although this variability in strength and direction may seem entirely erratic at first, there is usually an underlying pattern which can be detected—and it is the detection of this pattern which determines the success or failure of racing in northwest winds. The anemograph of such a wind shows that for any period of 2 to 3 hr (the duration of the average race, usually conducted during the warmest part of the day) the range of direction variation, though often great, remains fairly constant, *i.e.,* the direction usually varies to a specific degree either side of a median line with each shift! Few shifts produce winds at greater extremes, though occasional winds of intermediate directions erratically appear.

It is evident, therefore, that northwest winds, except for occasional minor variations, consist chiefly of alternating phases of winds to the north of northwest and to the west of northwest. There is, in addition, often a regular periodicity in the frequency of the shifting. The major changes in wind direction usually occur at approximately the same intervals, so that there are equal periods of wind from the north of northwest and from the west of northwest. Thus what is usually involved is a predictable alternation of wind phases from two different directions, rather than an erratic scramble of variations from many directions.

PRINCIPLES OF SAILING IN WIND SHIFTS

The advantage of racing upwind in a shifting breeze is that a shorter course may be sailed to the windward mark. In a steady breeze a boat must sail alternately 45 degrees to either side of the median wind direction but in a shifting breeze may almost always sail less than 45-degree angle to the median wind direction (taken as the wind direction midway between the extremes of the shifts). *That boat which is farthest upwind in relation to the median wind direction is closest to the windward mark, and that boat which sails the shortest course to gain true distance to windward in relation to the median wind direction will reach the windward mark first.*

There are marked differences in the gains to windward attendant upon a single wind shift which are dependent upon the location of the boats of a racing fleet in respect to one another at the time of the shift. Actual gains and losses are relative to the previous distance remaining to the mark, but in practice gains and losses are of course only relative to other boats. An actual gain may be a loss (at least temporarily) if another boat gains more—and vice versa. Such gains are immediately apparent to an experienced sailor as he surveys the fleet, translating positions ahead, astern, to windward, and to leeward into true distances from the windward mark. And it is evident to such a practiced eye that as the wind shifts forward on a fleet of boats, *i.e.*, heads them, the boat which is farthest forward and/or to leeward gains the most, the following boats losing greater

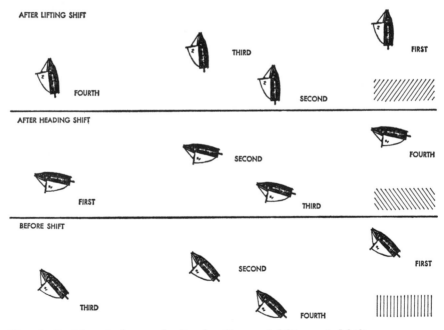

Fig. 1. Positions before and after heading and lifting windshifts.

increments, depending upon their distance astern. It is also evident that with a wind shift aft, *i.e.*, a lift, the boat farthest astern and/or to windward gains the most as the leaders lose (see *Fig. 1*). *Thus, when on a tack sailing toward an expected heading shift (a situation which should be continually applicable when sailing in a north-westerly), a boat should be sailed free and to leeward of the fleet.*

Do not pinch, keep her full and driving forward rather than to windward. If it is necessary to pass another boat, pass to leeward; when the shift appears the leeward boat, if previously even, will be ahead. And remember when checking relationships with other boats, *all those to windward will lose in an expected header—watch those ahead and to leeward!* Conversely, if a lift is expected, keep to windward and watch the boats to windward.

This is a demonstration of a rule formulated by Trevor and Calahan (*Wind and Tide in Yacht Racing*) to the effect that the boat nearest to the new lay line after the shift gains the most. In most races, contrary to some concepts, boats do not stand out far toward the lay lines until nearing the finish (often they are racing in a confined harbor and so must closely approach the mark before they can reach a lay line). Unless the wind shift is marked, no boats will actually reach the new lay line. This means that, for usual considerations, *the boat which is farthest to the side of the course from which the shift appears will gain the most.*

Utilization of these principles is simple enough if only a single shift of a predictable direction is involved. Only two tacks are possible: toward and away from an expected shift and every shift is a header if a boat sails toward it, a lift if a boat sails away from it. The shortest course to the windward mark requires tacking immediately toward a predicted heading shift (as the boat farthest toward the shift gains the most when it appears). Whether the heading shift is a static one which boats sail into one at a time or a phasic "northwesterly," one which appears as part of a sequence of shifts affecting all boats simultaneously, the arrival of the shift increases the distances between each of the boats, consolidating the positions of the leaders in direct proportion to their distances from the side of the course from which the shift appeared. In a race in which a single shift to starboard of the starting line is expected, the first boat to take the port tack after the start at the windward end will be the farthest boat to the side of the course when the shift appears and will undoubtedly be the first boat to reach the windward mark. Tacking with the header consolidates the gain, as the boat after tacking is able to lay a higher course, nearer to the median wind direction (the median of the various wind directions encountered), than she could before the shift. Tacking under these circumstances immediately moves her farther to windward; and, as it is the distance to windward rather than the distance toward the mark that determines the distance remaining to be sailed, she immediately reduces her true distance from the mark.

In northwesterlies unfortunately what is involved is not here and there a single shift but constantly recurring double shifts—each usually equal in degree but in the opposite direction to the last. This means that if all boats tack together with each major shift header, the boats farthest ahead for the northerly shifts will be the farthest behind for the westerly shifts, and the advantages of each shift for each boat will be exactly equaled and canceled by the disadvantages of the next! Therefore, for one boat to consolidate a gain or loss in a northwesterly and to permanently alter her position in relation to another, something else must happen besides "tacking on headers."

The time-honored precept for racing in these winds is to "tack when headed," *i.e.*, to tack as soon as the heading shift appears. A boat may do this, however, and subsequently note a boat behind continuing on, apparently falling off to leeward, and then tacking across ahead on a second, far greater header! *The boat which regularly gains is the one which tacks only on a major shift which permits her to point closer to the median wind direction on the opposite tack.* (Sailing closer to the median wind direction does not necessarily mean closer to the windward mark. Remember it is the boat farthest to windward, not necessarily the boat closest to the mark, that reaches the mark first.) *For this boat is immediately sailing away from the direction of the present shift toward the direction of the next, so as to be as far ahead and to leeward as possible when the next heading shift appears.* The boat which tacks with a minor header—one which still permits a better sailing angle on the same tack and which may be expected to be followed by a further shift in the same direction—is sailing away from the next shift and loses greatly when the next shift appears. The boat which sails the shortest total distance on the windward leg is that boat which always sails on the tack taking her nearest to the median wind direction, *i.e.*, the boat which tacks whenever a heading shift appears which permits a better gain to windward or a higher sailing angle on the opposite tack.

By tacking regularly with such major shifts but only with such shifts (and never with shifts which permit sailing nearer to the median wind on the original tack), a boat is always headed and advancing as far as possible in the direction of the next expected shift, prepared to take maximum advantage from it.

THE 1957 SEVERN TROPHY RACE

The long windward leg of the 1957 race for the Severn Trophy provided an excellent demonstration of the principles of racing upwind in a shifting northwester. This race was conducted over a 10-m. course at the mouth of the Severn River, the final leg being to windward upriver in a 15-knot northwester. The median wind direction was approximately parallel to the main course of the river, which gradually narrowed toward the finish line. The previous legs had been planing reaches on which the wind had shown a pronounced tendency to shift in both strength and direction—on the latter part of the last reaching leg the wind had shifted to the north (for the leaders), *i.e.*, aft on the starboard tack boats. An analysis of what the competitors did, and how they achieved their finishing positions will be necessary to determine what they should have done to finish most rapidly and in the best possible position.

Graeme Hayward and Glen Foster rounded the leeward mark first and second and proceeded upwind on the starboard tack toward the southern shore, as did Stuart Walker, rounding fourth, about 200 ft. astern, and Mark Coholan, rounding a very close sixth— presumably believing that the wind shift to the north noted in the latter part of the reaching leg meant a starboard tack lift which would be followed by a reverse shift to the west. George O'Day, rounding third, and Dave Kirby, rounding seventh, took the port tack immediately, hoping for a furtherance of the northerly shift phase and/or an additional northerly shift off the north Severn shore. Hayward and Foster continued on the starboard tack for about ½ m. until they encountered a major westerly shift phase and they both came about. Walker short tacked up the middle, tacking on each little header. By the time Hayward and Foster, still in the same relationship to each other, had crossed the center line of the river, they had gained considerably on Walker. Walker, however, had gained considerably on Moffatt, who had continued on to the south shore, ignoring the westerly shift, and on O'Day and Kirby, who had been on the port tack sailing away from the shift when it appeared. Coholan passed Moffatt, by tacking with this shift, as he was in a far better position when the next major shift to the north appeared.

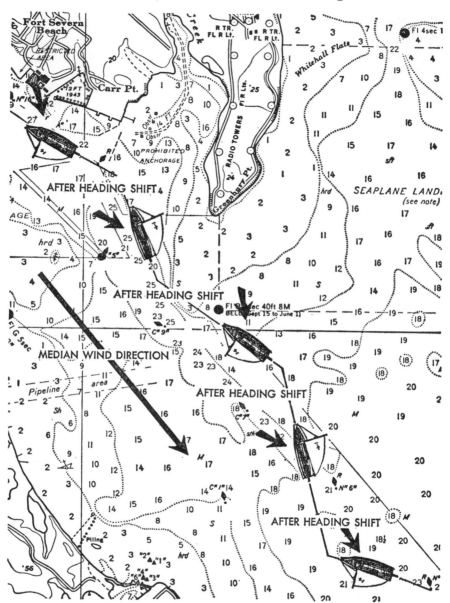

The 1957 Severn Trophy Race—Final leg. This course, taken by John Foster, demonstrates the technique of tacking with each major shift of wind to keep on the tack closest to the median wind direction.

By this time Hayward and Foster had made two-thirds of their port tack crossing and were well to the north. But O'Day, being farthest north, received the maximum benefit, with Kirby receiving a slightly lesser advantage. Neither gained nearly enough to overcome Hayward and Foster's initial advantage from the westerly shift while on the starboard tack. Walker, being farther north than Coholan and Moffatt, gained more on these two boats but lost considerably on all four of the boats north of the center line of the river. All boats continued on the starboard tack, which had been lifted to almost parallel to the center line of the river—the boats farthest north being lifted most, perhaps because of a greater northerly shift off the north shore.

When the leaders were approximately two-thirds of the way home, a major westerly shift occurred which had a maximal effect along the south shore. Moffatt and Coholan, being farthest south, dead to leeward of Walker and close to the south shore, received the maximum benefit, tacking and coming respectively from 100 and 150 yd. behind to even with and ahead of Walker. The four boats to the north received less of the westerly shift and thereby lost less than appeared to the southern boats but temporarily dropped behind. As the boats to the south came about to the port tack to take advantage of this shift they sailed off the south shore and were gradually headed. Walker, now to leeward, came about to starboard (after a partial northerly header) to seek a further westerly shift off the south shore and cover Moffatt and Coholan, who, proceeding farther on the starboard tack, sailed into the next *major* northerly shift well to the north of Walker. They thereby consolidated their gain, completing the two-shift phases respectively 50 and 100 yd. ahead of Walker! The boats to the north, having lost only a moderate degree with the lesser westerly shift on the north shore, now received the maximum benefit from the northerly shift and regained their lead over all the boats to the south. Hayward, having tacked out of phase once, as did Walker, was passed by both Foster and O'Day. Kirby, moving up to a close fourth, also passed all the boats to the south as the last northerly shift held with only minor variation to the finish. Finishing positions (for the first seven boats): Foster, O'Day, Hayward, Kirby, Coholan, Moffatt, Walker.

Foster won and gained on all other competitors (seventh place was half a mile back, rather than 100 yd. back as at the leeward mark—with each boat about 100 yd. ahead of the next) by (1) *tacking with every major header, (2) commencing the leg on the proper tack, (3) sailing chiefly along the north shore where the shifts gave less adverse effect when westerly and more beneficial effects when northerly, and (4) being to the north in a northerly shift at the finish.*

O'Day gained on all competitors except Foster apparently because he did as Foster did except for taking the wrong tack initially. The same may be said for Hayward, who, however, made a more serious error by tacking once against the phasic shifts, rather than merely ignoring one shift as did O'Day. Kirby made the greatest gain in positions by following O'Day and lost less to Foster because he commenced the port tack at the leeward mark when the westerly shift was about to appear, was therefore on the wrong tack for only a very short time, and was well to the north of Foster when the next northerly shift appeared. Coholan passed Moffatt, as Moffatt ignored the first major westerly shift, and Walker, as Walker tacked to the west in a westerly shift, but lost to all the others by short tacking up the south shore, missing the major gains of the northerly shifts, and being to the south when the final shift at the finish appeared to the north. Moffatt had the same disadvantages as Coholan, with the additional defect of having ignored the initial westerly shift. Walker took the right tack at the leeward mark but from that time on did almost everything wrong, *i.e.,* (1) tacked against a westerly shift, thereby losing almost 200 yd., (2) short tacked up the south shore, (3) and was to the south for the final northerly shift.

The above evaluation demonstrates the following principles of racing upwind in varying northwesters: (1) *Tremendous gains and losses can accrue from the shifts in wind direction so that all other factors may be disregarded. (2) The wind shifts tend to be periodic, with shifts in alternating directions of approximately the same degree at approximately the same interval. (3) Shifts of lesser degree and modifications of the shift dependent upon the proximity of a shore occur and may be confusing. (4) It is essential that each yacht tack in phase with each major shift,* i.e., *tack when headed, toward the direction of the next expected shift. (5) It is desirable to sail as far as possible and be as near as possible (within the lay lines to the mark), or at least closer than any other boats, to the side of the course from which the next shift appears. (6) It is necessary to take the favored tack at the initiation of the windward leg. (7)*

And it is necessary to be on the favored tack at the completion of the leg.

To summarize: *Gains and losses are temporary and will be equalized if all boats tack in phase (and if there are an equal number of alternating wind shifts of equal degree) but are consolidated when boats (1) tack out of phase, (2) take the wrong initial tack, (3) are affected by shifts of varying degree in different locations, or (4) finish after being exposed to an odd total number of shifts or a different total number of shifts from other competitors.* Or, as indicated by the statement generally attributed to Cooch Maxwell, *"The fellow who makes the fewest mistakes wins the race."*

TACK IN PHASE WITH EACH MAJOR WIND SHIFT

Tacking in phase appears to be the most important consideration, as when this principle is violated the greatest losses occur. Ignoring a major shift, continuing in the previous direction on the same tack when headed, is undesirable but the consequent loss is at least partially offset by the greater gain during the subsequent shift back (the third shift in the series), as the boat will be far nearer to the direction of this shift than the others which tacked in phase. It is far worse to tack against the shift—out of phase—as this not only decreases the gain from the initial shift but places the boat to windward, (*i.e.,* away from the shift) at the time of the next shift—consolidating the loss. Therefore, *when in doubt—don't tack!*

The doubt is obviously the problem—likely to be enhanced by the sight of the apparent gain of any boat to windward after a given shift. The temptation to tack to cover tends to encourage tacking on only slight headers, a tactic which actually allows the apparently gaining boats to continue on farther toward the direction of the next major shift. As constantly reiterated by C. Stanley Ogilvy in several books and articles—particularly in a varying northwester, "sail your own race." *Don't try to cover* under these circumstances. Covering is almost impossible, will probably cause a loss, and is usually unnecessary as a subsequent shift will probably restore the desired status quo. Anything which interferes with tacking in phase as indicated above can only result in harm. Covering can be successful only in a negative sense. If there is doubt that a major header has occurred and other boats are continuing without tacking, it will be safest to continue with them.

Another doubt often arises when approaching a shore because of the expected shift to a more perpendicular direction, which occurs in northwesters as well as all other shore breezes. This static shift may be mistaken for a northwesterly phasic shift, and a tack may consequently be made on such a header without regard to phase period. Though a slight gain may be made by approaching shore to take advantage of such a shift, the degree of shift will probably be insufficient to offset a failure to comply with the alternating directions of the northwesterly.

The usual cause for doubt as to tacking in phase is the occurrence of minor shifts at uncertain intervals throughout, between, and superimposed upon the periodicity of the major shifts. Fortunately two definite characteristics of the major shifts, their periodicity and equivalent degree of direction change, are usually helpful in their recognition. Every effort should be made prior to the commencement of the windward leg to determine the interval between these major shifts and the range or degree of direction change. This is usually not difficult to determine prior to the start if the first leg is to windward or if the same conditions exist during a subsequent windward leg as at the start. However, an evaluation of the period and degree of major shifts should be continued during the race prior to and in the early portion of the windward leg: How often was it necessary to jibe on the run? To what degree did the wind haul aft on the reach? How often did the planing leg become close-hauled? Once the periodicity and degree are determined and understood (determined as recently as possible, inasmuch as these factors can change), tacking may be judiciously withheld until a shift of the expected magnitude appears after the expected time interval.

Actually it is the shift of the expected magnitude which is important, as this is obviously the "major" shift; as soon as such a shift occurs it should be tacked on regardless of the time interval. *It is essential to conceive a median line representing the wind direction midway between the extremes of the shifts and to establish the direction of these extremes.* With such lines constantly in mind it is possible to note whether any particular shift is or is not of a magnitude sufficient to require tacking in order to maintain a course nearer to the median wind direction—*i.e.*, is or is not a major shift. It is possible constantly to locate the boat in relation to these median lines and extremes and so usually to be certain that it is heading in a direction nearest to the median wind line and toward the next expected shift.

Watch the other boats; if a significant shift has occurred their bearings will alter markedly—all those to windward will drop back if the shift is a header, and all those to leeward will gain. If this happens—tack; if the other boats seem little affected, particularly those ahead and to leeward who stand to gain the most, hold on. Watch out for being forced to tack; don't let minor tactical considerations tempt you into tacking out of phase. If you are caught in someone's blanket or backwind, but are on the right tack for the wind phase, hold on; you'll lose far more by tacking (when the next shift appears). And again, don't be tempted to tack to cover when you are already on the favored tack, particularly into a starboard tack "safe leeward" position from which you will be unable to tack back to the favored direction.

Northwesterlies are, unfortunately, not always regular in frequency of shifting. In light air major shifts occur erratically and with great frequency, but whenever shifts of major magnitude appear they must be tacked upon. However, unfortunately shifts of lesser magnitude followed by shifts in the opposite direction (which should be tacked upon) may appear and be impossible to evaluate. Under these circumstances it is best to withhold tacking which could produce major losses, particularly as tacking in shifts of small magnitude can produce only slight gains.

TAKE THE FAVORED TACK INITIALLY

If, as is to be expected in fleets of competent helmsmen, most boats tack in phase with each major shift, commencing the windward leg on the favored tack may be decisive. Thus, it is essential to be able to determine which tack is favored in advance. If the windward leg commences at the start, the favored tack may be readily determined (as pointed out by C. Stanley Oglivy in *Thoughts on Small Boat Racing*) by noting the favored end of the starting line and its relationship to the median wind line. The favored end of the line presumably indicates a recent shift in the direction of that end, *i.e.*, a header for boats sailing on the tack taking them in that direction; and it indicates that the initial tack should be away from the favored end, *i.e.*, port tack for a line favored at the port end and starboard tack for a line favored at the starboard end, in order to be heading toward the direction of the next expected shift (see *Fig. 2*). This seems to contravene the accepted dictum to start at the end of the line farthest to windward, but actually it does not. It merely expresses the far more significant tack or direction which should be sailed regardless of which end is favored for starting.

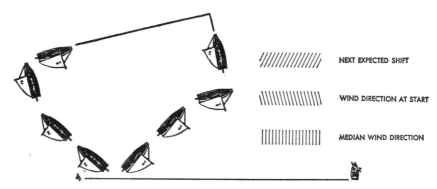

|||||||||||| NEXT EXPECTED SHIFT

\\\\\\\\\\\\\\\\ WIND DIRECTION AT START

|||||||||||||||| MEDIAN WIND DIRECTION

Fig. 2. The effect of windshifts on the favored end of the line and the favored tack for starting (leading boat always on the tack closest to the median wind direction).

If the windward leg is sailed later in the race, consideration should be given to a determination of the most recent shift during the latter part of the preceding leg. Are you easing sheets or taking them in just before rounding the leeward mark? If the wind has shifted forward, tack immediately after rounding, heading for the next expected shift—or vice versa. If the median line and the extreme range of the wind shift have been previously determined (before the start or during a previous windward leg), a comparison of the wind direction at the moment of rounding the leeward mark may readily indicate the favored tack, *i.e.*, away from whichever side of the median line the wind is then coming from, toward the direction of the next expected shift. This is, of course, usually the "tack headed most nearly to the mark."

TACK TOWARD THE WINDWARD SHORE

If shifts of *unequal* degree occur at different locations along the windward leg, positional advantage becomes distinctly evident. Those boats closest to the side of the course from which a shift of greater degree appears will gain more on such a shift and lose less with a lesser shift toward the other side. They will, therefore, consolidate their gain on those boats on the other side of the course which are exposed to shifts of lesser degree. The greater the degree of shift, the greater the immediate gain; and, in this instance, the greater the difference in the degree of the alternating shifts, the greater the permanent gain.

Northwesterlies are land breezes, usually stronger closer to the land, and do become more perpendicular to the shore line as they pass over it. This means that wind shifts more closely parallel to the perpendicular to the shore are enhanced along the shore and wind shifts less parallel to the perpendicular are dampened; *i.e.*, along a north shore northerly shifts will be increased, westerly shifts decreased. *Boats sailing close to the north shore will therefore receive the maximum gains on the enhanced northerly shifts and will lose less to offshore competitors in the dampened westerly shifts*—so acquiring a net gain even though all boats tack in phase (see *Fig. 3*). In the Severn Trophy Race, discussed herein, both shores seemed to demonstrate this characteristic but the south shore less consistently, giving a probable advantage to the north shore boats.

It may thus be desirable to hold on into a header for short periods

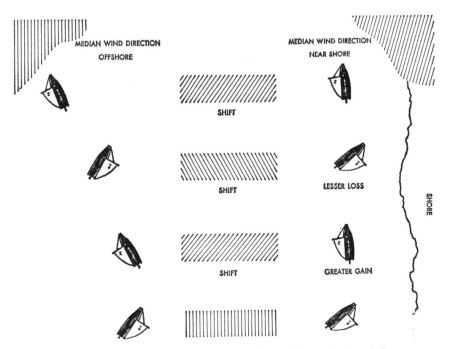

Fig. 3. The effect of the static wind shift produced by a windward shore superimposed upon the phasic shifts of the Northwesterly.

—temporarily ignoring shifts but never tacking against shifts— in order more closely to approach a shore off which a northwesterly is blowing. This is probably indicated when the shift periodicity and magnitude is uncertain, as in light air (particularly as these winds are usually strongest inshore) or when sailing in a narrow channel where the shore effect is greatly enhanced.

Inasmuch as the boat farthest to the side of the course makes the greatest gain with each shift, it is always desirable to sail on the outer edge of the fleet and to avoid tacking behind and within the fleet (except in obvious major shifts).

PLAN TO BE CLOSEST TO THE DIRECTION OF THE FINAL SHIFT

Although an even number of shifts of equal degree will cancel each other, if the total number is odd for any individual boat or different from its competitors major gains or losses can occur. The number of shifts to which a boat is exposed will obviously depend upon when the boat commenced the windward leg. It is possible for a following boat to round the mark in a different phase than the leaders, complete the leg with an odd number of shifts, and make either a major gain or loss in finishing position—merely because she rounded the leeward mark at a different time. Inasmuch as boats commence and complete a leg at different times, are exposed to shifts of different degree at different locations, and may tack out of phase occasionally, it is almost certain that they will not be exposed to an even number of shifts of equal duration. It is, of course, usually impossible to tell in advance in what phase the leg will be completed in order to time its commencement! However, a determination of the interval between shifts and of the approximate progress of the boat will usually indicate the shift which will be in effect at the termination of the leg. A careful consideration of the situation may demonstrate an opportunity to capitalize on the final shift—which will affect each competitor differently, depending upon his location.

As the boats farthest ahead (toward the new lay line) and to leeward prior to the shift will make the maximum gain, this position must be sought for the final shift in every instance. Tacking out of phase is certain to be harmful. Falling off to leeward in the preceding phase, however, may place the boat farther toward the new lay line (*i.e.,* farther upwind) in the final phase (see *Fig. 4*).

Inasmuch as the finish is a consolidating factor and finishing positions are obviously most important, the control of relative positions between close boats separated from other competitors becomes decisive. The only certain covering position for a leading boat is to carry her opponent out to the current lay lines. From this position the leading boat cannot lose if no further shift occurs or if a lifting shift occurs and will gain considerably with a heading shift. *Thus if only one other boat is in contention nearing the finish line, the leading boat should make every effort to encourage the contender to sail with her to either lay line, disregarding the next*

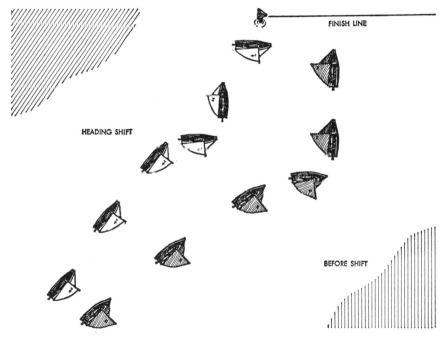

FINISH LINE

HEADING SHIFT

BEFORE SHIFT

Fig. 4. Effect of falling off to leeward so as to be further to the side of the course from which a heading shift is expected before the finish.

expected shift. If the leading boat is close to a lay line she should continue on course along it, not tacking with a header until the following boat tacks, as she will gain by any heading shift and cannot lose from a lifting shift (both boats then presumably laying the finish line). *Opposite tactics are, of course, indicated for a following boat, who should make every effort to avoid being carried out to the lay lines.*

If shifts are occurring at infrequent intervals or the windward leg is so short that it is possible to sail beyond the bounds of the expected new lay lines before a shift appears, it is desirable to short tack along the expected new lay line rather than overstand. This is most likely to happen at the finish, as any boat always seeking to get as close as possible to the new lay line before the next shift must eventually succeed! It is, however, undesirable to arrive in this position so early that there is time for another shift in the opposite direction, *as the maximum loss will be suffered by a boat already laying the mark when a heading shift appears.* In other words, tack in phase until carried to a position which is to be a new lay line after the next expected shift; thereafter tack along the lay line until the shift appears, and when laying the mark in this shift, hope that it is the final one! Fortunately, if the shifts are fairly regular in frequency, if the windward leg is of sufficient length to permit at least one tack on a shift prior to reaching a lay line, and if the boat does tack in phase with each shift, it will not arrive at a lay line until there is insufficient time remaining for a subsequent damaging shift to appear.

SUMMARY

When a northwest wind is blowing, there is one paramount consideration—to tack in phase with each major shift of wind. Evaluate the wind conditions thoroughly to determine the range and periodicity of the shifting, and whenever a major heading shift appears which permits a higher sailing angle (relative to the median wind direction) on the opposite tack, tack. Thereafter sail as fast as possible, falling off to leeward if necessary, to reach as soon as possible the side of the course from which the next shift will appear. If a windward shore exists, hold your tack a little longer than otherwise to obtain the advantages of the greater shifts near shore which will most favor the boats nearest to shore. Determine and take the favored tack at the commencement of the windward leg, and determine and place yourself in position to take the maximum possible advantage of the final shift before the termination of the leg. Above all, don't tack out of phase by accepting the temptation of a minor shift, the proximity of other boats, or the possibility of a lift from the static shift along a windward shore.

12. Reaching in Moderate Air

By ROBERT E. EMPEY,
San Diego

Reaching legs tend to be parades in moderate air, as all boats readily reach approximately equal maximum displacement hull speed. Thus, one of the primary, but frequently forgotten, considerations is distance sailed; and often the boat which sails the shortest distance arrives at the mark first. However, much can be done positively to increase speed, and unfortunately much occurs to decrease it— so that the shortest distance between two points, particularly when there are other boats around, may not always be a straight line. One should keep in mind, in addition, that a straight line may require a considerable variation in course steered if a significant current is present and that a transit between the mark ahead or the mark behind and a point on shore should be constantly checked to insure that you are indeed sailing a straight line.

BOAT SPEED

Maximum-displacement hull speed, chiefly determined by water line length (approximately 1.3 LWL), is unaffected by additional lift in the form of better sails, larger sail area, or more wind or reduced drag in the form of a smoother bottom, a refined centerboard, or less windage. However, whenever thrust falls below the threshold, the provision of relatively greater thrust or less drag than that of the competitor will make a difference. Thus, in moderate air every effort should be made to avoid a thrust reduction due to patches of decreased wind or the interference of other boats. Particularly careful attention should be paid to sail and hull trim during such periods.

In lighter air, of course, the basic hull, rig, and sail lift and drag factors become all-important. Maintaining a proper slot effect by the use of reaching jib sheet leads or by holding the clew of the jib out by hand is extremely valuable. It is under these circumstances that decreased wetted surface, proper hull trim and helm balance to decrease drag reach major importance. Well-cut, deeply arched, and properly trimmed sails are never more valuable than in a light air reach. Indeed, it is precisely this situation which demonstrates the fast boat most distinctly!

In moderate air reaching, however, the sailing angle is the chief variant of boat speed. Most boats increase their speed as they come higher on the wind from a broad reach to a dead reach to a close reach. Maximum-displacement hull speed is usually reached on a close reach about 2 points below close-hauled. This will vary with the individual boat, the wind strength, the wave formation, the crew's ability to prevent heeling, and the possibility of planing. Usually planing is more readily initiated and sustained on a dead reach because of the lessened side force. On the usual moderate air reach the boat which sails the farthest (or the greatest percentage of time) highest on the wind will achieve the maximum average boat speed for the leg. Therefore, being to leeward is most desirable and provides the greatest potential speed.

STRATEGY

It is generally better to take the slower portion of the leg initially, saving the fastest portion for the crucial period when approaching the mark. If it is feasible to bear away with clear wind, this should usually be done immediately. If well clear of other boats, the ideal course should be only slightly to leeward, counting on the straight-line distance to be the fastest. If closely followed by one or two boats, bear away more sharply immediately, as once they round and steer a course to pass to leeward you may not bear away below the normal course. In all probability they will luff out to weather, give you clear wind to leeward, and eventually sail a much slower course.

If there are variations in the wind strength, proper use of sailing angles becomes all the more important. The lighter and unsteadier the air, the more important clear wind becomes and the more risky it becomes to hold to leeward. The best solution in these circumstances is to *keep to leeward if not pressed and no further to windward than necessary to keep clear wind if other boats are nearby* (see *Fig. 1*). Always bear away in the puffs, taking every opportunity with stronger wind or clear wind to get to leeward. If no

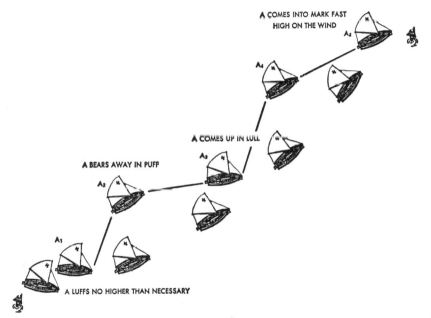

Fig. 1

opportunities are missed to bear away, adequate reserve will be available to come up in the light spots and keep clear air to windward by short periods of luffing without ever coming excessively high of the course. By bearing away in the puffs you also stay in better wind longer, and by coming up in the lulls boat speed is maintained despite decreased thrust.

If the general wind strength is dropping, it is particularly important to sail to leeward initially, using the best wind for the early slow angle and saving the fastest angle for the final stages when the boats to windward will be barely moving. If the wind is increasing, you can afford to go to windward initially, utilizing the fastest sailing angle for the period of least wind and bearing away later when the wind will be strong enough to sail at maximum speed at any angle.

If the course is a close reach always keep to windward by sailing close-hauled initially. This gives essential protection should the wind haul and the leg become a beat, and saves the fastest portion of the leg, bearing away to a close reach, for the final stages of the leg.

It is often desirable to use the spinnaker when reaching in moderate air, but when in doubt, don't. If the boat has reached maximum hull speed with the jib, additional sail won't help. On a dead reach or above, the spinnaker is a handicap as it limits maneuverability in adapting to varied wind strengths and gives a less effective slot than the jib. Even on a broad reach unless it produces additional speed, *i.e.,* in less than optimal wind strengths at less than maximum-displacement hull speed, it doesn't pay its way. Obviously with lesser wind strength or sailing angles approaching a broad reach or run its additional thrust is essential. If forced high of the course into a poorer sailing angle, decreased speed may necessitate its use. Or to maintain optimal speed in the initial bearing-off phase, the spinnaker may be of real value. In any case it should be suitably rigged and the crew be capable of its instantaneous use for short or prolonged periods on the reach whenever boat speed falls below the maximum and the sailing angle is a dead reach or below.

Few of the monster chutes in regular use are ideal for reaching, and it may be desirable in some cases to carry a smaller, flatter reaching spinnaker in addition. The reaching spinnaker is not used at the stall and must provide an adequate slot effect with the mainsail. It must be set far enough out from the main by easing the halyard and trimming in the main. Excessive easing of the halyard may be harmful, however, as it may produce or increase heeling and may cause a sloping of the foot back toward the boat. The lower edge must be kept vertical or sloping forward, if possible, so that the air flows out from under the spinnaker without hindrance. Additional pole length is particularly valuable on the reach, and therefore the pole should be kept horizontal so that it will protrude the maximum distance outward. In light air if the clew will not lift to the level of the tack and pole, the pole should be lowered on the mast. In moderate to heavy air the spinnaker should be encouraged to lift up and away from the mainsail by moving the pole to the maximum allowable height up the mast. This also reduces side force and heeling by enhancing the release of air under the foot.

Modern spinnaker handlers and their reporters in the press have become preoccupied with the speed of hoisting and breaking out the spinnaker after rounding the preceding mark. Although it is usually possible to determine the sailing angle of the subsequent leg in advance of the rounding, the efficacy of spinnaker use and/or the jibe on which it will be set are often in doubt. Premature hoisting on the wrong course may produce greater slowing than can possibly be offset by the few seconds saved on the correct course. The spinnaker is not the panacea for all reaching ills and its use on too close a reach, in too strong or too light a wind, may do far more harm than any expected good. In addition, the tactical vulnerability, the inability to respond to a luff, to move out to protect one's weather, or to jibe at the crucial moment when other boats are rounding near by may be extremely hazardous. Again when in doubt, don't—at least not until after careful consideration on the actual course.

If planing is possible at any sailing angle remotely approximating the course or by any conceivable sail combination, it should be sought without delay. Usually, in moderate air, planing requires sailing higher or lower for a portion of the leg and if so this faster sailing angle should be saved for the final stage of the leg. Often in puffy winds planing can be maintained almost continuously while bearing away in the puffs and riding up in the lulls. Here again maximum attention should be paid to bearing away as much and as frequently as possible without dropping off the plane so that one can come up in the lulls without getting too high of the course. Boats planing in from leeward at the mark can pick up a lot of places on those who enjoyed the early planing to windward too well.

Here again the spinnaker may be of value. Additional thrust may be of no value (beyond a threshold amount) for displacement sailing but if it provides enough power to plane will be of real significance. The exact range of wind strength on a dead reach between that sufficient to produce maximum-displacement hull speed under jib alone and that necessary to produce planing with the spinnaker is difficult to ascertain, varies with different boats, and may be too narrow to consider in such classes as the International 14—but is of real significance in classes of greater displacement. Thus, it may be desirable to plane up under jib and maintain planing thrust with the spinnaker on the way back down or to plane off under spinnaker initially and plane into the mark under jib. It may also be possible in planing boats, even though maximum-displacement hull speed but not planing is reached under jib, to increase thrust sufficiently to plane with the spinnaker on the base course. Mac Paschal discusses this possibility in detail in a later chapter.

TECHNIQUE

The board should be trimmed between a slight lee helm in the lulls and a slight weather helm in the puffs. Should the sea be right, opportunities for surfboarding may present themselves. A low board will quite effectively nullify many of these opportunities. One can ride down a wave, not quite getting the oomph that was in it, and chalk it up to the fact that there just wasn't enough power, when actually, had the board been well up, a good ride—and several lengths—most probably could have been gained. The best rule on trim of the board is probably—up to where you think it should be and then a little bit more.

A mast 1 in. to leeward of straight up is too much as long as there's enough air to fill the sails. Fore and aft the boat must be constantly trimmed to present the optimum surface and entry to every variation of the surface of the water, from the slightest ripple to a screaming wave. Trim of the sails too is anything but static. The jib must be constantly trimmed to every variation of wind and course. The crew should be instructed to keep it on the edge of a luff and watch every variation. I know of no better way to accomplish this than to pay off every few seconds to feel for a luff, then nail it just short of this point. Of course if a luff develops due to a shift or change in course, nail it right now. This constant trimming must be accomplished slowly, smoothly, but firmly. Any crew who cleats a jib in a planing boat for any reason short of retrieving a lost limb should be put out to graze. As in the case of the jib, the main should be constantly trimmed on the edge of a luff.

As variations in the helm appear, they should be trimmed out in the following sequence: first, "body English" on the trim of the boat, and then correction on the trim of the main. It seems to be universal reflex action to trim the main on a puff. This is at times almost involuntary and in most cases is good, as the apparent wind will move forward as the boat accelerates in the puff. The common tendency, however, is to forget to give it back as soon as the puff has been expended. Before long, and without realizing it, you will be sailing strapped down and wondering why you aren't moving.

A planing boat is ridden rather than sailed. The best way to stop a 14 in her tracks is to sit still. Consider the race horse. With 100 lb. of jockey she may win a race, but in the same race with 100 lb. of inert mass she'll trail the field every time. What we need to move is obvious: the shoulders and that part of the anatomy in most intimate contact with the rail. Athwartships trim or hiking is, of course, constantly carried out in order to accommodate the vagaries of wind and sail trim and to keep the boat level at all times. Fore-and-aft trim or ooching is a bit more subtle. Let us say it's to take advantage of the variations in entry angle due to acceleration and deceleration. Even more, fore-and-aft trim must be varied in order to take full advantage of hull configuration. I like to think of the 14 as a two-hulled boat. There is the relatively narrow entry for use when we want to dig in and the long flat run aft to get up and ride on. It isn't enough to say that we want to dig her in going to weather and get up and ride on the reaches and runs. *We have to ooch in order to present the best surface for each and every set of conditions and these conditions are constantly changing.* Another consideration, and one not generally recognized, is the effect of gravity. In any kind of sea, we're constantly climbing up and downhill. If we can vary the fore-and-aft trim so that the load is eased in climbing a wave and full advantage of a downhill ride is gained, we may be able to minimize the deceleration due to the climb and enhance the descent.

In a fairly close reach in moderate air the seas will be on the weather bow. In this case, any deviation from absolutely upright is fatal. Each sea will tend to take the boat to leeward and back. Weight fairly well forward is best in this case, relying on a good entry to break through. This again cannot be static, as it will result in slugging it out. A very slight movement of the weight aft to get a bit of a run between seas, with a definite lunge forward to help break through each sea as it hits, will yield the best over-all results. The motion will vary from a definite forward lunge from the waist to what might amount to a mere nod to break through a ripple. When confronted with a heavy, weather bow sea, a good rule is to come up slightly to meet the sea and run off slightly in the trough.

In a broader reach from abeam to on the quarter, the seas will be on the quarter. Under these conditions the seas can really be made to pay off as they invariably run a great deal faster than the boat. They'll run the boat ahead, they'll dump it, and they'll cause severe variations in the fore-and-aft trim. The major consideration is to maximize the length of time of receiving drive from each wave. It is essential to get the feel of the sea in order to anticipate the instant before the quartering sea begins to lift the transom. At this instant drive off and shift the weight aft very slightly to raise the bow. All will be lost if you overcorrect and dunk the transom. As the boat begins to derive power from the wave, it will be necessary to shift forward again to stay on or ahead of it and to present the best planing surface to the leading edge of the wave. This will be nose down in relation to the horizon. There is an instant here, just as the boat gets maximum power from the drive of the sea, when the bow will want to dig in. A rather violent correction aft may be necessary to prevent this. As the sea passes on, as it eventually must, all will go slack—or relatively so. The apparent wind will move aft due to deceleration and you'll experience a wallowing feeling. Trim fast and come up. Minimize this slow period and set yourself for the next sea. The rather wild peregrinations described above will take a lot longer to read about than to do, and the posterior will cover a large segment of rail in the doing. However, as George O'Day has illustrated time and again, this can be what separates the men from the boys.

TACTICS

Tactics must be subordinated to the strategy discussed above. Overconcern with tactical considerations will usually decrease the speed with which the course is sailed. In the negative sense, however, tactical techniques should be employed to achieve and protect a clear wind. The maintenance of a clear wind is obviously essential to the utilization of strategic techniques for maintaining or increasing boat speed. On a reach all boats must sail approximately the same course and therefore each successive following boat must sail through air which become progressively more disturbed farther back in the fleet. This is another reason why reaches tend to become parades, with each boat dropping farther and farther behind the one ahead.

Thus, if clear wind can be obtained only by tactical means, it must be sought. *Tactical techniques should not be applied merely to pass or prevent the passage of a nearby boat, but to recover or maintain maximum boat speed for as great a percentage of time as possible.*

Passing to weather is usually easier than to leeward and often not difficult for a following boat on a broad reach who may pick up a puff first. Usually it is attempted immediately after rounding the mark as the leading boat bears away to a progressively slower course. If only one boat is near, and particularly if the air is light, it may be better for the leading boat to forego the sharp turn to leeward and to hold high to keep her air clear. The following boat then may be better advised to shoot to leeward if the leader luffs too high. The leader should never luff any higher than necessary, luff only halfway if a single competitor goes high but is not close, and avoid luffing altogether if a whole mob of potential luffers rounds behind (except on a very broad reach when clear wind may be retained to windward and followed later by a jibe).

A successful attack by luffing requires a sudden increase in speed, usually gained by heading high or aided by a puff, combined with a slowing of the leader by blanketing (see *Fig.* 2). Blanketing extends to leeward in the direction of the apparent wind up to 7

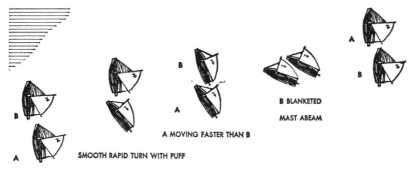

Fig. 2

mast lengths, depending upon the wind, but is most effective close aboard. Unfortunately blanketing is less effective and the detrimental effect of sailing in the leader's wake is greater in light air, so that passing to windward should be attempted at a distance without blanketing under these circumstances. In moderate winds, however, the following boat may and should come up close aboard the leader's transom (or even initially to leeward of him), turn suddenly high on the wind with proper sail trimming, surge ahead, effectively blanket the close leeward boat, and be "mast abeam" in a few seconds. The leading boat must be alert to this danger, ready to round up immediately and at the same rate with the same precision in sail trimming to avoid being blanketed. Neither boat should go any farther to windward than necessary, bearing away immediately as soon as it is recognized, whether the luff was successful or not. Often the leading boat, unprepared, rounds up too sharply or fails to trim properly, is blanketed, and must resume her normal course greatly slowed. If an obviously faster boat wants by, rather than initiate a prolonged luff high of the course, the leader may be better advised to bear away on a better strategic course and let the attacker go. A following boat in turn, once having established an overlap to windward, may find herself taken higher and higher off the course. If dealing with such an overzealous luffer, the attacker would do better to slow up and bear off to leeward.

Once slowed by a blanket a boat may be easy prey for an entire series of windward attackers. It is essential for a leading boat closely followed by a group to avoid being drawn into a luffing match and particularly to avoid losing one! *In general, the lead boat is best advised to keep to leeward and let the next boat take over the role of "defender of the wind."*

If concerned by but one other boat, it is best to avoid a blanketing attack until the crucial period at the finish line or approaching the mark when the blanket can be applied and the leader passed but insufficient time remains for him to regain speed and repay the blanket. It may be desirable to draw a leading boat gradually farther and farther up by continually feinting at his weather until the sailing angle is such that the following boat may gain an overlap at a mark or even pull ahead at the finish after bearing off to leeward without being blanketed (see *Fig 2*).

Covering is difficult on the reach because the worst place to be is in the middle where the wind will be most disturbed (unless well ahead). It may be best to stay directly ahead of the most dangerous competitor if in the final stages of a series, but in general it is best to pick the strategically desirable side or technique and sail the fastest course without regard to particular boats. One can't go both sides of the course to cover everyone, so choose—and, particularly on a broad reach, avoid the middle.

A very valuable technique for a boat following at a distance is a continual feinting attack to pass first to windward, then to leeward. If this is done smoothly, and particularly if it is adjusted to the puffs and lulls, the following boat will gain as the leader makes sharper and sharper course adjustments to cover and breaks the puff-lull cycle. Finally, close aboard a sudden but smooth feint to weather will bring forth a sharp luff from the leader, and the following boat can shoot off her transom through her narrowed blanket zone (as she luffs) and be in a safe leeward position before the leader can regain speed.

Subject to the strategy discussed above, plan to be on the inside at the mark. Particularly if it has been a reaching start, a large number of boats may reach the mark together. The loss of distance and of clear wind by the boats on the outside as they turn necessitates seeking the inside overlap by luffing across the sterns of half the fleet, if necessary, before reaching the mark. The greater the number of boats near by, the more essential the inside position. Do not be afraid to temporarily lose six places to gain eight! The delayed luff and blanket or the technique of driving the leader up by frequent feints to weather to provide clear air to leeward are particularly valuable techniques for gaining a last-minute overlap. The leading boat must be alert to these dangers, utilizing quick sharp luffs without being drawn too high, protecting her lee if that is inside, and avoiding speed loss consequent to ill-managed maneuvers in response to threats from astern.

SUMMARY

If boats are traveling at maximum-displacement hull speed, the fastest course on the reach is a straight line subject to allowance for tide and utilization of waves. If the wind strength is less or the sailing angle too low for maximum-displacement speed:

a) pay careful attention to hull, centerboard, and sail trim;
b) keep to leeward by
c) bearing off in the puffs whenever possible,
d) avoiding luffing any farther than necessary to keep clear wind;
e) use the spinnaker.
If the wind strength is sufficient to permit planing:
a) plane as much as possible by
b) bearing off in the puffs, up in the lulls,
c) keeping to the side of the course which provides the fastest

planing angle at the end of the leg,
d) *using the spinnaker, and*
e) *utilizing the waves.*
At all times keep your wind clear, retain the fastest sailing angle as long as possible, and aim to be inside at the mark.

13. Running in Moderate Air

By JOHN CARTER,
Nashua

On a dead run or broad reach sheer area of mainsail seems to be significant, but on a middling broad reach the draft of the mainsail starts to work. At this point unzipping the foot of the sail or easing the outhaul will throw helpful added draft into the sail. Reduction in tension on the halyard or vang may also increase and move the draft aft for greater effect.

The real money, however, is made or lost with the spinnaker. The first spinnaker we ever bought had large shoulders and a big head —we called it the "prune." The head was so deep that it kept falling in, making the shriveled appearance responsible for its name. Needless to say, we did better with the jib wung out.

I once had occasion to crew for a famous helmsman and sailmaker in a cup match. Like the threadbare tailor, sailmakers always seem to be relieved of all their best personal sails by friendly competitors. This time we had left a chute with a loose leech, causing a steady soft flutter all the way downhill. I'd never seen a chute with this trouble before and, mistaking it for some innovation, I commented on it frequently, finally evoking an embarrassed and exasperated comment that the damn thing was too loose and that I should tend to my knitting! We did relatively well in all the runs, the floppy leech notwithstanding. I was glad the leech was loose and not tight as I believe we lost relatively little by having the air flow out a bit easier than it might have otherwise. Perhaps it *was* an innovation and neither of us realized it.

The next time you are running with a spinnaker, try trimming it in close to the mainsail. You will notice immediately that the boat slows down. The air is being pocketed and not being allowed to flow out of the sail. Anything in the spinnaker's shape which tends to produce this situation is poor. The edges of the spinnaker are easily as important as the edges of a jib; they should be smooth and straight, without any cupping or bagging.

The lure of the deep head is added lift and spread to the shoulders: more area. Some sailmakers have added holes in this upper part to help relieve the choking action of the shape. At its most successful this shape pays its way only on a broad reach. The minute the reach tightens up and the pole goes all the way forward the lower part of the sail will flatten pretty well, but the upper portion will have a wondrous great bag in it. I prefer what might be described as a broad, flat-headed shape. There seems to be no visible penalty straight downhill and you can all but go to windward in a pinch. The foot should be clean, and sharp or slightly relieved, no matter what the head shape may be.

The first essential is to plan the rigging of the spinnaker (see *Fig. 1*) so that it is "outside" all other gear and out of the way when down. The halyard must be held outside all other gear too. Usually an old-fashioned wooden clothespin is the easiest answer. Sophisticates may prefer a small metal clip mounted on the breast hook. I like the clothespin as it is simple and large enough to make clipping the halyard easy and swift on taking the chute down. The spinnaker with sheets connected and led through the leads on the quarters of the boat is stuffed into a net or under shock cord loops on the bow tank. It is a good idea to see that the spinnaker is not twisted from one corner to the other and that the top corner is uppermost. Fancy packing and flaking in the best parachute tradition seems to me a waste of time. Before the advent of non-wetting spinnaker cloth it was of some importance to keep the chute dry even in moderate weather, but now covers or turtles are of little or no importance.

On a two-man boat the spinnaker can be hoisted either by the crew or by the skipper, but it seems better for the skipper to do the hoisting so that the crew can start opening the chute and get the jib tucked away. As the chute starts up, the pole is hooked into the appropriate clew and pushed outboard to open and sort out the sail. The skipper should be trimming the sheets (standing on the mainsheet and steering with his knees) while the crew puts the pole on the mast and hooks up the lift-down haul. Once the

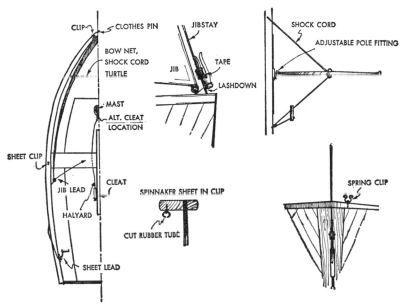

Fig. 1

chute is drawing, the jib is either rolled up (on a short leg or in a smooth sea and moderate air) or taken down (in a lumpy sea or fresh to heavy air). Consideration should be given to the likelihood of the jib's coming unrolled and the danger of the crew's going way forward to roll the jib. The heavy oily material in jibs and the "window" material seems to interfere with keeping the newer jibs rolled. The sure but slightly slower method of taking the jib down would seem to be preferable.

To take the chute down (after hoisting the jib), the sheets are let go and the pole is taken off the mast and pulled in so that the crew can grab the tack of the spinnaker without getting too far into the bow. This means that the spinnaker is flapping out ahead of the boat. The crew must gather in the foot and luff swiftly, pulling in and down so that the chute is muzzled. The crew should re-member that he isn't putting hospital corners on a bed. The im-portant thing is to get the chute down and in fast. Stuff it in the net or under the shock cord, clip the halyard in the clothespin, and get back to the jib sheet, ready to round the mark and off to windward.

One word of caution. If you use closed-eye spinnaker leads there is a danger that the leeward sheet may flip over the end of the boom—especially if the main is trimmed for a middling reach. The obvious solution is to get the chute in fast! The advantage of the closed-eye spinnaker leads is that once the sail is down and the halyard clipped it is also ready to hoist again. The loose sheets may get caught in the jib leads, so rubber clips outside the boat are needed. Open leads have the disadvantage that the sheet may jump out, but the advantage that the sheets can be completely cleared after the spinnaker is used. If you need to use the chute again, well . . . maybe closed leads are the answer.

Jibing should be done smoothly and swiftly without rocking the boat or collapsing the chute. Easily said! The helmsman should turn the boat only when the rudder is fully in the water; not just as a wave lifts the stern and rudder. The boat should also be level athwartships, as it tends to steer opposite the direction it is tipped. The crew should sit to leeward and hold outboard the leeward spinnaker sheet. He should then, as the boat crosses the wind axis, flip the boom across the boat. The helmsman can help by trimming in slightly on the sheet. The spinnaker will stay filled and the pole can be brought across leisurely. The spinnaker routine has been developed in considerable detail, as only by careful practice of a detailed system can the setting, jibing, and dousing become so automatic that the helmsman need not restrict his tactical use of this sail to situations in which there is plenty of time (and distance) to sort out the worst efforts.

Flying Dutchmen, with their very large jibs, find that increased effective sail area can be presented by keeping their jibs up and sheeting their spinnakers inside the jibstay with the wind aft. This apparent return to archaic flat spinnaker sheeting has long been effectively used in the tremendously overrigged Australian, New Zealand, and Bermudian dinghies and is not a consequence of limitation on spinnaker area or shape. The flow of air from the spinnaker leech is directed along the lee side of the jib as the spinnaker itself is sheeted only minimally inside the jibstay. When the jib is adjusted to this air flow, a major increase in drive from both sails results. In moderate air this technique will probably prove to be a safe and effective technique for many classes.

The purist will want to run with the centerboard up. While this is theoretically the swiftest way, the likelihood of having the boat skid or crab on its course is so great that I find it worth enduring the *very* slight extra drag to have the centerboard tip down 8 in. or so to insure the boat's staying in the "groove." In jibing it is usual to put the board down a bit more than is usual for ordinary running, again to prevent skidding. The lumpier the sea, the more board is necessary.

BOAT SPEED

The only aspect of flying spinnakers on which there is universal agreement is that they should never be allowed to collapse. One view is that the largest projected area possible is to be desired. This line seems irrefutable until one considers the necessity of disseminating the air around the spinnaker and mainsail. In order to facilitate this flow the spinnaker must be as far away from the mainsail as possible. My first forceful demonstration of this principle was presented by the California contingent to the 1948 National 14 Championships at Rochester, N.Y. The original rig of the One Design 14 included a head stay which seemed a great handicap to us, but the Californians ran the spinnaker halyard through a loose ring on the head stay. As this stay was a foot in front of the mast at the halyard sheave it effectively moved the spinnaker one foot *out* away from the mainsail. The results were devastating. The spinnaker pole by "rule" is supposed to be carried at right angles to the apparent wind. On setting the tack of the chute by "rule," the clew should be eased out as far as possible. This gets the spinnaker somewhat away from the mainsail; what else can be done? In the days before the current monster-size chutes the sail could be flown farther away from the boat by moving the pole up on the mast. To some extent the sailmakers have now done this for us by making the sail taller on the hoist. The halyard can be let off some. This will be a function of the wind strength; the harder it blows, the farther out away from the mainsail the spinnaker will fly. The "rule" on spinnaker pole trim must be modified in puffy weather or lumpy sea—any condition in which the spinnaker will oscillate.

It will be useful then to choke up on the sail, trimming it in closer to the boat. A spinnaker's most inefficient trim is still its collapsed state.

As a rule it does not pay to run by the lee, but to my chagrin Mac Paschal has shown me there are exceptions. The occasion was a race involving a dead run with a slightly swinging wind and a lumpy but fairly regular sea. The wind would swing so that alternately we could fetch the line or were above it. Whenever the wind let us off the boat went perceptibly better. Mac started from what should have been safely behind us and proceeded to work past and substantially to *leeward* of us. He was on the same tack and didn't jibe once. The trick he worked was to maintain his favorable angle to the waves, even though he was alternately by the lee, shooting steadily by us. Howard Boston, in winning the Thistle Nationals at Saybrook, Conn., used a similar technique of downwind sailing into the "holes"—the troughs of the waves. This technique more than compensated for the lack of efficiency of sailing by the lee for Mac and brought him past us.

The difference in speed on opposite jibes because of wave action was evidenced clearly in a race in Yankee One Designs (moderately sharp-sectioned, heavy-keel boats, 30 ft. LOA). We were running back across Buzzards Bay on the starboard tack with a dying southeast wind. Shortly before it had blown perhaps 35 knots. Our progress was very smooth and steady; the boat seemed in harmony with the wind and waves. As we came within a half mile of the finish line, it was evident that we would have to jibe to make the line. Although our pursuit was quite distant the wind was becoming steadily less reliable, so that we decided to make our downwind tack while away from the influence of the shore and before the wind died further. On jibing, the boat seemed to stop, and our erstwhile easy motion turned into a lumpy, irregular one. The boat seemed to force its way across instead of with the waves. Our pursuers on the original tack gained rapidly on us. Observers of the race said afterward that our speed on jibing initially was cut down to perhaps only a quarter of what it had been. It took considerable strength of character (helped by a strong lead) to hold on. After what seemed an endless period of time we made good a couple of hundred yards on the port tack and were able to jibe back to our fast course again. Sailing by the lee may have been justified in this instance also. The tactical vulnerability of being to windward and ahead on the fast tack and having to jibe to the slow tack across the course of the pursuing boat is extreme. It is the recognition and either avoidance or exploitation of this sort of tactical vulnerability which marks the expert racer and makes the limits of sailing skill infinite.

In a smooth sea and moderate air it rarely pays to tack strongly downwind. The factors which may make downwind tacking worth while are wave shooting and the ability to plane on a slightly tighter course. (Occasionally tactical and tidal factors must be considered.) On a long run in moderate air care should be taken not to sail by the lee. Usually the wind will move back and forth enough to permit averaging the desired course. If not, very slight tacks will be enough to keep the boat moving rapidly and on the most nearly direct course.

TACTICS

Tactics have variations and subtleties without end. Some situations and ideas will be outlined here, more to indicate an approach than to attempt an exhaustive treatment. Running tactics usually start at the weather mark or at the end of a beam reach. A smooth swing from the beat or reach to the run is essential to carry or pick up as much speed as possible. If you are ahead by 3 or 4 lengths you have little concern if the pursuers are not closely bunched. Should there be a great cloud behind you a windward position, as well as a smooth accelerating rounding, is necessary. Once the mob rounds the mark very little air will be available if you are too low. On the other hand, if there are only two boats close together but 3 to 4 lengths behind you, it may be best to swing more tightly to take up a leeward position as it is quite likely that the two boats close together will indulge in a bit of luffing and so move well out to windward off the direct line to the next mark.

There is an old axiom used in gravitational circles that "what goes up must come down." The same is true in running downwind. However, contrary to the gravitational situation, it is usually faster to go "up" than to get back "down," especially in nonplaning weather. As a general rule it is safer to keep low and come "up" at the mark ending the run. You approach the mark with clear air and more speed for maneuvering. You are also either on the inside (buoy room) or have speed enough to pick up the overlap going into the mark (see *Fig. 2*).

Another old axiom in planing boats is to get her going fast first and then worry about going in the right direction. In conditions of marginal planing he who planes will leave the nonplaner in another county. On starting a middling broad reach you may discover that by heading higher you get both a better angle to the waves and a speed increase natural to a beam reach. If you can make the boat plane steadily, this course will be preferable as long

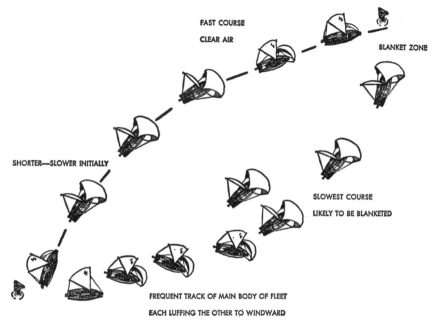

FAST COURSE
CLEAR AIR
BLANKET ZONE
SHORTER—SLOWER INITIALLY
SLOWEST COURSE
LIKELY TO BE BLANKETED
FREQUENT TRACK OF MAIN BODY OF FLEET
EACH LUFFING THE OTHER TO WINDWARD

Fig. 2

as it doesn't lead you too far from the normal course. In practice one would sail somewhere between these extremes—off in the puffs, up in the lulls—probably avoiding a jibe to the port tack as this will make you vulnerable until at the buoy.

One of my favorite devices for passing people is what might be called a double blanketing (see *Fig. 3*). The victim is blanketed

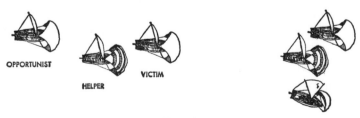

OPPORTUNIST
HELPER
VICTIM

Fig. 3

hard by the "helper" (this is the most difficult part). The "victim" is markedly slowed by this and, as the "helper" moves out to windward to pass, the "opportunist" takes up the blanketing chore, continues to slow an already slowed boat, and in effect passes him on back. Obviously there can be several opportunists and the results proportionately disastrous to the victim. The victim must be alert after the first blanketing to escape the second and fatal dose. This is a very useful tactic in team racing as well in regular racing.

The attack by blanketing is familiar to everyone. One way to avoid it is often useful particularly as a team tactic (see *Fig. 4*). B tries to blanket A. A draws B across in front of C and uses C's blanket

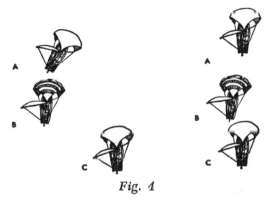

Fig. 4

zone to club B. B either gets blanketed or gives up trying to blanket A. In the event that all three get in line, B will still get blanketed and A will get away free as B's blanket zone is greatly diminished by the inadequacy of her available air. The one word of caution I would introduce is that if there are several boats in line with C look for another boat, C, with some room around it. Otherwise there is the likelihood of a large blanketing zone's being set up and A can fall into the pit with B.

An overlap may be acquired just before the mark is reached by flying the spinnaker a few seconds longer than the boat ahead and taking it down while rounding (see *Fig. 5*). Under these circumstances the skipper in the following boat should "talk up" his overlap to keep "out of court." The risks of this move are obvious, in that should the overtaking boat miss the overlap she will probably not be able to go under the leading boat and will either hit the buoy or get snarled up short of the buoy through a sharp luff. The maneuver should be used in critical situations, preferably well clear of pursuing craft, where its success means the winning of a series or a team race and its failure means either a modest drop in the series or the loss of a team race which can be won only by taking the boat ahead. It seems to me that one of the things that makes an A-1 racer is a knowledge of the percentages and a firm view of the final objective.

A less risky circumstance in which to retain the chute until the actual rounding is when leading in an attempt to break an overlap (see *Fig. 5*). If the overlap is not broken the worst result is merely a sloppy rounding. In team racing a trap may be set by luring a

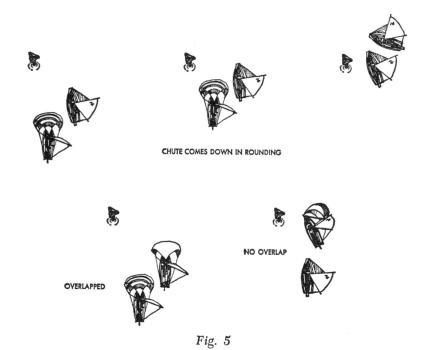

CHUTE COMES DOWN IN ROUNDING

NO OVERLAP

OVERLAPPED

Fig. 5

competitor into the inside position although he has no overlap and then tagging him out as you swing into the turn. In series racing, of course, the following boat should be warned to keep clear if his overlap is not properly established.

There is also a good time to take the chute down early. The leading boat may block a close competitor who has been staying outside but waiting for a chance to try for the inside overlap (see *Fig 6*). By dropping the chute early the boat may be slowed suddenly, catching the competitor overlapped on the outside and unable to swing across. With the overtaking controlled, the leader can hold slightly wide for a smooth rounding. If A, the leading boat, is successful in setting up the lap, she should be careful not to allow B, the following boat, to crowd her toward the mark. On the other hand, if B can entice A into a position from which she must make a sharp turn at the mark, B may, by a smooth turn, arrive at a position giving her clear air to leeward of A, turning an unbearable spot into a clear working position. A variation of this situation is for B to crowd A into a sharp turn and then make a wide smooth rounding on the approach, finishing up inside and to windward of A (see *Fig. 6,* lower diagram).

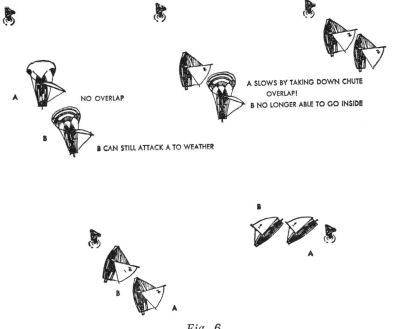

Fig. 6

Occasionally in team racing if luffing rights exist A, the leeward boat, may carry B, the windward, well beyond the turn until B passes the mast line of the leeward. B can escape only by passing A or tacking clear. A will not want to let B know immediately what is in store for her, as the longer the maneuver is prolonged the more effective it is in letting A's team mates through. It may be useful for A to lay off again after a short distance to suggest to B that the delays are over and that they are going back to racing. Anything that can be done to keep B from concluding that she must tack to get away should be done.

When the mark is to be left to windward and the leading boat has luffing rights, an attempt may be made to break the overlap by luffing just short of the buoy. If the luff is sharp, and particularly if it is unsuspected, it is usually successful for this purpose but does permit boats farther to leeward to move up rapidly, possibly to clear ahead, as the luffer bears off to the mark. If the luff is not successful in breaking the overlap and if it has been carried so far that there is danger of fouling the mark or the overlapped boat in a last-second rounding, the windward boat may be carried above the mark. The leeward boat must go above the mark as well but will be able to jibe and return much more rapidly than the thoroughly irate and confused windward helmsman. This technique ordinarily should be reserved for team racing because other boats undoubtedly will gain by it.

Another useful maneuver in team racing is to use a member of the opposition for protection. When boats are on opposite jibes approaching a mark to be rounded to starboard, a starboard tack competitor may try to pick off a port tack boat. The port tack boat A may be able to fall off toward the mark, letting another port tack competitor B blanket her. A can then hide behind B so that C on starboard is unable to get at A without fouling B in the process. A then gets a protected path around the mark!

CONCLUSION

There is much speculation as to what constitutes the top racer —why does he win? The answer is very simple to state but harder to achieve. The equipment must be the best available. The level of competition should be such that no amount of hard and skillful sailing will bring a mediocre sail in ahead of an A-1 sail. Naturally this applies to the boat's condition too. As top sailors will have top equipment this leave the onus on the skipper and crew. Let them both be strong, well trained, and coordinated so that the boat is always well sailed. There must be continuous concentration on the trim of sails and boat necessary to keep the boat always at top speed. That which usually separates the competent from the steady winners is the matter of generalship. *Both skipper and crew should be constantly observing the opposition, the wind and the tide, and the location of the marks. The acuteness of their observations and ability to see a situation developing, and the adroitness and subtleness of their tactical execution will determine their final success. The hardest thing is to know what to look for and to recognize what it is that you are looking at.*

PART III

The Techniques in Heavy Air —Planing Conditions

Preface

With excessive thrust available, which to windward may decrease boat speed if improperly managed, and off the wind may increase boat speed, limited only by capsize, boat speed becomes (as in light air) the crucial factor. In contrast to light air, however, where thrust and drag factors integral to the sails and hull determine boat speed, in heavy air, helmsmanship, the ability to "make the boat go," regardless of the equipment, is the determinant of boat speed.

Here the crew becomes of equal if not greater importance than the skipper, and the skill of both working together dissipates the fury of the gale, stands the boat up, and drives her to weather. Off wind the slightest movement of the tiller, adjustment of the sheets, or movement of the weight distribution, is fraught with the danger of a capsize or a dramatic increase in boat speed. The start, the course, the distance sailed, the tactics at the start or around the marks pale in significance to the necessity of sailing the boat— well and fast. One boat may be inherently better adapted to these conditions than another, but the variations in ability of skippers and crews make heavy-weather racing the opportunity for the aggressive sailor.

14. Starting in Heavy Air

By LIVIUS SHERWOOD,
Ottawa

The importance of a good start, regardless of the strength of the wind or the size of the fleet, cannot be exaggerated. The good helmsman after a bad start in heavy air can catch up to the inexperienced and less able helmsmen he would have beaten in any event, but he will never catch up to the other top helmsmen in the race and generally finishes right behind the leaders or just in front of the second-raters. The combined disadvantages of blanketing, backwinding, disturbed sea, inability to tack at the proper time, and the reduced manuverability consequent to the heavy wind are too much for anyone to overcome.

THE PREPARATION

The groundwork for a good start begins before you leave shore. For heavy weather select your flattest sails. If you must use a full mainsail, pull it out as far as possible on the boom and the hoist. Set your traveler at the full width of the transom. Set up the boom vang tightly. When a mid-boom mainsheet is available much of the reduction in draft may be accomplished by tightening the sheet.

Every effort must be made to reduce the total thrust produced in the presence of excessive available force by reducing the draft of both main and jib. Simultaneously the draft must be moved forward by stretching the luff as tightly as possible to move the center of effort forward. This is necessary to reduce the weather helm which will accompany the increased heeling and increased angle of inclination consequent to the strong winds. It is much easier to make these adjustments ashore than out in the howling gale when you need both hands to stay afloat.

In all winds strong enough to require hiking both skipper and crew should don their life jackets before embarking, whether or not they think the race committee will order that they be worn. Pleasure can become tragedy in a moment. A dinghy sailor drowned in Canada in 1948 and ten years later one drowned in the United States. Both would be alive today if they had been wearing life jackets when they were thrown clear of, or let go of, their dinghies. It is impossible to put on a jacket safely under way in heavy weather so do it before you start.

The centerboard should be set at the first opportunity. The luffing of a large portion of the mainsail has the effect of moving the center of effort of the wind aft. It heeling is unavoidable (although it should be prevented by every means possible), weather helm will be produced or increased. To maintain balance, the centerboard may have to be slightly raised for windward work, thus moving the center of resistance aft.

From the time you leave shore until a few seconds before the start, the dinghy should be sailed with the mainsail luffing. Many dinghy sailors leave their jibs down until the 5-minute warning gun and the writer has done so on occasion but does not recommend the practice. The dinghy is less maneuverable without the jib and there is also the possibility of difficulty raising the jib in heavy weather through halyard trouble or because the crew must place himself in a position in which he cannot assist in the management of the dinghy. In a strong wind both skipper and crew will need every ounce of their strength after the race starts, hence maneuvering until a few seconds before the start gun should be with sheets eased and the crew sitting inboard. In addition, it is desirable to keep the boat as dry as possible until the actual start. By keeping weight well aft you will avoid digging in the bow and rounding up in gusts and will reduce the amount of water taken aboard.

Strong winds necessitate several changes in normal sailing technique. It is important, while trying to sail the dinghy as easily and drily as possible, to maintain good way so that part of the force of the wind is absorbed in the forward movement of the dinghy and so that the dinghy will not become a helpless victim of steep seas and gusty winds. This can be accomplished by keeping the jib working at maximum efficiency while easing the mainsail until all of it is luffing or backwinded by the jib except a small area at the leech. A surprisingly small amount of main with a sheeted-in jib will keep your dinghy driving and maneuverable. The jib should be eased only in the most extreme circumstances to avoid capsizing. Even in a violent gust, try to stay upright by working to weather and ease your jib only as a survival measure when your lee rail starts under.

More room than usual is needed for tacking and jibing. A quick tack which is easy in moderate conditions may not work in heavy weather because the reduced headway caused by the excessive wind strength and the big waves can stop a dinghy and leave it helpless. Your tack must be delayed until you can find an area with at least one boat length clear to leeward and two to windward. If necessary, tack a bit earlier or later than you had planned—you can readjust by luffing or sheeting in and bearing off onto a plane as necessary. As you near the point at which you plan to tack, tell your crew to be ready to tack (and hike), bear off slightly, and sheet in your main to pick up way. As soon as good way is acquired and preferably just after your bow has cut a wave crest, you should tack. Do not hesitate once the decision is made, slam her about! Avoid moving too far aft while tacking. This drags the stern and frees the bow to be blown back on the original tack.

If by trying to tack without proper way you end up "in irons," don't panic. As you begin to make sternway, rudder action is reversed, so you should, assuming you wish to complete the attempted tack, push your tiller to what will be the leeward side of the dinghy. At the same time the crew should hold out the jib on what will be the windward side and, as the dinghy falls off onto its new tack, the mainsheet should be allowed to run until the dinghy is well off the wind. At this point the crew should release the jib and sheet it in on the new tack. Thereafter (and no sooner) you may sheet in the main gradually and hike as necessary until you are well under way on the new tack.

If you must bear off to clear an obstacle or keep clear wind, ease the mainsail if necessary to avoid heeling. In trying to break through the blanket zone of a windward boat, bear off early and get the dinghy planing before you enter it. You will break through quite quickly but must be prepared to move quickly outboard as you bear off, inboard as you are momentarily blanketed, and outboard again as you burst clear.

Hardening up at low speeds to change course or avoid obstacles can be accomplished in the conventional manner by simultaneously altering course, sheeting in, and hiking. If you must harden up suddenly while moving fast, you should make your course alteration before sheeting in and be prepared to hike as necessary.

An additional heavy weather enemy is the sudden puff which causes the dinghy to heel, bury its bow, build up a lee bow pressure wave, and round up rapidly to windward. Such puffs are dangerous only when they are completely unanticipated or when crew weight is too far forward. The writer has twice capsized in such circumstances by attempting to luff up, thus combining the forces of wind pressure and centrifugal force. *Luffing along on a beam reach in a strong wind is particularly dangerous as the bow is immersed, side force maximal, and speed to dissipate thrust unavailable. The sudden puff increases heeling, increases the pressure under the lee bow, slows the forward progress, and combines heeling force with centrifugal force to cause a capsize. The remedy is to throw your weight aft and out while pulling your tiller to windward, forcing the dinghy upright again.* Be prepared to move back inboard quickly to avoid entering a series of violent yaws. As much as possible, yawing should be corrected with the tiller (steer in the direction in which you are heeling), rather than by shifting weight which is easily overdone.

STARTING POSITION FOR WINDWARD STARTS

The two essential factors in a good start are starting at the right point on the line and proper timing. The entire first leg should be carefully planned before the start and the start should be executed to best carry out the plan. Avoid tacking away from the line later than 2 or 3 minutes before the start as tacking may be temporarily impossible in very heavy air, thus negating all plans.

For a start to windward, even if the leeward end of the line is favored because of the wind direction, you must decide whether the advantage in starting at that end will overcome the disadvantages of being unable to tack across the bows of the dinghies that have started farther to windward. If the wind is shifty, it is probably better to start at the windward end of the line to permit tacking readily in response to the shifts. If a heading shift occurs, changing the conditions to favor the leeward end, an immediate tack is indicated, while a lift will favor the windward boats on the original tack. In a leeward-end start, additional room must be allowed to clear other dinghies after tacking because your dinghy will be slow to tack and regain headway in heavy weather and steep seas. When the dinghies to windward finally tack, thus clearing you to tack, you will have to carry on for an additional distance because a lee bow position reverses itself when both dinghies tack. A late start at the leeward end is hopeless—there will be no clear wind or water anywhere (see *Fig. 1*).

Authorities seem to agree that the ideal start under most conditions is made by the helmsman who is on the line, under full way, close-hauled on the starboard tack, right at the windward end of the line when the start signal is given. He has full rights over all dinghies to windward and need not give them room to pass between his dinghy and the mark. There can be no one ahead of him to affect either his wind or the water through which he must sail unless a heading shift occurs. He is free to tack at any time if he has sufficient way and the dinghies astern do not outpoint him. However, unless the wind direction definitely favors the start at the windward end, the windward boat will suffer from the backwind of boats to leeward and should probably plan to and actually tack at the earliest opportunity.

Entry lists in regattas are becoming bigger and bigger as more sailors recognize the merits of small boat sailing, but as a necessary result the proportion of relatively unskilled helmsmen is also increasing. In modern regattas there is almost always a serious jam at the windward end of the line. Helmsmen who have been attempting the perfect or near-perfect start are frantically screaming, "No room!" or "Get up!" at the other helmsmen who are bearing down on them on a wild barging plane. All too often the situation ends in a tangle of boats and rigging, profanity and excuses, with perhaps one boat emerging relatively unscathed. One must also consider the helmsman who arrives at the line early and, although without rights, bears down on the leeward dinghies to avoid crossing. The degree

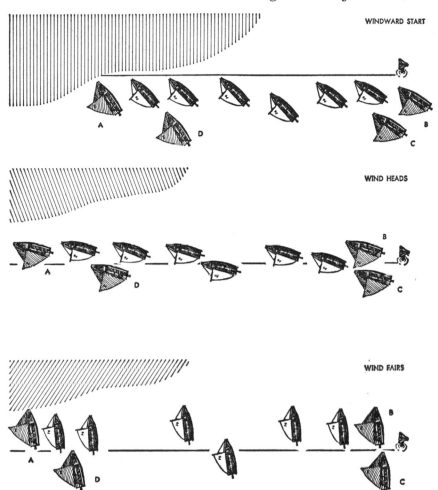

Fig. 1. A appears to have an excellent start as does B. C's start is fair at best. D is in a very bad position. When the wind heads, A should be able to tack momentarily and lead the fleet. B should tack at once to have clear wind and water and be in a position to take the lead on the next shift. C should tack at the first sign of the heading to try to clear her wind on the new tack. D is in a nearly hopeless position and can only carry on starboard in the hope that the heading will become worse and permit her to tack later to greater advantage. When the wind fairs, A is in a precarious position and, unless the wind again shifts, will cross astern of all boats to windward when she tacks for the mark. B is in a commanding position and leads every other dinghy by the distance she was to windward at the start, wind and water are clear, and she may tack when she chooses. D is now in a completely hopeless position. C can remain near the top of the fleet. She should be ready to tack at once at the slightest sign of a heading. A short tack at once to clear her wind is of doubtful value because two extra tacks in strong winds and high seas would be quite costly and would be in the wrong direction to take advantage of the next heading shift.

of control which helmsmen have over their dinghies in strong winds also varies widely, and capsizes on the start line are not infrequent.

The good helmsman, who is fighting for top honors in a regatta, will find little consolation if his excellent start is ruined by flagrant barging or other fouls arising out of the inexperience of other helmsmen. The race is lost no matter whose fault it is. As long as these problems remain, the perfect windward-end start should be considered with some misgivings. If you are just an average starter, you would do well to consider starting slightly to leeward of the windward mark, where you may very well be able to clear your wind and water and have a start second best only to the one man at the windward end who made the perfect start.

There will always be confusion at the windward end of the line unless the barging rule is enforced by disqualification of any barging dinghy which hits a leeward dinghy or forces it to alter course without making every effort to stay clear. Barging dinghies and other dinghies to windward must be disqualified if they do not respond to luffing by dinghies to leeward. In this way every helmsman who attempts a barging start will know that he faces almost certain disqualification if he interferes with any leeward dinghy. He should either be wise enough to avoid such starts or, if he finds himself trapped between a windward and a leeward dinghy, harden up and hit the windward dinghy rather than sail down on the innocent leeward one and ruin its start. Dinghy sailors and protest committees should remember N.A.Y.R.U. Appeal No. 37: "We would not hesitate to disqualify an intervening yacht that connived in a windward yacht's failure to luff by using her lee side as a refuge and by making little or no attempt to force her to luff."

In general, if the windward end is strongly favored by the wind direction or if the wind is shifting frequently as in a northwesterly, start at or near the windward end. If the leeward end is definitely favored and there is no advantage in an early port tack, start at the leeward end. If the line is well laid out with little advantage to either end and no necessity of an early port tack, start at the most uncongested area of the line, avoiding particularly boats on your lee bow. If the wind is shifting, take the tack which is lifted in relation to the median wind direction of the day. If this is the port tack, start on starboard in a position from which an immediate tack may be made to port—or, in a small fleet, start on port. Under these circumstances, or if the starboard side of the course is favored for other reasons, the first boat to take the port tack may often win the race.

There are several methods of timing a start. Large boats generally make a timed run of about one minute away from the line, allowing time to tack and one minute to return to the line. This system is not as satisfactory for dinghies, particularly in big fleets where blanketing or backwind may seriously slow the final run to the line. If you do use a timed start, you should not go more than 30 seconds away from the line because a dinghy, unlike a larger yacht, can be quickly maneuvered in close proximity to the line and there will be less danger of unexpected speed variation's producing major effects in the short distance involved.

Other methods include "luffing" near the line until the time seems ripe to go for it, or shadowing a helmsman you know is a good starter and trying to start on his lee bow or weather quarter. The former method is bad in heavy weather because it involves too many dangerous maneuvers in a crowded area with limited steerage way. The latter method is not likely to make you popular with your subject and you may, by your proximity to him, ruin both your starts. A fourth and better method is to select a point from which you want to start your final run, try the run to determine the time it requires, then start at that point, leaving a bit of extra time because there is likely to be some interference on your final run. Remember that leeway is excessive while luffing along at slow speeds approaching the line. A boat may drift 50 ft. to the side while moving 100 ft. toward the line. Starting the approach above the lay line to the windward end is essential. A nice hole may open as the entire fleet drifts to leeward.

The most frequent cause of a bad start lies in the timing and since the majority of starters, probably out of an abundance of caution, arrive at the line late, it is recommended usually that helmsmen do their best to be early. This advice seems particularly appropriate in a dinghy because it is easy to luff up and kill way if you do indeed approach the line too soon. A dinghy can pick up speed so quickly from a dead stop that you can luff almost to the line, laying off or sheeting in only at the last moment. However, a premature start in heavy weather, with several tacks or a jibe required to restart, may be extremely hazardous.

RECOMMENDED START—TIMED RUN FROM PRESELECTED POINT

The writer usually prefers to start from a preselected point and head for a point on the start line at or close to the windward mark and on starboard tack. To accomplish this, the following method is suggested. Make a few early runs from a preselected point about eight boat lengths from the line on a course which will permit you to lay the windward mark on a close reach. Having determined the time necessary to reach the windward mark on this course, get yourself to the preselected point and on course to the windward mark about 5 seconds early (see *Fig. 2*).

As you approach the windward mark, take careful note of the dinghies to leeward. If there are none close, bear off slightly until you just lay the windward mark and arrive there at the gun for a fine start. If dinghies appear on the lee bow, which will later be able to force you above the windward marker, kill way, then plane off under them and harden up as soon as your wind is again clear and you have some room to leeward. If dinghies approach from the lee quarter and their course will affect you before you reach the line, bear off across their bows to a point just to leeward of them. These maneuvers will consist of a series of bearings off during which you will accelerated rapidly, and therefore you will have to luff violently after each bearing off to avoid arriving too soon. As long as your timing is right, pay no attention to dinghies to windward except to hail any that bear down on you. As soon as you have cleared a space of a few boat widths to leeward, lay a close-hauled course for the windward end of the line and luff as necessary to avoid being early. If this procedure is followed you should either be able just to lay the windward marker or, as is more frequently the case because of the repeated bearing off, you will be making your start at some point up to one-quarter of the length of the line from the windward mark. This should leave you at the start signal on the lee bow of boats to windward and a sufficient space to leeward to prevent any other dinghy from getting on to your lee bow. Both your wind and water should be clear and you should be free to tack fairly early, because only one or two, at most, of the windward boats will have started well enough to provide interference. (see *Fig 2*).

It is desirable to time the run so that your sails can be sheeted in hard about 5 seconds before the start signal is given. At the

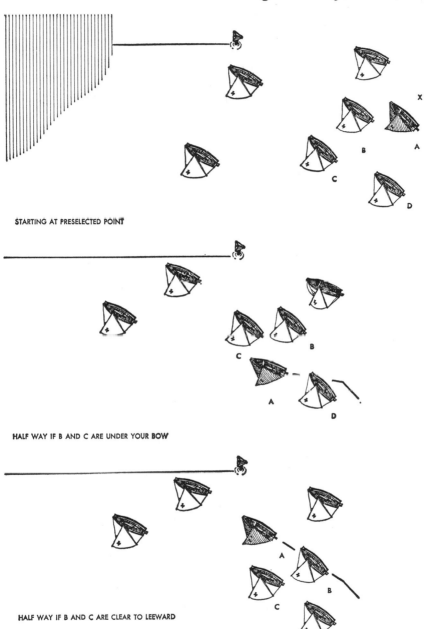

STARTING AT PRESELECTED POINT

HALF WAY IF B AND C ARE UNDER YOUR BOW

HALF WAY IF B AND C ARE CLEAR TO LEEWARD

Fig. 2

same time, it is essential that skipper and crew hike hard. Failure to hike promptly in strong winds will leave your dinghy "on its ear" at the start and other, better-handled dinghies will sail through you to windward and leeward.

LATE START AT WINDWARD END

Many helmsmen who like to start at the windward mark, but wish to avoid either being early or being jammed at the start line, like to start on a somewhat barging course and a little bit late at the windward mark. This generally leaves them free to tack whenever they choose, and while they can never get the best start in the fleet they are generally in a contending position at the end of the first leg. See dinghy "C" in *Fig. 1*. If you find that you are going to be late, never try to pinch to windward because the combination of the pinching and the blanketing effect of boats starting on time will leave you wallowing far astern at the gun. It is far better to lay off and reach the line farther to leeward but sooner and with better way.

Starting position and timing should be determined chiefly by the strategy of the first leg. It is not the dinghy first across the line which is first at the weather mark, but the dinghy which arrives at the offshore wind shift, or reaches the new header of the north-westerly, or sails out of the adverse tidal current first. Freedom to tack to port or being farthest to leeward in a gradual header may be far more valuable than a well-timed start. And don't be afraid to give up temporary advantage to seize the real opportunity. If port tack is indicated, tack and bear off behind half the fleet if necessary, but get to port.

Second in importance only to the over-all strategy is getting clear wind and maximum boat speed as rapidly as possible. In the first few minutes after the start the majority of the fleet is either blanketed, backwinded, or sailing in another's wake. Boats moving at proper speed may gain tremendous and ultimately insurmountable distances during this period. *It is this ability to get moving immediately after the start which distinguishes the top helmsman in any fleet and which usually determines the general outcome of a series.* Such helmsmen usually make well-positioned and well-timed starts, but even if they are unable to do this they shoot for free air, driving to leeward or hiking with every ounce of strength to break away from a competitor on their lee bow or tacking behind a blanketing boat to windward. They make every effort to avoid being backwinded by avoiding boats close to leeward like the plague—before and after the gun. Often, when starting at the windward end, they are able to produce that little extra bit of speed which enables them to pull enough ahead of the closely packed boats behind, or to pinch enough to windward, or to acquire good way before the boats behind and to windward so that they are able to tack, safely, alone and free, leaving the fleet to wallow astern.

REACHING AND RUNNING STARTS

Although most races start with a windward leg, there are still occasions when a start must be made to leeward. In such a case you should usually prefer the end which will leave you on the inside at the first turning mark, even if the line slightly favors the other end. If the other end is strongly favored, however, you would do better to start there and count on a combination of a shorter course and clear wind and sea to put you in the lead by the first mark. If other factors are more or less equal, you would be well advised to start at the end which will put you on your dinghy's fastest planing angle to the next marker. Approach the line on a close reach on the tack on which you will sail the first leg.

If the first leg is a dead run, it should always be approached on a starboard tack reach. Your dinghy will move faster than on a run, you will have much better control in strong winds and steep seas, and you will have the right of way over all dinghies starting on a run or on a port tack reach. Never set a spinnaker until you are well clear of the line and have some room for maneuvers. A dinghy with spinnaker set before the start is a fair target for every dinghy in the fleet.

THE PREMATURE START

The premature start is a serious problem. It has been truthfully said by many racing authorities that to start consistently well a helmsman must occasionally be over too soon. An occasional premature start is far more desirable than invariably arriving late at the line. However (it has already been pointed out that it is very easy to kill way in a dinghy and luff to the line), every effort should be made to kill way at the last moment because the cost of a premature start in heavy weather is very high.

The early starter has no rights over dinghies that have started on time and must frequently stall his dinghy head to wind until dinghies to windward and leeward have passed him. He must then contend with a jibe or a tack, or both, which can be hair-raising at any time, but even more so when they must be done in a hurry by an overexcited helmsman and crew. Remember the earlier remarks on boat management—at low speeds tacking is safe, but at high speeds a jibe is safer.

Occasionally a restart can be made by simply bearing off onto a broad reach to get back across the line, then hardening up to restart. This has the advantage of avoiding the jibe and tack; however, it starts a boat well to leeward and astern of all competition and eliminates almost any possibility of making up for lost ground.

A premature start on a run is tragic. You must tack or jibe under dangerous conditions, then tack back to the line, avoiding the entire oncoming fleet which is speeding off on a plane to the first mark.

Premature starts in major regattas have become more and more common, usually because of a few helmsmen who push over the line early at the windward end. Leeward dinghies are also drawn across when they try to keep their wind clear. This practice leads to a series of restarts, especially in strong winds, when a hail by the race committee can be heard for only a limited distance.

The race committee often cannot identify the more windward dinghies in a clump of premature starters in time to recall them or in some cases cannot identify any of them. The starting gate system used in some parts of Europe has found little support in North America, where helmsmen feel that it would kill initiative and do away with one of the most exciting and skillful parts of the race. The only answer would seem to be to place a committee boat at each end of the start line and perhaps a third boat under power, which could be sent out by the committee boat right after the start to identify the premature starters. Every effort should be made to hail the culprits as soon as possible, and all who can be identified should be disqualified. Some hardship might result, but it is believed that in a very short time the standards of starts would be vastly improved. Many premature starters know that they were over too soon but think or hope that they will not be seen because they were hidden under the lee of another boat, and they carry on in the hope that they will not be identified or because they fear that some of their opponents may escape detection. Such conduct is hardly consistent with Corinthianism and should have no place in one of the few sports which still values sportsmanship at least as highly as success.

CONCLUSION

Now you have made your start. Remember your plans carefully laid with calm consideration long before the start. Do not abandon them in the excitement unless a wind change or a badly executed start have made them obviously impractical.

In accordance with the above, you will be well advised to remember three basic rules:

1. *Never stray too far from the line.*
2. *Remember the strategy of the first leg.*
3. *Keep your wind clear.*

15. Beating in Heavy Air

By JACK KNIGHTS, Philadelphia
and JOHN HARTLEY WATLINGTON, Bermuda

No one can call himself a proper small boat sailor until he can sail in a breeze of wind, for it is then that a boat really comes to life. It will be the races in big winds that will live in your memory, not the days spent in the lee scuppers with one eye on the jib, the other on the telltale, and zinc oxide on your nose. Another thing: when the wind blows briskly it usually blows steadily. Anyone who excels in these conditions can count on winning every time. But light air is usually flukey too, and even the best light weather expert is vulnerable to bad luck.

THE SAILS

For windward work in heavy air, the jib should be long on the foot to provide maximum area at a low level with least heeling moment. It should be close along the deck or gunwale to reduce the severe wing-tip eddy of the triangular sail plan. If the boat is kept upright as it should be, the lower area of the jib remains effective; but if heeling is permitted, a major portion of jib effectiveness may be lost. The jib should be cut flat and kept flat—the harder it blows, the tighter the sheet.

To further reduce heeling moment and to improve the slot effect, the head of the jib should be cut away. The head should be at least 15 in. down the jibstay on an International 14 and probably even lower if the main is particularly full. The leech of an overlapping jib should be hollow to avoid closing the slot. *The parallel alignment of jib and main with maintenance of an equally wide slot throughout is of the utmost importance to windward work.* Careful adjustment of jib sheet leads and mainsail draft (chiefly with the vang) for each jib and each main, with further adjustment for varying wind conditions, is essential. It may be necessary to recut the jib (or even get a new one) if the slot cannot be made perfect.

Experiment, not only with the fore-and-aft position of your jib fair-leads, but also with their athwartships position. The nearer you can bring them to the center line—without sacrifices in other directions, such as mainsail interference—the higher you will be able to point your boat. And remember that as open classes grow beamier, so will the jib leads need to be farther from the gunwhale.

The mainsail is a balancing sail only in a blow. It should be flat and kept flatter to improve the slot and reduce the produced thrust. It should also be of reduced aspect ratio ideally, as a tall plan increases heeling moment upwind and is less efficient downwind in strong breezes. With the adjustments available in a modern rig even a large full main can be lugged to weather without significant harm, however.

There is a new trend in mainsheets. They are moving forward, away from the end of the boom and the transom, toward the center thwart and the center of the boom. In this latter position they do the right thing automatically. A heavy flow of wind encourages them to bend down the center of the boom while allowing the outboard end to bend up and out to leeward. This takes some of the draft out of the sail while easing the leech. As a result, small boats are sailing to windward with less playing of the mainsheet than used to be necessary. Many people now cleat the sheet, relying entirely on the rudder and this automatic boom bending to take them safely through hard puffs.

In effect, most modern small boats now have two mainsheets. One adjusts the track position of the lower sheet block and thus hauls the sail in horizontally. The other, the standard mainsheet, hauls the sail down and by this means controls mainsail draft and set. During an average race both will have to be adjusted frequently when on the wind. Practice, racing experience, and sensitivity for the "feel" of your boat will have to be your guides. In general, the stronger the wind the more the block is eased to leeward on the track. In light air it may be best to pull the block to windward, keeping the sail amidships but easing it upward to increase draft. Even in strong winds it should never be eased more than a few inches from the center line (when going to windward), or pointing will be seriously impaired. *The more amidships the block is kept, the harder it is to sit the boat up but the better she points.*

THE RIG

The mast must be strong—strong enough to stand with the minimum staying. Tight shrouds and a tight forestay seem essential in an International 14 as a starting point for a straight jib luff. The jumpers (if present) should be fairly loose to permit the tip of the mast to bend aft under vang and mainsheet tension.

The degree of bend of the mast and flattening of the mainsail are chiefly controlled by the boom vang, which should be extremely strong. The vang itself should be of wire and of at least 6 power, but preferably should run to a winch which will permit adjustment when already loaded. The vang not only flattens the main but tightens the jibstay. It is the *sina qua non* of sailing to windward in a breeze—*the stronger the wind, the tighter the vang.*

The boat should be balanced with the centerboard full down, possibly canted a little forward to achieve the proper angling of the board to weather. Ideally the mast should be located in the position desired and the centerboard pin position adjusted to balance the boat with the board full down rather than fixing the centerboard and moving the mast. Not only will the twist of the board tend to make the boat eat out to windward, but also the boat can be sailed more nearly upright without having a lee helm. Most small boats are designed on the theory that they will be sailed at, say, a 5-degree angle of heel and are balanced for this angle. Many small centerboarders, however, seem actually to go best when they are heeled 2 or 3 degrees to windward. This is probably because the hull shape itself then becomes an asymmetrical hydrofoil, tending to pull the boat upwind. Unfortunately the average boat will carry a bad lee helm at such a heel, causing the loss of all other benefits. Moving the board well forward tends to correct this and allows one to sail the boat really flat. In a blow some skippers move the board aft of vertical in order to relieve the weather helm which tends to develop if the boat heels. I believe that a better policy is to work a little harder at keeping the boat really flat and thus not develop the helm in the first place. If all efforts at keeping the boat level fail, however, by all means move the board so as to relieve the helm.

Practically all racing skippers like a bit of weather helm, varying from just the slightest whisper to a good healthy tug. I believe the amount of pull in pounds is immaterial; the important consideration is the angle of helm. Since the water foil has been shown to work best at low angles of attack, say about 4 degrees, I think that the helm should be enough to cause the rudder to assume this angle. Then the skipper knows he is getting all the lift to windward possible out of his rudder blade while still allowing a few more degrees of helm before reaching the stalling angle, which really causes drag. Of course, the skipper tries to avoid abrupt movements of the rudder which will cause separation of the flow on the low-pressure side of the blade.

Windage and weight are the twin enemies of windward efficiency. Hunt them down constantly, harass them ruthlessly, volley and thunder. A thicker mast with a little rigging is to be preferred to a thinner mast with much rigging, but masts at all costs should be light. The light boat with the light gear will show up best in a blow, *providing nothing actually breaks.*

Keep weight away from the ends of the boat. The bow has to climb over the waves and the stern has to cause as little interference with the flow of the water as possible. For the same reason, concentrate crew weight as centrally as possible. Leave ashore everything not absolutely required by the rules or by the need to go fast. The neat little lockers and bags that some boats carry are pernicious collectors of extra pliers, screw drivers, shackles, and associated supercargo.

THE TECHNIQUE

Stand her up, straight up, heeled a bit to windward if possible —and keep her up! Feather her along the edge of the wind, pinch her a little if necessary, but keep her upright! Hike as hard as possible, and a little harder if necessary, ease the main if you absolutely must, but keep her upright! This means, in effect, that you must *hike, hike, hike for most of the time when on the wind.* You should practice to anticipate changes in wind speed. After a time you and your crew should be able to keep your boat upright and steady through wind variations, simply by moving a fraction before the wind strikes.

Some helmsmen and their crews move in and out in unison. Personally, I prefer to hike all the time and call on my crew for help only when my own weight is no longer enough. I find it easier to sail upwind when I am as far from the sails as possible. In this position I can see more, and the boat transmits its feeling to me more clearly when I am perched on its gunwale rather than crouched in its belly.

You can keep your boat upright either by giving the boat sufficient power to resist the heeling effect of the wind or by easing the sails. Clearly the first is preferable because the sails are your engine and you must keep your foot on the gas or be left behind. Yet do not forget the second course. It is often the only way of keeping a boat on her feet when a sudden puff strikes or when you are already hiking out as far as possible and she still heels.

Take a serious look at the way you hike your boat. Then take a studious look at your class rules. Some classes, such as Stars, prohibit hiking straps altogether. This is a mistake because hiking straps are cheap and they make hiking safer and easier.

If your class rules do not prohibit hiking straps, find out what arrangement would enable you and your crew to hike out most effectively and comfortably. In the early days, hiking straps were always fastened along both sides of the centerboard trunk. You slipped your toes under them, placed your posterior on the narrow gunwale, and leaned back until muscular collapse or sheer pain brought you in. Then a young man from Denmark named Paul Evlstrom, who was used to sailing Dragons, took up small boat sailing with an open mind. He placed his toe straps on the floorboards under where he sat, and proceeded to win three Olympic Gold Medals, once in the Firefly and twice in the Finn Monotype.

His hiking strap arrangement didn't make him go any faster, directly, but it was more comfortable. It enabled him to sit farther outboard for longer stretches of time than anyone else. If you can hike out an inch or two farther than before, you will gain more speed to windward than you could have gained any other way.

Hiking straps should be adjustable. Short crews need them higher and nearer the side of the boat than tall ones. And remember, you are not hiking properly unless most of you is outside the boat. Side deck sitting is not enough.

Two modern classes—the 5-0-5 and the Flying Dutchman—allow trapezes for the crew. These offer tremendous possibilities for adding extra power to your boat, but to exploit them fully you need a regular crew and an agile one, and you need lots of practice. Other things being equal, your crew should be lighter than is desirable without a trapeze.

POINTING

Whether to point or to foot has plagued helmsmen ever since the first vessel tried to sail to windward. In terms of the lift generated by sails, centerboards, and rudders, pointing at the expense of speed through the water doesn't make much sense. Since speed is the only factor in the lift formula which is squared, *any improvement in speed will add lift far more quickly than anything else.* A little more speed will mean much greater efficiency, which spells less leeway.

The only way to be certain that the boat is sailing as high as is advantageous, is to keep prodding the boat experimentally into the wind, watching the while for reactions on the sail luffs, particularly the jib luff. Catamariners are finding that they go best to windward in a series of swoops. They first let their craft romp good and full, and then squeeze them slowly up into the wind. Before the speed is lost and the boat stalls, they bear away again to regain speed. This technique holds good, in lesser degree, with small sensitive sailboats. *You should nibble your way to windward, luffing up for a bite to weather and then bearing off for a speed-regaining breath* (see Fig. 1).

Going to windward in a light sailboat, the rudder should be in constant use, to thread the best course over the waves and to work out to weather of the competition. By weaving alternately off and into the wind your boat can at one moment be given a little extra speed so that at the next moment you can feather your way more closely to the wind. You luff up until you feel your speed wavering to such an extent that a wave might stop you altogether. Before this can happen you bear off enough to get your boat romping again.

This technique is most effective in heavy airs and considerable waves. Naturally such weaving should be subtle. It shouldn't be carried too far. It is all a matter of that mysterious intangible "feel." Some craft, particularly short boats, cat-rigged boats, and overcanvased boats need more of this weaving than others.

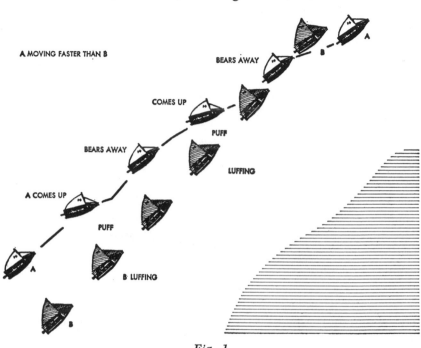

Fig. 1

Rudders can be used in another way to help keep a boat upright. On puffy days, when the wind strength varies every few seconds, the boat can often be kept on a more even keel by use of the rudder than by moving crew weight in and out of the boat. This is done by luffing slightly but sharply when a puff dies. This little luff, because of centrifugal forces at work, tends to make the boat heel momentarily and this is sometimes enough to help keep the boat from heeling to windward from one puff to the next.

Modern small sailboats, with their good hull lines, efficient lateral planes, clean rigs, and smooth synthetic sails, will sail high on the wind. Don't be afraid to let the luffs of your sails shiver spasmodically. If you use the weaving technique your boat will quite often be higher on the wind than optimum. Providing you don't fall into the error of "pinching" by continuing on that too high course for too long, such experimental "prodding into the wind" is all to the good. It helps you detect freeing puffs quickly, and every time you prod you get a little nearer the weather mark.

Steer the boat on the jib, keeping it almost on edge but never actually luffing. *With almost full hiking power exerted continuously sail her as high as necessary to keep upright.* The more power available, the more she can be eased off and driven and the faster she'll go. Sail up in the puffs off in the lulls to match power and thrust. Play the main as necessary to make the final adjustment, in tighter as the wind decreases and eased out as the wind increases. The main is only a balancing sail in these conditions; do not be afraid to ease it. Remember, however, that pointing depends upon the main; and the closer to the center line it can be kept, the higher the boat will point. Never ease the jib except as a last resort when the rudder is no longer in control.

The bow should be kept well immersed by keeping crew weight forward, usually crowded against the shrouds. Here also weight is most effective in controlling heeling by being directly opposite the center of effort of the side force. The immersed bow seems to get a better grip on the water, reduces the tendency to pitching by cutting through the waves, and reduces the wetted surface and drag of the less immersed stern. The degree to which the bow should be immersed can be determined only by trial and error. It may be carried to excess with the occurrence of cavitation in boats with fine bows.

Avoid being thrown about by the seas as much as possible. Head more directly into the biggest seas to avoid being knocked sideways. Ease the main as a wave comes under the boat, lifting her into full exposure to the wind, and tighten the main as the boat settles into the trough to avoid heeling alternately to leeward and windward.

Learn to tack well. In an average race you tack, say, 30 times. Gain a mere 3 ft. each time you tack and you will give yourself a 30-yd. lead. Different boats need different techniques, but always use as little helm as necessary. It hardly ever pays to throw the helm hard down or to let go of it and catch it again on the new tack, but you see this done again and again. It is far better to press the tiller down progressively. Start turning slowly and increase the tiller movement as you go through the eye of the wind. (You need only a little helm when you are moving fast, but as you slow toward the end of the tack more helm is needed.)

An interesting test in helping to improve your tacking is to leave your self-bailers down and watch the amount of water that enters through them each time you tack. The best tacks are surprisingly quick, quicker than I would have thought advisable before I took the self-bailer test, and quicker than a normal crew can handle a big jib.

Be certain that the boat is bolt upright, moving at maximum speed, just before you tack. Give an extra hike and bear off a little if necessary. Tack as quickly as possible; light planing boats will not shoot to weather and can easily be blown or forced by the waves into stays or back onto the original course. Let the jib go immediately. Except to insure that the head comes around in extreme conditions, holding the jib merely slows the boat unnecessarily. The crew should insure that the sheets are clear, indicate that he is ready to tack, release the sheet on command, move rapidly across the boat with the new sheet in hand, pulling it in as he moves, and get it in as tightly as possible as soon as possible before the tack is completed. The windward sheet may be fed through the fair-lead by the skipper as the boat comes about. Both skipper and crew should hike immediately and strongly to prevent heeling as the boat settles on the new course with the main slightly eased. Once the boat is stabilized and heeling controlled, the jib should be strapped in as tightly as possible, the skipper assisting the crew on the sheet if necessary. Finally the main is brought in and the boat feathered up to her ideal coure.

TACTICS

The start and the 3 minutes or so following are by far the most important part of the race. So give them everything you've got. In a foot race the sprint comes at the end but in a yacht race you should start with the sprint. Then, when you are ahead with a clear wind, you can settle down and take life easy while your rivals are scrapping in each other's disturbed air.

In general, if the wind is offshore it is best to go inshore on the beat where the wind is usually stronger, the sea less, and the possibility of a lift available. In an onshore wind, everything else being equal, keep to starboard of the fleet so that you approach both the other boats and the mark on starboard. If you are taking a hosing from another section of the fleet, because your wind has lightened or headed, whereas theirs has freed them or strengthened, do not despair. At a time like this, many skippers believe in taking their medicine, in other words cutting their losses by tacking toward the favored boats even though it means they will end up behind. It is better to stick to your guns. If you are religious you may pray for your wind to come back. More often than not it does and then it is the other's turn to lose ground. In this case the boat that "took its medicine" loses twice.

Don't be too clever—by which I mean, don't go hunting for hypothetical airs that your higher intelligence has told you should be there. In Marblehead they tell you they sail toward the clouds for wind. To my way of thinking that sounds like chasing rainbows. Small boat races are too short for the grand strategy; more important are correct minute-by-minute tactics. Be a platoon commander rather than a general. There may be one time in a hundred when it will pay you to head off to sea because the sea breeze is expected. But at all other times it is better to mark your main opponents and make your tacks as the wind heads. Some helmsmen continue sailing into a header, long after they should have tacked, because they feel they are sailing farther into the new wind and will stay in it longer when they do finally put about. This may sometimes pay if you are sailing toward a shore whose topography alters the wind permanently. At other times tack just as soon as you are sure the header is more than momentary. Take advantage of the wind as it comes, bending it to your purpose by tacking on every header and singing at every freer.

All things being equal, tack onto other boats' lee bows rather than their weather bows. It is a much safer position and one which will inflict more damage. Backwind from sails does more effective harm than straightforward lack of wind in the lee of sails.

Until the closing stages of a race or series, do not overdo the boat-covering bit. Sail your own race and let others sail theirs. If a boat hails when you are on port tack, bear away under her stern rather than tack. If you tack you will be taken away from your original course, sailing someone else's race and not your own. And if you do go under her stern you will be hailing her next time you meet. Cover the major group when ahead, staying in the middle of the fleet if the fleet is equally split to the sides of the windward leg. *Don't tack more often than necessary and certainly no more often than the other boats.*

If trying to pass another boat close ahead, try to pinch up to weather. If you are gaining it is probably because you are sailing the boat better, more upright, and with more power. If so, you have but to continue, hike a little harder, and you'll soon be past. If other boats interfere to weather, passing to leeward may be possible (see *Fig. 2*). Work up to the leading boat's weather quarter,

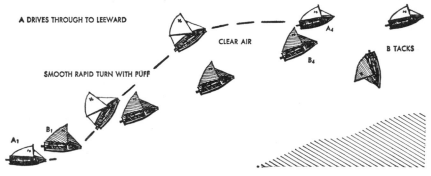

Fig. 2

if possible, then bear off sharply, hike hard to keep her flat, shoot through the blanket zone at about a 45-degree angle to the course, and then sharpen up about 1½ to 2 boat lengths to leeward. If you are sailing the boat more effectively from this safe leeward position, you will soon be dead ahead. If caught above someone else's lee bow, try pinching and hiking momentarily; but unless immediate progress is evident, tack! Always check to insure that you don't go from one interference to another before tacking, however.

Avoid reaching the lay line too soon, else every wind shift will help the other boats and you may soon find yourself in a parade with greatly disturbed air (see *Fig. 3*). Keep to the long or major

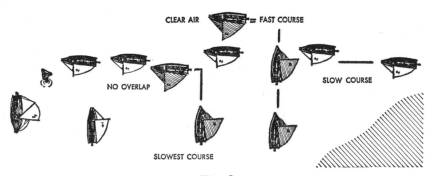

Fig. 3

tack until it is no longer the major tack by 5 to 10 degrees, then tack. Plan to hit the lay line close to the mark, never sailing excessively far to the side of the course. From here the mark can be laid accurately, without overstanding, and clear wind can be retained to the last minute. Usually, if a parade of starboard tack boats is approaching the mark on the lay line, it is best to tack into a safe leeward position, but if this puts you dead in another's backwind it may be wiser to sail through the line and tack in clearer air to weather. In heavy conditions it is always wise to allow a little extra room to avoid difficult extra tacks or hitting a bobbing mark as the boat is tossed about in a seaway.

Don't become overconcerned with tactics in heavy air beating. If the sails are well trimmed, the helm balanced, and the boat kept bolt upright by good strong hiking, there won't be any other boats near by to fight with.

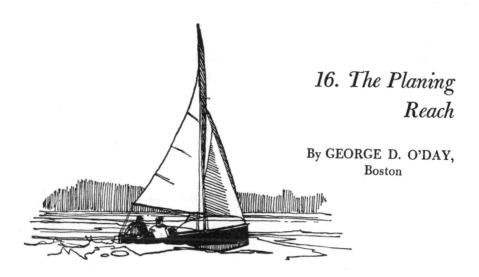

16. The Planing Reach

By GEORGE D. O'DAY,
Boston

To understand planing, we must know what it is. In the case of true planers, like hydroplanes and scows, planing is easy to understand because the planing hulls are skimming over the surface, displacing very little water, if any, and the resistance of the water is practically nil. In this situation the speed of the hull is controlled only by the power of the wind in the sails and the boat's ability to stand up to the force exerted. However, this chapter is concerned with the more common type of planer, such as the International 14 from which many light-displacement boats have evolved, such as Thistle, Highlander, Jolly, Flying Dutchman, Bantam, Firefly, and others.

BASIC FACTORS

There are three basic factors that provide clues as to the possible speeds of boats under sail. These are: (1) *the speed-length ratio,* (2) *the displacement-waterline ratio,* and (3) *the sail-area-to-wetted-surface ratio.*

Under the speed-length ratio the best estimated speed for normal displacement boats is approximately 1.3 to 1.4 times the square root of the waterline length ($1.3 \sqrt{\mathrm{LWL}}$). The controlling factor here is the bow and stern waves. A "heavy" hull fits down between them and, no matter how much additional power is poured on, she cannot be made to go any faster than 1.4 $\sqrt{\text{LWL}}$. In the case of light-displacement keel hulls, and the heavier centerboarders, the factor immediately jumps to approximately 1.6 to 2.0 $\sqrt{\text{LWL}}$, which produces speeds in excess of the bow wave and the boat tends to lift onto the wave, giving mild planing. In this group there are 110's, 210's Lightnings, and the light-displacement cruising boats.

The light-displacement centerboarders, such as the International 14, Jolly, Thistle, Highlander, 5–0–5, Flying Dutchman, and Raven, immediately jump the ratio range anywhere from 2.0 to 5.0 $\sqrt{\text{LWL}}$. There is actually no control on the speed of this latter group, except from power and durability. The more power is applied, the more speed results, provided the boat can hold together and keep afloat.

If the speed-length formula were the only valid rule, the question would naturally arise: why doesn't a 110 plane as fast as the International 14? Her speed-length ratio is better than the minimum of 2 and she gets up on her bow wave. Of course, there are other limiting factors, one of which is the displacement-waterline ratio, expressed by the formula

$$\left(\frac{D}{\frac{L}{100}}\right)^{3} \qquad (D = \text{displacement in tons of 2,240 pounds; } L = \text{LWL in feet})$$

This works out at a ratio of about 95 for the International 14 and 70 for the International 110. The upper limit for planing boats is in the vicinity of a ratio of 160 (International 12), and a good planer is around 80 to 120. According to this formula the 110 contradicts our figures as she should "take off," but she doesn't so there must be still another determining factor.

This factor is the sail-area-to-wetted-surface-area ratio. The International 110's ratio is approximately 1.4 to 1 while the International 14's is 2.8 to 1. For this reason, plus her good displacement-to-water-line ratio, the 14 will get up and go while the 110 lags behind. Investigation of other full-planing boats will almost invariably show the sail-to-wetted-surface ratio to be in excess of 2 to 1. A ratio below this will only give "surfboarding" or short planes if there is enough wind (power). Thus there must be the right combination of displacement, length, sail area, and wetted surface to get a good planing hull. Satisfying just one formula will not suffice. Hull shape also plays a vital part, although a boat of almost any shape will plane after a fashion if it satisfies the other requirements.

EQUIPMENT

Now for the technique and requirements of planing. First, the equipment to be used must be up to snuff and should include the following: (1) Wire kicking strap (boom vang), (2) roller reefing gear (not a top necessity), (3) Adequate mainsheet arrangement, (4) hiking straps, donkeys, or trapezes.

Boom vang

The kicking strap or boom vang is the most important single item on the boat for planing, yet is the most neglected item. A keyhole slot or traveler on the boom should be strong enough to take the strain, and the boom should be reinforced with metal or wood to keep from breaking. The best position on the boom is about a third of the way back, but this will vary for each boat due to cockpit limitations, centerboard trunks, cabin tops, etc.

Bill Cox, of Long Island Sound, designed a kicking strap for a 14 which was one of the best I've seen. It consisted of the usual boom fitting and wire, but instead of going to the base of the mast the vang led to an aluminum track which was laid out directly below the boom fitting and reached from side to side. A small trolley with roller bearings of 500-lb. tensil strength was fitted to the track and the kicking strap taken up directly to it. With this gear in use, there was no appreciable forward thrust exerted on the boom, as all the strain was perpendicular, therefore no undue strain on the gooseneck fittings or the mast.

Most boats, however, cannot rig an athwartships track. Therefore I recommend using a six-part tackle, or a small winch and a three-part tackle. The location of the lower end of the tackle should be at the base of the mast if possible, unless the trolley track can be used. The less thrust put on the mast, the better. In International 14's the vang winch is often built into the thwart. The correct strain on the strap should be taken when setting your sails. To do this, pull your boom amidships with your sheet. Pull until the leech is tight; take up on the strap so it is taut; then release the sheet, and with a little pressure your boom should be able to swing from one extreme jibe to the other. If it cannot, then the position at the base of the mast might be wrong and should be changed. However, if the position cannot be changed, I recommend easing off on the strap even though you will lose some of the sail efficiency.

You are probably wondering why all the emphasis on the boom vang. The answer is simple. The main purpose of the boom vang is not to keep you from a goose-winged jibe but actually to hold the surface of the sail as flat as possible and reduce the twist of the upper part. By doing this you gain sail area, which is important because it is the means of capturing power and provides a better airfoil for the mainsail. One effect of the boom vang will be to permit you to let your boom out another couple of feet without luffing the main. Also, your boat will be easier to handle and more stable; your rudder will not constantly act as a brake; you will go faster and the mast will stand straighter, removing some of the tendency to bury the bow.

The best illustration I can give of this is the fact that the faster you plane a 14, the more stability you get and the less hiking you have to do. Several years ago I was on a flat-out plane in Buzzards Bay, leading the fleet and opening water on two Canadian boats about 100 yd. astern, when my vang disintegrated. We stayed upright and kept the mast in the boat, but the Canadians started to close rapidly. In less than a mile to the finish, they all but caught me; another 25 yd. and they would have done it. We just did not have the power and the resultant speed that they did, although we were still planing.

Reefing gear

If you have good gear, you can roll in a reef to windward and roll it out again just before the windward marker, giving you the necessary power for the downwind legs. If you cannot roll the reef out, then you are better off not to put one in, because most of the fleet will pass you on the leeward legs. Bruce Banks of England has effectively attacked the problem with his automatic reefing gear, which enables the crew to lower the main halyard and reef all with one crank and at the same time. This gear has enabled him to win the Prince of Wales Trophy several times. Within a few seconds he could reef for squalls, and roll it out as quickly.

Another school of thought on this reefing business, however, is that when it is blowing hard enough to require the gear most race officials will call the race off. But even when a race is sailed, most of us have found that by taking our vangs down hard to flatten out our big sails, we are able to feather the boat to windward and survive. This feathering is a technique of setting your boat up as straight as possible (within 10 per cent), driving almost directly into the wind in the puffs, and falling off in the lulls. It is now being used brilliantly by the top helmsmen in the world and the technique is permitting them to carry bigger sails to windward in a breeze without reefing.

Mainsheet arrangement

The next item, which is constantly overlooked, is the mainsheet arrangement. Most American planing boats are inadequately rigged in this department, as they do not have enough purchase to control the sails, or the system is so complex with blocks that it doesn't work. International 14's have a four-power arrangement and the Jolly a five-power arrangement and the pull is directly from the transom to the skipper. If the skipper is going to handle the main (and he should), this arrangement gives him the leverage across his body, as he is always pulling the sheet by his forward arm. He can also pump the sheet when that last ounce of power is necessary to set the boat onto its bow wave. Though this arrangement is awkward for most at the start, it becomes a necessity once you get used to it.

I never thought much of leading the sheet along the boom in a two-man boat, because pulling on the sheet only performed the function of a pseudo-boom vang and did not trim the sail fast enough. Unless a block was used on the bottom of the boat or on the centerboard trunk, pulling the sheet just curved the boom to windward and pulled the sail out of shape without getting a proper trim. Absolute control of the main is vital on a planing hull because the apparent wind changes so rapidly that power may be lost in a space of second, which could mean 50 to 100 yd. difference —the difference between dying in the trough and screaming off on a plane.

Hiking Straps, etc.

Other necessary items are hiking straps and a donkey. Though not absolutely essential, the straps make the effort of hiking a simple task and provide a feeling of security with your toes tucked under. The "donkey," for those classes that will permit it, is nothing more than a stick that sits upright on the gunwale, secured at the base so it won't jump off, and supported by wire to the centerboard trunk. The crew uses this to hold onto when hiking out. In Bermuda it is better known as the "Ladies' Aid." This gear is not an outrigger, but is a contrivance for supporting a crew and, therefore, may be outlawed in your class. Flying trapezes are also outlawed in many classes but in those which permit them, such as the Flying Dutchman, they afford most efficient and reasonably effortless hiking.

TECHNIQUES OF PLANING

Now that all the gear is assembled, how about some "planery"? Don't forget that you are not a hydroplane on the surface, but rather a displacement hull that has to use the bow wave to get up and get. Thus, all efforts must be to getting the hull up. Reaching along on a puffy day, steering a normal-displacement boat, you create a bow and stern wave and are sandwiched in between, probably at a speed of 1.4 $\sqrt{\text{LWL}}$. A puff hits and its normal tendency is to heel the boat more and push the bow into the bow wave, creating tremendous resistance. However, if you want to plane, there are two ways you can do it. *First, you must see the puff coming, head up a bit to get the bow out slightly, and trim the sails to gain speed before it hits. As it hits, you and your crew should hike as hard and as fast as you can to keep level, then head off as your speed increases, without having to change the trim of the sails as the apparent wind shifts forward as you go faster. Once planing, trim your sails for maximum effort, making sure to keep them full. Trimming too flat or letting the sails luff can knock you off the plane quickly.*

The second method is to await the puff without changing course, then, when it hits, trim or pump the sail hard and hike sharply. This normally will break the bow out of its wave and shift the wave back to the shoulders of the boat, thus getting you planing without changing course. This technique has to be used in close quarters, and effectively done does the same job as the first. Its one drawback is that you can miss getting any advantage from the light puffs which just don't have enough strength to lift the hull. In sailing to leeward, the cardinal rule, "up on the lulls and off on the puffs," holds especially true on planing boats. On a flat-out plane it is easy to get to windward of the course to the next mark because once you start to plane you almost forget about the race and boats around you. In order to maintain speed you must come up in the lulls, and you probably will not go off enough in the puffs to compensate. Thus, you will have to run off for the mark. You might have to set a parachute, and if you do the boats that held a leeward course will plane right across your bow and beat you to the mark. This, I can assure you, is the height of frustration.

Your next task is to stay on the plane once you have got there. It is a constant sail-trimming job, the most important sail being the jib. If this is trimmed too hard it is like putting on the brakes. It has to be right on the breaking point, and the crew must constantly adjust it for the course and speed of the boat. The board should be at least three-quarters of the way up, and taken up more if need be. (Of course, you pulled the board up to at least the three-quarters mark as you came around the windward mark.) On broad reaches, I usually take the board up all the way, using only the rudder and keelson for directional stability. If you keep absolute control of the sails and rudder, you won't need the board. Your weight in the boat should be so placed that her wake is perfectly flat and her bow just lapped by the water. Increase or decrease of speed will change this fore-and-aft trim, so you must change your weight. Uffa Fox's Mark I International 14 usually had to be sailed by sitting on the transom in a flat-out plane to keep the trim proper, but this has changed in his later designs. If, as you plane, you are throwing a "rooster tail," you may look pretty but you are not getting the maximum out of your plane.

The next thing to consider is the riding of the waves, a technique all unto itself. By using waves, you can easily break onto a plane, because a good wave, as it moves under your hull, supplants the bow wave and gives you the lift you need. You instantly have little resistance left in the water, and the slightest effort will send you surfboarding down the front of the wave. You can ride this perfectly straight or at angles to the wave motion, whichever you prefer. I choose to ride the angles in order to keep speed and my bow out of the wave in front, but this can be dangerous, especially if you get by the lee and broach. Practice alone will teach you how to get the most out of wave riding, but to be tops you must get the most out of each wave. Paul McLaughlin, the Canadian dinghy and Olympic skipper, once opened up a 75-yd. lead when we were racing neck and neck on a planing leg. He caught a wave just right while I hit it wrong and I watched him disappear, to capture a race and a series. Linc Davis, of 30 Square Meter and 210 fame, is a master at riding waves and he will pick up as much as 100 to 250 yd. on his opponents just by driving his boat up and down waves. One important thing to remember when riding waves is to keep your boat 90 degrees upright, if possible. Give your best planing surface to the wave and ride the daylights out of it, while shifting your weight to keep the stern, then the bow, from burying.

This whole chapter has dealt with how to get the boat going. How do you stop it? Well, to slow a planing hull down takes a lot of technique, especially when you have to jibe around a mark onto another plane. So much skill and timing is required that sometimes it is easier to pass the mark and come about rather than jibe and then plane to the next mark. This is the easy but safe way out. Ordinarily the best way to slow down and jibe is to drop the board three-fourths down and let both the jib and main luff. As the boat slows (point her up slightly if you have to), put the helm down and have the crew pull the boom across. If this is done too late, you will be swimming. The boat should be kept on as even a keel as possible, and when you time your maneuver, make sure that you are on the up side of the wave. This will keep your rudder in the water during the jibe. Make sure you hang onto the tiller so as not to go out of control and that the mainsheet is clear to run as soon as the boom comes across. Both you and your crew must shift simultaneously and fast, but not before the boom has reached dead center. According to Charlie Bourke of Toronto, you should start the jibe with a slight heel to weather and make a slight luff and then come around; but whatever your method, be sure to pray —it does more good than all the technique.

Other than by luffing or jibing, there is no way to stop a planing hull. I know of a Raven and a 14 alike that could not break off the plane; both ended up riding right onto the beach—a quick, but hardly pleasant, conclusion to a flat-out plane.

17. Planing with Spinnaker

By S. M. PASCHAL,
Bermuda

From my experience in sailing 14-foot. International Dinghies, I have decided that the planing reach with the spinnaker is the most satisfying and exciting leg of the course. Yet unfortunately, although conditions which should give a good planing spinnaker reach are often found and although most boats set their spinnakers, only a few of them seem able to plane steadily. The majority seem to be floundering around, having trouble keeping upright, and in general expending a great deal of effort with very little effect. After the race you hear remarks such as: "We couldn't point high enough, so doused the spinnaker"—"But did you see so-and-so go by us— what did he do to that boat?"

In a race of the 1957 Princess Elizabeth Series in Bermuda, in which it was blowing about 15 m.p.h., as we approached the reaching mark the International One Designs were rounding and setting spinnakers on the next leg with their poles about 2 ft. off their headstays. I had 340 lb. of live ballast and decided that we could carry the spinnaker, which we hoisted as we jibed around the mark. It was a nice reach and, without too much strain on the stomach muscles, we planed by the I.O.D.'s to windward and caught the leading I.O.D.'s at the leeward mark, having caught up over 200 yd. in a mile and a half leg. We also opened up a good lead on the next International 14.

240

In the afternoon in a team race we were well down in the fleet with the same course but with the wind a little closer on the second reach. With spinnaker we could barely lay the mark. The rest of the fleet did not set spinnakers and held high. We passed four boats on that reach by holding low and planing with the spinnaker. But Norman Roberts, who had a light crew, did not use a spinnaker, rounded the reaching mark behind us, and planed past the same four boats to windward, arriving at the next mark ahead of us. I felt sure that I had done the correct thing by carrying the spinnaker, but this shows that a jib is a more effective sail than a spinnaker for planing if there is enough wind to keep the boat moving in the flat spots.

SPINNAKER HANDLING

The spinnaker-handling arrangements on my 14 *Cardinal* are as follows. The halyard is permanently fastened to the spinnaker. The sheet and guy are led around the boat, passed under the hiking strap that runs aft from the centerboard box, and firmly knotted together. When down, the spinnaker is carried on the bow air tank and held down by being tucked under shock cord stretched across the tank. The halyard is adjusted so that it clips on a cleat in the bow and is held taut along the headstay. The sheet and guy are kept from hanging in the water by taking a turn around cleats on the inside of the gunwale on each after quarter. The downhaul is permanently fastened to the pole and leads through an eye in front of the mast to a cleat on the centerboard box for easy adjustment. The topping lift is shock cord from the lower spreaders which hooks onto the pole when needed.

The crew hoists the spinnaker and secures the spinnaker pole. The skipper handles sheet and guy and sets the spinnaker initially. The crew then lowers the jib and takes over the spinnaker guy and sheet.

If you think you may be able to carry a spinnaker on the next leg of the course to advantage, but are not certain, take the easiest way out: wait until you are on the new leg and then decide. When in doubt, don't set the spinnaker. The following rules of thumb are generally correct. To use the spinnaker effectively:

1. *The wind must be at least slightly abaft of the beam.*
2. *If the jib is drawing well the spinnaker should not be set unless the wind is too light for sustained planing with the jib.*

3. *If the jib is not drawing well* (i.e., *reach too broad*) *set the spinnaker* (*unless it is really blowing and you are certain you will be overpowered*).

If the spinnaker is already set, keep it set unless you cannot lay the course or are overpowered when laying the course. In either of these cases, bear off to keep the boat on its feet while the crew takes down the spinnaker. You will probably be at a better reaching angle when you came back with your jib set.

ESSENTIALS

But what makes one boat go and another get into difficulties? The following minimum requirements are essential to spinnaker planing:

1. *A hull that will plane.*
2. *A wind strength within certain limits which will vary according to class, hull design, weight of crew, and size of spinnaker (for a 14-ft. International between 10 and 20 m.p.h.).*
3. *A boat kept on her planing surface i.e., upright or with only a slight angle of heel.*
4. *A course at the correct angle to the wind. (This requirement varies with the wind strength, weight of crew, etc. i.e., a broad reach, almost up to a beam reach in moderate winds and down to a run in stronger winds.)*
5. *A slot effect working as the wind blows across the spinnaker.*
6. *Sufficient lateral resistance.*

Requirement No. 5 presents the problem in a nutshell, or more correctly in a slot. Once you have discovered how to keep the slot effect working you can plane with a spinnaker. On a reach the spinnaker is a big bag pulling nearly straight across the boat, leaving very little room between the leech of the spinnaker and the mainsail. So how is it possible to achieve a slot effect? Take down the spinnaker and put up the jib? Yes, sometimes; but you *can* use that big bag as efficiently as a planing sail.

First trim the mainsail and give the wind room to flow between spinnaker and main. The usual answers to this are: "We've tried that but only kill ourselves laying out and fighting the boat and she just doesn't want to go"—"sometimes she seems to get going but can't keep it up."

Second, remember that keel boats often carry spinnakers successfully on reaches in planing winds. The usual responses to this statement are: "But they have all that lead in their keel and can sail on their ear"—"You can't compare a keel boat with a planing centerboarder." But when one asks, "Where was your centerboard?" the answer is, "Oh, as usual halfway up." "Did you try pulling it right down?" "No, why should I on a broad reach?" *Because the pull of the spinnaker is mainly across the boat, unless the centerboard is almost all the way down the boat will sideslip.*

With the board only a quarter down as a puff hits, the spinnaker pulls harder, the boat heels over, the crew lays out, and the boat is forced sideways through the water. Although the spinnaker is pulling hard the boat is not moving. The forces in action are very similar to those in affect when you are on the wind and the board must be down to provide a fulcrum against which you can apply crew weight to counteract spinnaker pull.

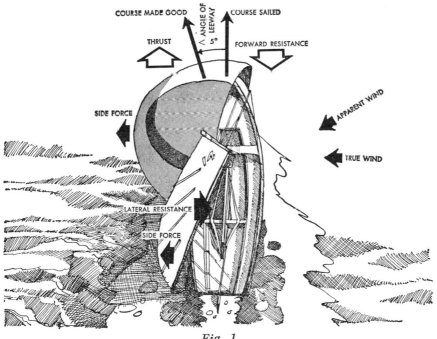

Fig. 1

Under ordinary planing or nonplaning conditions side force is a relatively slight component of the total aerodynamic force provided. However, when a spinnaker is hoisted with the apparent wind abeam or even forward of the beam (drawn forward by the boat's planing speed, which may reach 12 to 14 knots), side force is greatly increased. To prevent an excessive leeway angle with a consequent major increase in forward resistance due to oblique forward movement, lateral resistance must be increased by pushing the centerboard down (see *Fig. 1*). As noted in the chapter on sails, increased speed may be obtained only by increasing lateral resistance in the presence of excessive thrust. Thus the maximum speed on a planing spinnaker reach is achieved (as it is close-hauled) at the time the increased angle of leeway with board full down becomes unable to maintain the normal forward/lateral resistance ratio.

I seem to have taken a long time to get to this point but feel that the beginner may recognize in the questions and answers some of the feelings of frustration that we have all experienced before learning how to handle a spinnaker reach.

The position of the centerboard cannot be overstressed and as a general rule in reaching with a spinnaker it should never be less than three-quarters down, and if in doubt pull it down a bit farther.

SUPPLEMENTARY FACTORS

With the board down you will find it easier to keep the boat upright. When a puff strikes, the forward acceleration is increased and the wind starts moving across the spinnaker, the beginning of the slot effect. This effect can be increased by easing off the spinnaker halyard 6 in. or more. (Don't do this in heavy winds, however, as the spinnaker may oscillate more, making the boat unsteady.)

Now, skipper, is that mainsail really working? Can you feel it in the mainsheet? Pull it in and try to feel it. There is a tendency to leave the main too slack, just as there is a tendency to have the board too far up. If the spinnaker pole is just clear of the headstay, the main should be almost close-hauled.

Pull the jib down completely out of the way. Do not merely furl it. Anything that might stop the flow across the spinnaker is a menace.

Gear must be simple but adequate and adjustable so that skipper and crew can work together to keep the spinnaker trimmed perfectly. Small centerboarders do not provide a stable platform for meticulous sheet trimming. The crew has to lay out, adjust his weight, bail, trim the sheet and guy, and adjust the centerboard. I have found that the best arrangement is to cleat the spinnaker guy in its approximate forward position. The crew or skipper can then make slight adjustments by pulling back when necessary without uncleating. *The skipper should watch the luff and sail the boat on the spinnaker, at the same time, if there is a sea, sailing off the seas to prevent them rolling the boat to leeward. He must remember the golden rule—up in the flat spots, down in the flaws.* With the guy cleated the crew may have a spare hand to do other odd jobs that may need doing.

Cleated or not the guy must be played for maximum effect. Modern flat spinnakers must be stretched across the bow to produce the greatest possible exposure of surface and this means constant adjustment of the pole. It has to be kept nearly at right angles to the apparent wind at all times. With changes in the speed of the boat due to wind variations and with changes in the true wind direction due to shifts or to course alterations, the guy must be tightened by cross pressure or eased from the cleat. *Major adjustment, however, should be accomplished by varying the course, bearing off under the spinnaker as the wind increases and the apparent wind moves forward, and easing upwind as the wind decreases and the apparent wind moves aft.* This usually coincides with wave-riding techniques, as the maximum boat speed and apparent wind are produced as the boat bears off down the face of a sea and the least boat speed and apparent wind when the boat comes up to force its bow into the back of a sea.

In our annual long-distance race in 1957 the wind was gusty with squalls of 18 or 19 m.p.h. and an average of around 15 m.p.h. On a long leg of about 8 m. we were carrying a spinnaker with the pole about 3 in. off the headstay. In the squalls both skipper and crew were laying out flat to keep the boat upright on the course. But by bearing off in the squalls we found that we could have a fast but comfortable ride. With the spinnaker guy cleated we could adjust the pole by leaning on the guy when necessary. The leg was an almost constant plane but skipper and crew each had a hand clear and ate lunch on the way. These conditions were ideal for spinnaker planing, as the extra area kept us going in the flat spots while we could still carry it comfortably in the squalls. On this leg we gained a lead of 600 or 700 yd. on the next boat. My crew called it "a real sporty leg."

If you own a planing boat that carries a good-size spinnaker, get out on the water and practice. See how close you can point with the spinnaker and find out if I am right about that centerboard. If you disagree with my theories, tell me why. Although my wife says I'm getting too old to sail a 14-ft. International, I hope I will never be too old to learn something new about sailing.

18. Running in Heavy Air

By RICHARD W. BESSE, Syracuse

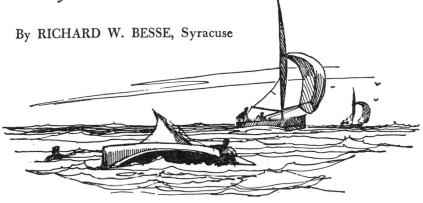

Running in heavy air may be a blessed respite from a cold, wet, strenuous beat, or it may be the most perilous leg of the whole course; but in many cases it provides unsuspected opportunity for getting on with the race and home ahead. A few years ago, in an International 14 series off Manchester, Mass., a rather disappointing race for me was turned into a most exciting one at the beginning of the final long run. Over the low rocky islands and cold May water suddenly came a sharp squall, announced only by trouble among the tail-enders. There was no chance to watch. We jibed accidentally with the sudden shift and took off on a wild plane. Some ahead did not get their weight aft fast enough, others luffed and even with all sheets slacked were overpowered. Suddenly we were well ahead with nobody threatening!

The principal considerations, as demonstrated in this instance, when running in heavy air are the development of maximum planing speed by proper utilization of the sails in the presence of the tremendous available thrust and the proper management of the hull to prevent capsize in hazardous circumstances. Tactical considerations are usually subordinated to the strategy of assuming and maintaining the fastest possible sailing angle.

THE MAINSAIL

The mainsail, especially in boats such as the Moth, Comet, or Star, will provide the major drive on a run. Since the simple aerodynamic principle involved is demonstrated by the effect of the wind upon the broad side of a barn door, the essential point is to get the whole sail out as far as possible. Probably an approximately 75-degree angle between the plane of the sail and the axis of the wind is ideal, 15 degrees less than perpendicular to allow the air to slide off, yet with very little reduction in the area presented to the breeze. It is often difficult to get the sail out this far because of the interference of the lee shroud with the boom. Incidentally, watch for chafe here as it cannot be readily seen until you are on the other tack and the damage is done. My brain saver for years in this respect has been to tie a figure-8 knot in the mainsheet so that the boom will automatically stop just short of the shroud.

If, as an unusually hard puff hits, you roll to windward, the top of the sail goes way forward, the boom rises up into the sky, and your heart is suddenly in your throat, you need a boom vang! If you don't have one on your boat resolve to look into this alarming deficiency as soon as you get ashore, and in the meanwhile rig a preventer or sacrifice one of your crew to ride the boom. By holding the main down you maintain an appropriate angle of inclination at all levels of the sail, spread a larger effective area, decrease the tendency to roll to weather, and spare some chafe in the bargain. You probably can't hold it down too hard and probably will have difficulty in holding it down enough. A crewman sitting on the boom may put weight too far forward in a 16-footer, while in a larger boat one man cannot do the job any too well. A strong vang properly tightened in advance is an absolute essential. On an International 14 a six-part tackle of wire leading to a winch is not excessive.

THE JIB

The best way to treat the jib (if a spinnaker is not to be used) is to wing it out on a whisker pole if class rules permit. It will provide excellent drive trimmed this way and will steady the boat better than an idle jib or any spinnaker rig. The maximum length of pole permitted is usually desirable. For instance in the Rhodes Bantum, with a genoa jib 7 ft. 9 in. on the foot and a 48-in. foretriangle along the base, a pole between 7 and 8 ft. long keeps the jib adequately spread out and at an angle of approximately 75 degrees to the wind. To keep the clew from kiting up, raise the pole's inner end and/or hold it down by leading the weather jib sheet from farther forward. Rigging the whisker pole with identical fittings on either end will facilitate setting it out and jibing without your having to reverse the pole end for end. The latter operation can get the sheets well tangled up, lose the pole overboard, and even give the helmsman a well-deserved jab for not providing something better. If the pole is overboard, out of commission, ashore or out-lawed, you'll have to hold the clew out by hand, an ineffective and miserable job to behold or perform. Don't overlook the run as an excellent opportunity to tighten the jib luff with the halyard or downhaul while the mainsail is taking the strain off it and you have the chance to get at it. It's also a good chance to change the jib, if you consider it necessary. But be careful, there are many small boats which don't take kindly to a crew member's going far forward, and some that don't allow it at all without going under or rounding upwind due to the steering effect of the deeply immersed bow.

THE SPINNAKER

Although undoubtedly overgrown and inefficient, the modern flat spinnaker is the most effective sail available on a run, often making the difference between ability to plane and no ability to plane.

If the spinnaker can be hoisted in stops, it will be possible to have everything and everybody prepared before opening the wild beast. Also the sail will be much less likely to fill out with a twist which will be exceedingly difficult to clear. If you are unable to stop the sail, try to hoist it to leeward, where the mainsail affords a lee, by rigging the sheets with the sail to leeward or by pulling the lee sheets and sail around the jibstay prior to hoisting. With the spinnaker up it is essential to check that the halyard is securely cleated, yet free to run whenever it is to come down, which may be sooner than you expect. The most spectacular event of a series of international team races off Toronto between U.S. and Canadian 14's, from the point of view of the sports writer covering the series, resulted from my disregarding this advice. By the time my wife grabbed hold of the slipping halyard, most of the sail was under the keel and all of it in the water. She performed an unprecedented feat, pulling the sail up and out of the water by tailing on the halyard, but not without the benefit of some colorful encouragement from aft.

The downhaul, or foreguy, on the spinnaker pole is essential in heavy air. This should be rigged before the sail is set or immediately thereafter. The sail must be kept square to the wind for maximum effectiveness. For the same reason and to keep the boat from rolling, the halyard should be fully hoisted, the pole pulled aft as far as possible, and the sail well flattened across the axis of the wind. When a slack sheet and guy and high pole allow the sail to go forward and up in a deep belly and sway from side to side, the boat will probably follow suit.

A large spinnaker like the Lightning's can produce a severe heeling moment in a heavy puff or squall even though the wind direction is only a few degrees over the quarter from dead astern. Provided you have the sea room, it is best to follow the spinnaker with a sure hand on the tiller, bearing off as the spinnaker swings to leeward and heading up as it swings to weather. Weight should be as far aft as necessary to keep the bow from showing any tendency to bury during such oscillations. Few boats will sail under this way; but, if the bow buries deeply, the rudder will be of no avail, pressure will increase against one side of the bow, and the boat will broach and go over.

It is often surprising how you can carry on with a spinnaker, making remarkable haste, when you probably couldn't get it down without running into serious trouble. But sooner or later it must come down, and again the best place is in the lee of the main. With the sail off the pole the spinnaker can be pulled into the cockpit by the clew as the halyard is lowered. It can be very costly not to take down the sail in sufficient time to square away for the next leg. A spinnaker which isn't fully down, a pole left unsecured on deck, a guy fouled around a jib sheet are not only costly in themselves, but take a crewman from what he should be doing in rounding the mark and from where he should be on the weather rail. The psychological effect on the helmsman can be the most damaging factor of all. The jib re-enters the picture here because presumably it has been idle during the run with the spinnaker hoisted. It seldom can do any work under these circumstances, so must be dropped, rolled, or tied up to the jibstay. Of course it can remain set, sheeted gently to leeward, if it will not detract from the spinnaker. The choice among these alternatives should depend considerably upon the time you intend to take, or want to spend in setting the jib again at the end of the run and before the next leg. The higher the course on the wind, the more damaging will be the effect of the unlowered jib on the spinnaker.

THE CENTERBOARD

While running in heavy weather the centerboard can be of help in three respects. The further down it is, presuming it is a metal or a weighted board, the greater will be its righting moment if the boat should receive a knockdown (although its effect may easily be insufficient to save the day). Secondly the farther down the board, the more lateral plane is presented to dampen the boat's roll. Rolling is not only disconcerting but can slow the boat considerably and cause a lot of unneeded activity. Third, and most important, the centerboard can greatly increase rudder control, especially in hulls like those of Comets and Lightnings. The lateral resistance of the board acts as a fulcrum around which the rudder can turn the hull. Trying to alter course sharply with the centerboard fully up is like trying to swat flies with a swatter but no wall. How much centerboard will provide the best control must be determined by experiment, but half down is a good place to start. It is desirable to have the centerboard rigged so that it can be lowered quickly in case the situation needs to be stabilized. Someone in the crew should be placed and deputized to make the grab that may save the day. A knot in the centerboard pendant rope that will fetch up in a fair-lead is one way to keep a heavy board from parting the wire pennant or splitting the keel by swinging forward of vertical. As noted in the chapter on planing with the spinnaker, the higher the course on the wind the more lateral resistance, *i.e.*, the more centerboard, is needed to prevent an excessive leeway angle.

TRIM OF THE HULL

Wherever you are you should be able to move quickly. You will want to keep the bow high enough to avoid burying, whether planing or not. A wave under the stern or a harder puff may force the bow down to where the boat starts to take water aboard, by which time the boat is nearly impossible to fight with a rudder more in the air than it is in the water. You should have been farther aft to begin with, so get there quickly, right aft to the transom if necessary. If your bow deck is under and acting like a diving plane, as the old Wee Scots used to do so enthusiastically, an angle of heel will help you shake the load and surface again. Try to keep her at an angle of heel that minimizes the helm by shifting weight athwartships, though this is a nicety that cannot always be practiced in a blow. Here again mobility is important, for even one crew member, moving in or across, or back and forth, can do wonders to steadying a roll, if he doesn't lose his footing. It is preferable if possible to have a member of the crew on or near each gunwale to dampen oscillations before they begin and to avoid rapid over-correction by weight shifting which may actually stimulate greater oscillations.

HOLIDAY ROUTINE

This sounds unglamorous and so will your suggestions that your crew had better get busy bailing. However, the run may be the only opportunity, and a situation already bad will probably deteriorate rapidly once you come on the wind again. Besides bailing, by suction or with honest labor, you should check for standing rigging that is backing off or starting to let go, glance over your running rigging and leads, look aloft over your sails for the beginnings of a tear, straighten up the cockpit, especially the halyard coils, and check the course yet remaining to be sailed. Sometimes such a survey will result in your withdrawing from the race, but only when you probably were not going to be able to finish anyway and didn't need a broken mast to prove the point.

JIBING

Jibing in heavy weather is like parachute jumping; you have to do it right the first time to get a second chance. But there is one advantage to jibing; the technique can be studied and practiced in mild weather. Before starting the maneuver, obtain adequate sea room from other boats and the mark. Insure that your board is down sufficiently for good control and that the mainsheet is free to run. Whether planing or not, the crew should be well aft, ready to move quickly to either side, the bow should be high, and the boat sailing on its flat after surfaces. Bear off until you are dead before the wind (see *Fig. 1*). A masthead wind indicator is especially help-ful to determine this. Then when the stern is down in a trough, the bow up, and the speed at a consequent minimum, bear off a few degrees farther and bring the boom across. If you have the strength it is quicker and therefore safer to throw the sail over by pulling the boom itself or by grabbing the boom vang or all the parts of the sheet in one hand. Either of these techniques necessitates a boom vang. If the strain on the sheet, or a running backstay rig requires that you pull in the sheet in the usual way, then this must be done quickly. In any case, bearing off even farther by the lee will reduce the strain, distance, and time involved in waiting for the wind to catch the lee side of the sail and to take the boom across. As soon as the boom crosses, the sail should be allowed to run all the way out at once. The rigging must be constructed to

Fig. 1. Jibing procedure in advance of rounding.

stand the shock of the boom's suddenly fetching up against the slack sheet. Most important as the boom swings over, the helmsman should alter course slightly to oppose the centrifugal force of the swinging boom, and return to the dead downwind course rather than rounding up. The crew should shift his weight rapidly but cautiously to dampen rather than accentuate the expected oscillation to leeward as the boom fetches up.

The two worst and most common miscarriages of this maneuver are being caught with the sheet in before the jibe, and heading up after the jibe. The first applies a tremendous heeling moment to leeward as well as a turning moment into the wind. The other produces the heeling effect of centrifugal force in addition to the normal heeling moment of the beam wind, and does it when the crew is least prepared to sit the boat up. Either situation is likely to send you swimming. Success requires a sure hand on the tiller, no hesitation, and decisive action at the right moment, admittedly difficult when confidence is lacking. As in the old square-riggers, however, a jibe can often be accomplished in extreme conditions when a tack is impossible.

The use of the centerboard when jibing has been controversial because lowering it increases the heeling moment by lengthening the arm of the heeling couple (increases the vertical distance between the center of effort of the sails and the center of lateral resistance of the hull and fin). However, the heeling moment is less significant than the rolling tendency. The more she rolls, the more she wants to roll as the sail arcs laterally, producing a thrust component in the direction of the roll. In addition, the tendency of the boat to turn opposite to the direction of the roll due to pressure against the submerged bow is usually counteracted by rudder pressure in the opposite direction. This rudder pressure below the surface then operates to increase the roll still further. Beyond a certain critical point, shifting of crew weight can no longer keep up with a roll potentiated by these factors and capsize is inevitable. Reduction in rolling can be accomplished by spreading of crew weight laterally, keeping it low, steering in the direction of heeling, keeping the bow up, and *keeping the centerboard down.* This reduction in the speed of the roll by the lowered centerboard, permitting control of the roll by the shifting of crew weight, more than offsets the disadvantage of the increase in heeling moment.

The jibing technique presented here seems to be the safest for strong winds and necessitates continuing on an essentially straight course throughout the maneuver. The jibing technique with board up described in the chapter on crewing is necessary if the jibe is to be accomplished while rounding. However, it is far safer in strong winds when on a run to sail above the course so that the jibe may be completed on the approach and when on a reach or beat to delay the jibe until after the rounding when the wind and waves seem propitious—and to jibe with the board down.

PLANING

There are two aspects of planing which are experienced almost solely when running in heavy air. Even in a heavy squall, when you wish to carry on without reducing or dropping sail, or when you have no choice and are fearful of capsize, it should be possible to continue planing and stay upright. However, you may be forced to sail considerably off the course or past the mark. In such conditions the boat should be steered directly before the wind, so that there is no heeling moment. It is essential to keep the bow up to maintain control, and to alter course with the wind as it shifts and tends to produce heeling. Heeling will produce a turning moment into the wind, a weather helm, and a capsize if not immediately corrected. The controlling technique is similar to the steering required to bring the rear end of an automobile out of a skid. Only in this case you are putting the hull back under the rig (like the seal balancing the ball), continually moving the hull to follow and stay under the sails. If you are not planing, you are in more danger of driving under or losing the rig than you are of rolling over.

The major likelihood of capsize is consequent to a sudden rounding up to windward. While surfing down large waves and exposed to varying apparent wind strengths, deviations of heading and heeling are continuous with a constant tendency to build up a lee bow pressure wave which checks forward progress and deviates the bow to windward. Skipper and crew must be constantly alert to this problem, shifting weight to prevent heeling, steering in the direction of heeling to keep the boat under the sails, and, most important, keeping the headsail (jib or spinnaker) full and its sheet tight at all times. Prevent heeling as assiduously as possible; but if heeling occurs, avoid sudden weight shifts and use the tiller and particularly the headsail sheet to pull the bow off.

The other aspect of planing peculiar to running in heavy air is the use of waves to enhance speed. There will surely be some moving in approximately the same direction as the wind. The length of waves between crests determines their speed, so that you may easily be traveling faster than the shorter ones. In this case they are more nuisance than fun, for the boat will be alternately overtaking one and falling off its crest and burying her bow into the back of the next. However, waves going faster than the boat can almost certainly be ridden. To catch the ride be on the course of the wave with your weight suitably forward in the boat. As the stern is lifted onto the face of the wave, head up a bit to free your bow and then move your weight quickly aft. As your speed approaches that of the waves, bear off and ease your pole forward to compensate for the increased apparent wind, and shift your weight forward to avoid dragging the stern. Stay with the wave as long as possible, attempting to keep the hull absolutely level without dipping the bow or dragging the stern. *In broken seas always dive into the holes, bearing off immediately toward the deepest trough around.*

Lateral stability while riding the waves may be difficult to maintain. Marked variations in effective wind pressure result from sudden variations in boat speed, and therefore rapid adjustments in weight distribution within the boat may be necessary to avoid capsizing to windward or leaving a crew member floundering in the sea.

SAILING THE LEG

Getting Free Initially

When you have rounded the weather mark and are prepared to bear off onto a run, you will probably be confronted with a number of boats beating up to the mark. Some of these will have right of way over you if you are on starboard, and all will have right of way over you if you are on port. In small boat classes this problem is often increased by the large number of entries and, in certain classes with genoa jibs, the poor visibility to leeward. Heavy weather compounds the difficulties because of the high relative speed of the converging boats and their limited maneuverability. Decisive handling is required to avoid trouble. Defensive maneuvering is indicated, as you can be put out of the race by being disabled as effectively as by disqualification. A wide berth should be planned, as the boats on the wind may be changing course drastically and often to adjust to the wind and sea. Also, one boat heeled over and another rolling can cross masts when their hulls are surprisingly far apart. When clear of the worst of the mess, consider whether you are on the right jibe. Even if a jibe obviously is required by the course from the mark it may not be possible immediately, due to the press of competitors. Plan the early phase of the run before the rounding, bearing off to either side of the course as indicated to reach a position from which the remainder of the leg may be sailed at maximum speed.

You must have a good reason to deviate from the rhumb line to the leeward mark. However, tacking downwind may be profitable if the strength and direction of the wind and sea are such that the boat will acquire enough additional speed to make up for the extra distance to be sailed. This may be accomplished if planing can be achieved by sailing slightly above the course. Another possible benefit to be obtained by deviation from the direct course to the leeward mark is the advantage of a tide or current condition that is elsewhere more favorable, or less unfavorable. A third sufficient reason to deviate somewhat is to keep one's wind clear. The harder the wind blows, the longer is the shadow of disturbed wind in the lee of a sail. If you are unable to free your boat from the disturbed air of a slower boat, you may waste the whole potential of a run. Get free early and let the remainder of the fleet bother one another. One other good reason to favor one side of the course is to achieve a more favorable approach to round the leeward mark or finish. Boat speed is the determining factor, as marked variations in the speed of individual boats are to be expected in these conditions. Get free, get on the fastest possible sailing angle, and keep her planing (see *Fig. 2*).

Set the Spinnaker?

Unfortunately you can't always wait to see how someone else makes out with the sail or assume that you will be able to handle it as well. The question is not whether if will fly, but whether you can handle it without getting into difficulty, especially hoisting and lowering it. With the crew forward and the bow in the water, every oscillation, every additional puff brings the hazard of capsize.

How much faith do you have in your crew? In your gear? If something goes wrong, fully hoisted or only part way up, the spinnaker may throw the boat off balance and over. Hoisting to leeward or in stops will help, but don't hoist at all unless you are certain you will be able to get it down without excessive risk. If the race finishes with the run you may be more daring, as this particular problem won't arise during the race. Obviously your decision will be influenced by the tactical situation. When your competitors are comfortably astern and either not attempting spinnakers or flying them without success, you remain watchful and ready but should not innovate. When astern and dissatisfied with your prospects, however, you are justified in daring. A Lightning District Championship I officiated presented a beautiful contrast on this point. The leader, A, began the run with a 100-yd. lead. The second crew, B, in a fleet of 35, waited perhaps a minute, then set the spinnaker perfectly, as we had come to expect from this marvelously drilled threesome. The leader had not been faced with this problem previously because the wind had been so heavy during the first lap that no one had wanted to drop the first bomb. Now, after the run, a reach remained to the finish, and B was making a strong bid for the race. A waited a few moments, hoping his disadvantage would not prove too great. Then, seeing that he was sure to be overtaken unless he did something, he proceeded to do everything, including the setting of his spinnaker, wrong. Eventually he was lucky to salvage second place.

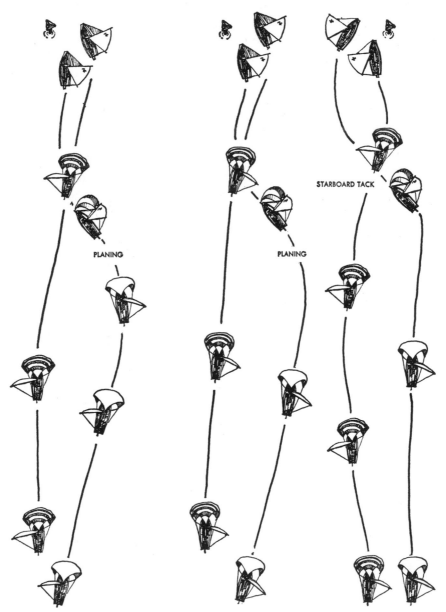

Fig. 2. Some maneuvers to gain an overlap.

ENDING THE LEG

If the finish ends the leg you will have the finishing problems common to any race, chiefly deciding which appears to be the favored end of the line (see Chapter 9).

On the other hand if the race continues beyond the run with a reach or a beat, you will have other problems. As you near the mark, set the jib, lower the spinnaker, secure it, and pull the board down. If a jibe is to be required, try to plan so that it may be done at least 50 yd. in advance of the rounding, sooner if possible. This greatly simplifies both the jibe and the rounding and produces a safer and more effective job of each. Remember that the inside boat has right of way while rounding even if on the port tack with an outside boat on starboard. Maneuvers to gain an overlap at the leeward mark, or at the favored end of the finish line, should be planned well in advance, especially in heavy weather (see *Fig. 2*). The actual maneuver, whether it be a luff, a blanketing, or the application of starboard tack, should be held until the precise moment when the temporary advantage gained (and that is about all it can be) will win the cherished overlap for the rounding, or enable you to slip across the finish line inches ahead.

PART IV

Race Management and Rescue

Preface

The racing skipper and his crew should be occupied with the adjustment of their boat to its maximum potential for the day's conditions and should devote their full attention to strategy, tactics, and technique of sailing the planned course faster than any competitor. However, they must recognize that the creation of race conditions suitable to testing their boat's speed and their abilities is dependent upon capable race management. Such recognition implies sympathy and understanding of the frequent variations from the ideal in starting and finishing conditions, course layout and adjustment to adverse circumstances and provides insight into probable intervention—"expecting the unexpected."

No Race Committee can be successful unless its membership includes experienced sailors and all sailors should expect to assume such responsibilities periodically for the benefit of the sport. The need for competence in this field is as essential as in the competition itself.

The major limitation on speed in planing boats is capsize, but all planing boat sailors should be prepared to push their boats to the utmost with the realization that capsize though a limitation is not a disaster. They must insure that adequate arrangements are made for assisted rescue but develop their boats to be capable of rapid self-rescue to continue the race without excessive loss.

19. Race Management

By D. W. JEMMETT,
Kingston, Ontario

Part V, Paragraph 35, of the NAYRU rules reads, in part, "Under the direction of the organization sponsoring a race, the Race Committee shall be responsible for making arrangements for and managing the race . . ." The arrangements for the race will vary greatly, from few and simple for most club races to very elaborate for a large regatta, especially if many entries come from a distance. But in every case the managing of the race should always follow the drill laid down in Part V of the NAYRU rules, the position of the starting point well chosen, the starting line laid with care, a good course laid out with a poper finishing line, and all signals correctly made and made at the proper times. It is not enough to try to do these things well when visitors are present, they must be learned by constant practice in club races for the double purpose of teaching young sailors the correct procedure and also of developing good race committee material. Not otherwise will a club be able to stage a good race or train its sailors to win races in open events.

INITIAL ARRANGEMENTS

For a small-craft regatta there may be up to 100 or more entries in one class, most of them coming from a distance and needing to find suitable stowage for boats, gear, trailers, and cars. This is the first problem of the race committee, as the solution must be incorporated in the regatta circular issued long ahead of time, perhaps about the New Year. Top-ranking sailors in the class will add greatly to the success of the regatta and an invitation to them should be early, otherwise they may make other plans. The boat yard should be as close as possible to the probable starting area. It should be near the club and the conditions such that all boats can be launched and taken out of the water in a short time. It should also be clean. Emergency repairs to hulls, spars, rigging, and sails must be possible at any time. Suitable craftsmen should therefore be on at least stand-by notice. The car park should be near the boats, so that spare gear and sails may be stowed in car trunks. Otherwise some other safe shelter must be found for them. The location of the boat yard and routes to it should be clearly stated in the circular, along with any information to assure the entrant that he will be well looked after. Unless a club has had previous successful experience with boat stowage, the race committee may have a hard time finding a satisfactory solution. The deadline for entreis, also the place and hour of the briefing session, should be included. These things mark only the beginnings of arranging for a race. There is still much to be done.

THE RACE COMMITTEE

If the race committee is not yet complete, suitable members should be invited. Above all, each individual should be reliable. The chairman should feel sure that if a promise to serve is given, that promise will be carried out to the letter. Members should also be familiar with race committee work on the water and willing to work as a member of the team. The race committee should consist of:

1. *The chairman,* to supervise and pinch-hit if necessary.

2. *The timekeeper,* armed with a good timepiece, with a sweep second hand and correct rate. A good stopwatch as a check and for emergency use. Probably several members of the Committee will have their own good stopwatches.

3. *The gunner,* with a double-barreled shotgun, No. 10 gauge for a long line or a noisy day, otherwise a 12 gauge with a heavy charge will do. A shotgun is far better than a cannon, as it is safer and can be fired with split-second precision. It is true that the rules state that the flag or shape is the signal and that the gun merely draws attention to the signal. But in small centerboard boats, particularly in heavy weather, no sailor is able to watch for signals. He depends entirely on the gun, which therefore should be exactly on time.

4. *The signalman,* to hoist and lower signals (correct signals, and at the exact time).

5. *A line judge,* with megaphone and a good pair of lungs. *Two or more clerks,* to keep track of everything needed for the record. They will also help the line judge by spotting and recording boats over too soon.

The judges (three will be enough) will also be appointed early. They will usually have a boat of their own, to carry them where they will. They settle all protests and see that all rules are observed. They are *not* members of the race committee but may be consulted by the race committee on any matter. They should also feel free to make suggestions to the race committee.

THE RACE COMMITTEE FLEET

The race committee fleet must also be found. Each boat should be suitable for its task and many of them, together with a shore station, should have a walkie-talkie and operator. All must carry suitable marks or flags, described in the racing instructions, so that everyone will know who they are and that they have authority to be where they are.

The race committee boat should have deck space and room below for perhaps eight people over and above any crew on board. The shelter below deck is necessary for paper work, if not as a refuge from the elements. There should be a high mast to form one end of the starting line and on which to fly the race committee flag. There must be a yard or other means of rigging several, perhaps six, signal halyards. A 35- to 40-ft. sloop, a beamy cruising type with an auxiliary, will probably do very well. It will lie well at anchor and a line from mast to standing backstay will give room for the various signal halyards. It will have lots of deck space around the mast for those watching the starting line and also for adjustments of the anchor line to get the starting line exactly where wanted.

A very important piece of equipment is a wind-direction finder. A masthead flag is hardly good enough. Boats of this size seldom have good telltales and the best portable wind direction finder is an ordinary cheap bamboo fishing pole with some woolen yarn streamers or very light baby ribbons. This can be held high overhead away from the influence of hull and mast and works well. Only be sure to read NAYRU Rule 29, lest some impudent skipper protest the race committee.

The judges' boat will need an operator for the boat and for the walkie-talkie, unless the judges themselves perform these duties in the interest of privacy. There should be shelter from the sun, wind, and water and some degree of comfort for these very necessary and presumably venerable gentlemen.

The mark-laying boat should have a fair turn of speed and be equipped to lay, shift, or lift buoys quickly and on occasion act as a mark itself. It will need the speed if it must lay marks ahead of a fleet of planing boats, otherwise it may be out at second base. Its walkie-talkie will keep it in communication with the race committee boat so that marks may be shifted or replaced quickly if necessary.

Another important preliminary is the provision of suitable ground tackle, with spare parts. Spares should be provided on a generous scale but in the last resort a boat may be anchored as a mark of the course or a government buoy used as one.

If the marks are placed ahead of the fleet after the start, *a pathfinder* will not be necessary as the mark-laying boat serves the purpose; but where the marks are all laid out in advance, the Pathfinder will be necessary, to give the strangers an equal chance with the natives. In most cases the mark layer could do double duty as mark layer and pathfinder but both should be present at a large regatta just in case the need arises.

Rescue boats will be needed to pick up crews and disabled boats and otherwise make themselves useful. Some may be assigned to various stations with respect to the racing fleet so as to cover as much of the fleet as possible. This should all be discussed beforehand. Another one or two should carry walkie-talkies and have roving commissions, reporting to the race committee and taking instructions from it.

Police boats armed with the civil authority will be necessary to keep overenthusiastic spectators from crowding in on the course and interfering with the racing boats. They may have to warn commercial craft to alter course, slow down, or even stop, but where possible the race committee should keep the course away from the fairways or be prepared to accept some interference. A police or Coast Guard officer might well be posted to the race committee boat to insure better cooperation from the police or Coast Guard boats through the walkie-talkie.

One or more *messenger boats*, small outboards, to carry perhaps food and drink to the race committee fleet, or to put some poor seasick soul ashore or to bring someone out, are always needed.

The above-mentioned craft comprise the working race committee fleet, and all are more or less necessary for the proper conduct of the race. *An auxiliary fleet,* for the wives and friends of the sailors, club members and visitors, the press and press photographers, is also desirable. A few of the larger boats in the club can be pressed into this service. By means of a suitable notice posted on the regatta notice board and with someone to round up these spectators and put them on board, the race committee should have no further trouble with them.

THE INSTRUCTIONS

The racing instructions must consider everything mentioned in Part V of the NAYRU rules. Since the race committee will answer no questions out on the water it must be able, by signal, to alter the course and/or the time of start and to postpone, cancel, or shorten the race. The distinguishing marks or flags worn by each unit in the race committee fleet must also be described. The details of the start and of the starting line, and any other information that the sailors must know, must also be included. A chart of the course, not over perhaps a foot square, with the location of the marks of the course, government marks, and prominent landmarks, is also needed. It should also show all bad water, shoals, obstructions, and any buoys marking them. Any printing of the chart should be clear and legible so that it may be read under stress of wind and water.

PRERACE PROCEDURE

Registration. The boats begin to arrive on the day before the race, are properly stowed in the yard, and the sailors passed on to the registration table. Here the skippers get their copies of the regatta information other than the racing instructions, in exchange for the entry fee and some information. This information should include the owner's name, names of skipper and crew, sail number, colors of hull, spar, and spinnaker, color of crew's uniforms, and any other special details to aid in rapid identification, plus, of course, a satisfactory measurement certificate. Registrants can now be reminded of the place and hour of the briefing session, shown the official clock, and turned over to other committees where they will find out the places to eat and drink and sleep and other such necessary but minor matters.

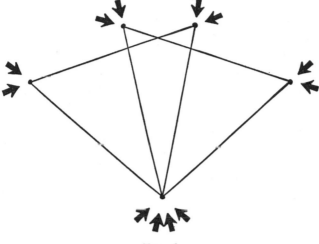

Fig. 1

The briefing session will probably be set for after dinner on the day before the first race, during which the racing instructions will be distributed to each skipper and crew member, each judge, each member of the race committee, and the skipper of each unit of the race committee fleet. Other copies go to the information desk for distribution to interested spectators. A free and full discussion of every question raised will now follow and then the visitors will be told of the local currents, probable wind shifts, and other information to put them on more even terms with the natives. Finally the weather predictions for the morrow are given and the session dismissed.

Before morning the race committees clerks must have ready, lists of all the boats that have registered, with their distinguishing marks and colors, in the order of their sail numbers.

LAYING THE MARKS

The race committee boat should be on the course at least an hour before the warning gun. Let us consider some of the problems which must now be solved. The solutions are all-important, as they can make or mar the race. Some race committees prefer to lay the marks for possible courses a day or more before the race. This allows time to lay them accurately and securely, particularly if the water is very deep—several hundred feet. The course should if possible not interfere with commercial traffic, possible starting points should be to weather of the shore to get a more constant wind direction, and there should be good weather legs for any direction of wind. In addition the probable starting point should be near the clubhouse for the benefit of the veranda sailors. Many of these conditions can be met if the prevailing mind is onshore at the clubhouse. A favorite plan is to use five marks which make two equilateral triangles of the desired size, say one mile to the side (see *Fig. 1*). These two triangles have a common vertex, the probable starting point for the prevailing wind. Each triangle has a side lying on a median of the other, and this gives a fan of four one-mile legs 30 degrees apart, spreading from the common vertex out into the prevailing wind. We thus have two triangles with six corners; and, as we can use any corner as a starting point and go around the triangle in either direction, we have twelve starting legs each 30 degrees apart and are therefore able to pick a good weather leg wherever the wind may be. If mark laying is difficult or slow for any reason, some such plan is mandatory. But it has a few disadvantages. If the wind is uncertain and variable the starting line may have to be moved to any of the five marks, and not only once but twice or even thrice before the wind finally settles down. This is extremely annoying, to say the least. Then when the wind is steady and the proper corner chosen, the first leg is not necessarily a true windward leg. It may be up to 15 degrees off the true wind if the five marks have been accurately placed as described, and more than 15 degrees if they have been badly placed or have shifted. This may not seem a very serious thing, but suppose a boat can make good 45 degrees off the true wind and that the weather mark in still water is truly upwind. The boat will travel 1.414 m. in making the mile to weather, half this distance and half the total time on each tack. But if the weather leg is not true and is 15 degrees off the wind, then the boat will sail 1.366 m. with 63.4 per cent of this distance on one tack and only 36.6 per cent on the other. The small loss of distance is immaterial, but the long and short legs make defense easier than attack and most good sailors prefer as true a weather leg as possible. Where there is a current with a component across this weather leg the desirable direction of the leg is that one which will give equal times on each tack. The exact direction of the leg is therefore a function of current velocity, wind velocity, and the characteristics of the boats. The third objection is that the triangle chosen may require passing the marks to starboard. Race committees are supposed to favor passing marks to port, because if they are passed to starboard there are frequent occasions when a port tack boat near the weather mark can gain an advantage over one on the starboard tack. This is alleged by some to be flying almost in the face of nature but seems to others to be only poetic justice. It probably produces the odd extra protest and this usually justifies the Z flag at the start.

There is another method of laying out a course which has been tried with good success. It needs comparatively light marks easily handled and water less than perhaps 100 ft. deep. But the only essential factor is the ability to lay, shift, and lift marks quickly. The mark-laying boat starts straight upwind just before the starting gun and therefore ahead of the fleet. Its compass course is given by the race committee boat and any necessary corrections can be made by walkie-talkie. The distance is measured by an engine tachometer calibrated in miles per hour and by a stopwatch. The mark-laying boat thus also does duty as a pathfinder. The other corner of the triangle is then laid and the job is done. Be sure that the mark layer has the speed to reach this second mark and lay both buoys before it can be overtaken by the planing fleet in good wind. This second method is probably the best in most circumstances. It involves a minimum amount of travel in looking for a starting point, gives a course requiring buoys to port, and as true a weather leg as the committee can provide. This triangle can give either a triangular course or a Gold Cup course. A windward-leeward course is even more easily laid, and indeed any random course of several legs can be laid as desired and depending on the conditions of the day.

The choice between these methods will of course have been made beforehand, but if buoys have been lost or shifted just before the race, new ones can be laid under the second plan as soon as the course is decided and before the start.

STARTING LINE AND FINISH LINE

The next decision is very important, the length and exact direction of the starting line. For small boats the line should be about as long as the fleet would be if placed stem to stern. Thus for a fleet of forty 14-ft. boats, a line 600 ft. long is suitable. Many sailors will say this is too short, but remember that it is difficult to judge one's exact position from near the middle of a long line. Also not all the boats are going to make perfect starts. There will be room for all those on time if the boats spread themselves along the line and do not bunch at one end. The race committee should set the exact direction of the starting line so that even the best skippers will be quite uncertain of the best place to start. The race committee boat should now anchor tentatively so that the starting line is about at right angles with the wind. If the line is exactly perpendicular to the wind, then the sailing distances from any point on it to the weather mark are all equal provided only that both tacks must be used by all boats. From this point of view such a line is ideal. But other factors enter in. The starboard tack has right of way and boats will crowd to the right-hand end, cross on the starboard tack, tack when they please, and deny that right to those boats ahead and to lee of them. To reduce this crowding at the right-hand end, the other end must be made more attractive. It can be somewhat farther upwind and thus closer in sailing distance to the weather mark. Suppose the starting line is 80 degrees off the true wind with the left-hand end the higher. For a 600-ft. line the left-hand end is 104 ft. farther upwind and therefore 147 ft. sailing distance closer to the weather mark than the right-hand end. This gives a 14-ft. boat starting at the port end of the line more than a ten length start over a boat starting at the starboard end. Quite an advantage—perhaps too much. Again currents, and small changes in wind direction, may be found off one end or the other. A helpful current or wind heading, off the port end, might make that end the desirable one even if it meant that the port end was lower than the starboard end. A cross current will also alter the relative desirabilities of the two ends. The race committee must weigh all these factors, set the line at the best angle, and hope that the boats scatter equally along the line. If they do it is indeed a tribute to the race committee. With a large fleet the mast of the committee boat and the mark give the direction of the line but its length should be cut short by another mark on this line and near the committee boat. Boats start between the two marks. This will reduce the number of protests at the start and lessen the chance of a serious accident through collision with the committee boat.

If the wind shifts just before the start so that the line is no longer at a good angle, the committee should not hesitate to hoist the P signal, reset the line, and start all over again. Another problem arises when many boats are over the starting line too soon and only some can be positively identified. Should the race be canceled and restarted, or allowed to proceed with several guilty boats at large? It is a difficult question. The answer would be easier if more of the delinquents could be caught. The judges' boat might be stationed at the other end of the line and the tall mast of the committee boat, with a bosun's chair, used as a point of vantage. Probably there should be no restart unless too many unidentified boats are over too soon. Remember too that the committee must protect the rights of those boats which have started properly.

Before the start the clerks must list all starters and the fleet should be counted by several of the committee so as to be sure of the exact number. This insures that missing boats will be identified at the finish and a search made for them. If the weather is heavy all crews should be ordered to wear life jackets.

When, as is sometimes necessary, the first leg of the course is off the wind, the starting line should be roughly at right angles to the first leg of the course but the exact angle determined so as to make both ends equally attractive. A start off the wind is bad, as the boats will certainly arrive at the next mark very close together and protests will be numerous. A short weather leg should be set to sort the boats out and prevent this trouble at the leeward mark.

A finish line should be set at right angles to the last leg if that leg is off the wind, but if it is a windward leg the finish line should be at right angles to the wind.

FINAL DETAILS

As the boats finish, the committee calls the numbers of the boats approaching and over the line, take the times of each, and the clerks record it all. One person should get the finishing sail numbers in order of crossing, regardless of the times, to be sure that two boats' positions are not interchanged.

With small centerboard boats, protest flags should not be required. Any boat with a protest should report to the committee boat as soon as it has crossed the line, giving the protested boat's number as well as his own. The written protest goes to the information desk by a certain hour stated in the racing instructions, all parties to all protests must meet the judges at the designated time and place, the judges do their work, and the final standings are posted. When the last race of the regatta is finished, the race committee must compile a list of the prize winners, arrange the prizes, introduce the V.I.P. who is to present them, and steer him or her safely through the entire list.

Three important duties remain: (1) to bid the visitors *bon voyage;* (2) to thank all those who have given their time and their talents, their services and their boats, to the race committee to help make a successful regatta; and (3) to write a report, noting the mistakes as well as the better parts of the race committee's performance, to the end that the next regatta will be under improved management.

20. Rescue

By
STUART H. WALKER, M.D.
Annapolis

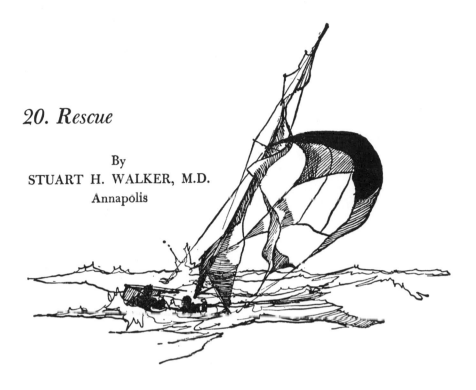

The fastest possible sailboat is probably the small light crew-ballasted centerboarder. Today the International 14, classic example of the type, is growing rapidly in popularity throughout the world and many new classes developed on similar lines (Thistle, Jolly Boat, Firefly, 5-0-5, Flying Dutchman, etc.) are appearing in increasing numbers. These boats (like the scows and other more radical types) are designed to apply the maximum possible thrust, in the form of very large sail areas, to an extremely light hull which can overcome the wave-length speed limitation of displacement hulls. They are able to rise up on their own bow waves to plane at speeds of 10 to 18 knots. (International 14's have been clocked to 16 knots and Jolly Boats, 5-0-5's, and Flying Dutchmen can plane even faster.) Freed of the usual waterline length-wave of translation speed restriction, these boats can be driven to almost unlimited speed save for one difficulty—capsize!

The only control of the tremendous thrust applied to these light hulls in a strong breeze is the movable crew ballast—the placement and weight of which has obvious limitations. Such ballasting may be inconsistent with the strength of the wind or the sea wave formations or the desired maneuvering of the boat. Control sufficient for a planing reach in protected water with the thrust controlled by luffing may be inadequate for running in rough seas or jibing or for the sudden increased thrust of a gusty northwester. Thus, when these boats are utilized in conditions suitable for their maximum speeds, capsizes are frequent and must be expected. In the two-day 1957 Lake Skiff Sailing Association Regatta, conducted in the periphery of Hurricane Audrey, there were approximately 48 capsizes among the 35 International 14's entered. Yet this regatta provided some of the best sailing of the year and none of the participants would have wished it called because of "too much wind." As more planing boats become available and more regattas are conducted in winds suitable for their best performances, more and better arrangements for the management of the capsized boats will be necessary.

Previous attitudes (and previously published articles) have considered capsizes as catastrophes to be avoided at all costs—catastrophes which could be avoided if skippers stayed ashore in strong breezes, reefed, tacked at the jibing marks, eased the main in the puffs, and generally behaved as if they believed that capsizes were catastrophes. Whereas capsizing can never be considered desirable, winning a race in a planing class against good competition nowadays requires driving the boat to the utmost, using the biggest possible sails, kept as full as possible off the wind, and strapped in tight and cleated to feather upwind. Skippers do not want to sit ashore when planing is at its best and are not going to lose 3 places by tacking at a jibing mark or 10 places by reefing. Modern boats and modern racing techniques necessitate taking the risk of capsize.

Although these boats are attracting many of our finest sailors, beginners, particularly among crews, must often be expected to place their foot in the wrong place at the wrong time. Only the long experience of the top helmsman can prevent at least occasional capsizes. (George O'Day, the 1957 Mallory Trophy winner, capsized his International 14 five times this year while chalking up 10 firsts in 24 starts and Walter Lawson, the Mallory runner-up, who had never capsized in 20 previous years of sailing, capsized his 14 three times in the same year.) The sudden pressure increase under the lee bow of a boat planing at 10 to 15 knots consequent to a sudden turn, dipping into a wave at a poor angle, or an awkward movement of the crew or the sudden increase in heeling moment when the mainsheet catches on a jibe or the jib gets caught aback in a shifty northwester, can capsize the best of them.

Consideration of the limitations on speed and joy in planing boats must be carried one step beyond the capsize—to the rescue. Unless self- or assisted rescue facilities are adequate, the race committee will not permit a regatta to be run in the presence of stormy winds —and rightly so. And unless rescue facilities are adequate the skipper will not drive his boat or take risks to the extent he would otherwise. Thus the limitations of performance and of opportunities for the most exciting planing are not necessarily the capsize itself but often the rescue facilities. In rough or cold water prolonged exposure in a capsized boat can be a serious threat to life and, although the actual capsize is rarely harmful to the boat, the rescue operation can be a significant danger if improperly managed. Race Committees undertaking the management of planing boat regattas must, therefore, in order both to permit the best possible racing and to avoid the inherent dangers of mismanaged capsizes, be prepared to provide the essential rescue facilities.

Even nonplaning centerboarders capsize occasionally and the commonly used 11- to 12-ft. dinghies of the frostbite circuits not infrequently, so that adequate preparation for assisted rescue from capsize should be an integral part of the management of any small boat regatta. The following is an outline of recommendations to sailors and rescue craft operators for the proper management of an assisted rescue of any small sailboat incapable of complete self-rescue (based partly upon recommendations of the Royal Yachting Association and published in their yearbook).

Skipper and Crew
  1. Recommended equipment
    a) Wearable life jackets
    b) Buoyancy apparatus up to maximum permitted—styrofoam, plastic air bags, etc.
    c) Gravity and/or suction bailers
    d) Tow line—preferably fastened to bow ring at all times—30 ft. or more in length, preferably nylon.
    e) Winch handles and pliers secure and available.
    f) Loose gear securely attached.
  2. Procedures (if self-rescue is impossible)

a) Lower centerboard and stand upon it to hold mast from going down.

b) Keep mast floating by attaching float to tip or by swinging bow around to face hull interior to windward (if standing on centerboard is insufficiently effective).

c) Don life jackets.

d) Lower sails and furl securely (fasten boom securely).

e) Right boat—by standing on centerboard and pulling on gunwale. Crew should be on opposite rail as counterbalance as boat comes up. This procedure may be assisted by rescue craft's gradually lifting mast or jibstay as weight of man on centerboard supplies force.

Rescue Craft Operator

1. Stand clear until boat is righted and organized for towing. The boats will not sink and there is no hurry. Avoidance of damage to hull and spars is an important consideration.

2. After boat is righted and the skipper signals, approach to leeward and at the bow end.

3. With the crew in the rescue launch, the boat's bow should be lifted as high as possible to empty water.

4. Crew may be able to get into boat, finish bailing, and sail home.

5. If rescue craft is too small to permit lifting of boat's bow, tow line (from boat or rescue craft) can be secured, the boat's bow slowly pulled into the wind, and the boat pulled upwind at idle speed until sufficient water has drained from over the transom to stabilize her. In open dinghies or in boats with transom bailers the speed of towing may then be increased to eliminate the major portion of the water over or through the transom. The crew may assist this operation by keeping weight aft until drainage is maximal, and then shifting forward to avoid inflow when tow ceases. Thereafter the crew may finish bailing and sail or be towed home.

6. In rough or cold water, the crew may be unable to lower sails. In this case they (the crew) should be taken on board the rescue launch. The launch should then get hold of the masthead, unshackle the head of the mainsail (letting it drop), work down the mast while gradually elevating it, unshackle the head of the jib, and work down the jibstay while righting the boat—so ending up with the boat upright and held by the bow. (The stem can then be lifted and the water emptied.) The crew can then return to the boat, finish bailing, and be towed home. The boat should NEVER be towed on its side.

It is essential to recognize the dangers inherent in capsize, to have life jackets available in the boat at all times, and *to wear them whenever capsize is likely.* (Race committees should require their wearing under the latter condition.) If the boat cannot be immediately self-rescued, they should be donned immediately after capsize. The crew must remain with the boat. Equipment carried within the boat should be securely fastened, or if it floats away should be disregarded when not within easy reach. If drifting is dangerous (near rapids or at sea, for instance), the sails may be used as a sea anchor by a controlled deflection of the mast beneath the surface in the direction of the drift. It is essential to avoid complete inversion of the boat as it becomes extremely difficult to right thereafter and in shallow water may cause the mast to stick in the bottom. The only solution to the latter problem is to pivot the boat about the mast tip, ending up with the boat downwind of the mast. Most important in any assisted rescue is the avoidance of overzealous rescue craft which rush in under little control to tear up sails, smash hulls, and wreck rigs in a misguided attempt to save the bewildered crew. The sailboat skipper should maintain control of the situation, if he is capable, and insure that he, his crew, and his boat are assisted to recovery rather than overcome by confusion. In many cases the U.S. Coast Guard Auxiliary provides the rescue services during sailboat regattas and may be depended upon to do a sensible and efficient job.

Unfortunately, despite the best planning, rescue craft may be inadequate for the task when there are a large number of boats, the boats are well spread out, or a large number of boats capsize simultaneously. For instance, the organizers of the British Cross-Channel Dinghy Race felt that it was necessary to have one rescue craft assigned to each competitor! It is of course unlikely that any race committee could often provide such facilities and it would be a major limitation on regatta opportunities to require such protection. An additional consideration is NAYRU Rule 26, which requires that a yacht shall render assistance to any vessel in distress (and this is often necessary when rescue craft are not immediately available). This requirement actually creates another limitation on racing in conditions likely to result in capsizes, as races must consequently be resailed or prove unfair for yachts rendering assistance. Thus, even the best arrangements may be inadequate and *the only completely satisfactory solution is for the capsized boats to be capable of rescuing themselves.*

Self-rescue capability is now being built in to many small boat classes, and many boats are rescued by their crews during races with significant advantages in their final standings. The Chesapeake Bay Men's Championship for 1957 was determined by the ability of the winning crew to rescue their Jolly Boat and finish after capsizing in a 50-knot squall. In the 1956 Viscount Alexander of Tunis Trophy Race in Ottawa, I was able to rescue my International 14 with the loss of but one position and lost only three positions after a similar downwind capsize in the L.S.S.A. race near Toronto. George O'Day capsized while in the lead upwind in a 1956 Princess Elizabeth Cup Race in Bermuda and was still able to finish seventh. Sailing canoes have for many years regularly capsized and righted themselves with minimum loss in speed or distance.

In order to accomplish these feats, boats must have two essential features: *buoyancy apparatus and self-draining equipment.* Buoyancy apparatus in the form of wooden or Fiberglas air tanks is being built in to many of the planing classes, while others rely on styrofoam secured in a wood framework or on plastic air bags lashed in place. Self-draining equipment is of two types: gravity drains cut into the transom or Venturi suction bailers operating through the bottom. Except for the sailing canoes, none of the modern planers has developed completely self-draining cockpits with full buoyancy tanks above water level, apparently feeling that this would be both more expensive to build and less seamanlike to sail than is warranted.

Buoyancy apparatus must be properly located with respect to the center of gravity of the boat, inasmuch as it serves to provide both lift (or displaced water) and stability or enhanced righting moment. The maximal lift effect is achieved by placing the buoyancy apparatus low along the center line of the boat where it will produce the most effective displacement of the least amount of water. Buoyancy apparatus high in the bow or stern or along the sides of the boat will have little lifting effect until a major amount of water has been taken aboard, but will be essential to maintaining stability by limiting the movement of such water. In addition, buoyancy apparatus located along the sides is essential to the production of a sufficient righting moment, displacing the maximum amount of water in the lowest portion of the boat when it is lying on its side. Unfortunately it becomes progressively less effective as the boat capsizes beyond 90 degrees. Such buoyancy apparatus should be securely fastened, inasmuch as it is subjected to great strains during capsize and rescue and inasmuch as its fixed position is so important. Most classes which utilize buoyancy tanks require at least annual testing to insure continued effectiveness. Wood tanks readily develop leaks where the tank meets the hull, styrofoam degenerates, and the plastic bags may easily be punctured. Fiberglas tanks probably make the most dependable apparatus available today.

The most effective self-draining equipment for elimination of the large amount of water taken aboard in a capsize is the transom gravity bailer. If the boat is provided with sufficient buoyancy, it will acquire considerably more water in a capsize than it actually displaces. A large hole in the transom will therefore permit the run-off of a considerable amount of water even with the boat at a standstill. When in addition the boat can be sailed at a significant speed, the water level at the transom is lowered by the creation of a wave of translation which permits far greater amounts of water to drain out the transom bailer. Transom bailers are usually constructed as bilateral openings low in the transom covered by metal or rubber flaps. They are used to maximum effectiveness in the Jolly Boat and 5-0-5, where the hull shape has little rocker, permitting water to run aft easily, and where the buoyancy tanks are arranged to funnel the water through the bailers. Transom bailers should be designed in respect to the particular boat, as they will be of varied effectiveness depending upon these factors of hull shape and buoyancy tank location, and the ability of the boat to move at significant speeds when filled with water.

Venturi suction bailers operating through the bottom may be either cylindrical or trap-door types. Both have openings on the after face of the exterior portion which, when exposed to the decreased pressure of water flowing past the bottom, drain water from the interior of the boat. Except for gravity run-out they are useless after capsize until the boat is sailing at significant speed. A minimum speed of 2 knots is usually required for operation with the boat empty, while higher speeds are necessary with the boat filled and the bailers submerged further under increased hydrostatic pressure. In a fully submerged International 14 with full buoyancy apparatus, they will not commence operation until speed is in excess of 5 knots. Speeds of this sort in a water-filled boat are of course only possible in a planing hull under planing conditions. If transom gravity drains (and buoyancy apparatus) are sufficient, however, water content may be reduced to a level which will permit operation of the suction bailers at lower speeds. In any case, as the interior water level (and degree of submersion) is reduced, the suction bailers become progressively more effective, operating at lower and lower speeds and eliminating water at a more and more rapid rate.

Location and total cross-sectional area of suction bailers are significant factors in their operation. The deeper they are located in the hull, the greater the speed necessary for their operation, but the more completely the water will be cleared. The greater the cross-sectional area, the more rapidly water will be eliminated but the greater the underwater drag. Probably one of the best solutions is to have several small bailers located at various positions with respect to the depth of submersion. Those high in the bilge will operate at the minimal speed of the completely submerged boat, while those deep in the bottom will clear the remaining water after higher speed and less submersion are achieved.

It would seem desirable to include some of these self-rescue facilities in all small boats. Star sinkings, for instance, could be prevented by the inclusion of buoyancy apparatus, while the assisted rescue of any centerboarder would certainly be greatly aided by both buoyancy tanks and self-draining equipment.

The technique of self-rescue in a boat adequately equipped for the purpose will depend to some degree on the type of boat and the wind and weather conditions, but certain general principles seem to be essential. It is sometimes possible to rescue the boat before the sails touch the water by a nimble crew's leaping overside to the centerboard. This, of course, is highly desirable, as the wetting of the sails and the submersion of the mast as well as the acquisition of increased water within the hull greatly increase the difficulty of righting. Some boats, such as Cadets, are so designed that, if the crew leaves the boat as it capsizes, they will float on their sides with the cockpit clear of the water and are therefore very easy to right.

In any case, *righting should be done at the earliest possible moment*, not only to get the boat back into the race quickly, but because it is most easily accomplished immediately after capsizing. At this time the boat will still be heading in the desired direction, the crew will be on the above-water side, and the sails will be to leeward of the hull. If the centerboard is not almost full down it should be lowered immediately (and here a centerboard lead to the side is invaluable). By standing on the centerboard (avoiding pressure too far out which could break it), the crew can not only keep the mast from submerging (it should preferably be of wood or other buoyant construction) but can, by pulling back on the gunwale, with or without the aid of the reversed jib sheet caught in its lead, readily right the boat. The sails thus come up toward the wind, the pressure of which prevents the boat from capsizing again to the opposite side, a common occurrence in boats with inadequate or poorly located buoyancy apparatus. The jib sheet must be seized immediately or, preferably, already in the hand of the crew, be tightened immediately to cause the boat's head to pay off, while the skipper frees the mainsheet. If the boat is allowed to come head to wind, in addition to agonizing moments waiting for her to bear off and the likelihood of her bearing off in the reverse direction, she may easily capsize again. She will probably drift aft and then suddenly sheer to the side, filling her sails, and, lying at a standstill, be completely exposed to the force of the wind. *By all means get in the jib sheet and get her head off immediately!*

It is preferable not to try to climb aboard until the boat is moving forward and stabilized. The crew should be in the water, hanging on to the windward gunwale and the jib sheet, giving a hard yank whenever the boat tries to come upwind, while the skipper drags along in the water astern holding the tiller. The skipper may at this time reach into the boat to open the transom bailers, which are usually released by a hooked shock cord (they may be already open if they are uncovered transom openings). When the boat seems sufficiently stabilized (usually in just a few seconds) the crew should clamber aboard, open the suction bailers, retrieve the spinnaker or any other gear which may be dragging or fouled, and position himself to best maintain stability. Finally the skipper should slide aboard, position himself to enhance the speed without interfering with the stability, and take in the mainsheet.

The boat should be steered on course if the leg was a reach, or on the fastest possible reach, without excessive deviation from the course, if the leg was a beat or a run. In wind conditions productive of capsizes, such courses should permit the boat to plane even though filled with water. In boats with adequate buoyancy apparatus and planing ability, large transom bailers will permit complete emptying in a few minutes. In the 5–0–5 complete recovery and clearing of all water after a capsize can be accomplished in 45 to 50 seconds! In an International 14, even with the small transom bailers permitted, the suction bailers will completely empty the boat in

5 to 7 minutes (dependent upon wind strength) and permit returning to the course in 3 to 5 minutes after capsizing. The danger of additional capsize and the tremendous reduction in speed occasioned by the filled boat necessitate obtaining maximum speed as soon as possible, even if in the wrong direction. Planing must be continued until the water is reduced to a level which the suction bailers can handle at the slower speed of the original course.

If the original course was a planing reach (which it is likely to have been, inasmuch as most capsizes occur while planing), the boat may be up and continuing on course in less than a minute. The subsequent speed differential for the few minutes involved will probably mean the loss of very few opponents. If the original course was a beat, the necessary deviation from the proper direction for several minutes may cause a significant loss in distance but even in this instance can be modified by the ability of the boat to plane on a closer and closer reach as the water is eliminated. The major time loss usually occurs during the righting procedure as this is often delayed by a variety of complications or a failure to recognize the necessity of immediate recovery. If the crew and skipper are prepared and/or experienced in this procedure, they can right the boat with jib in, main out, and rudder under control almost as soon as the mast hits the water and save major losses in time and crucial points.

CONCLUSION

It must be recognized that there are certain defects in this self-rescue business which may obscure the obvious advantages. It is possible that it may provide unjustifiable advantages to a poor helmsman who, unable properly to control his boat, capsizes and yet is able to continue the race. Although this factor is stressed by a few "old salts," it is difficult to believe that the penalties of distance and/or points lost from a capsize could ever be reduced to a level which would "encourage" poor helmsmanship. Actually the seamanship involved in a satisfactory recovery from capsize should probably be given credit; *i.e.*, the quicker the recovery, the fewer the boats lost. A significant disadvantage, however, does exist in the time involved in self-rescue by the inexperienced or poorly equipped which may cause a finish long after the remainder of the fleet. This may seriously delay the start of subsequent races of a series. When this possibility exists, the race committee should issue previous instructions to the effect that subsequent races will be started without regard to boats rescuing themselves from capsize. Under these circumstances, if his rescue efforts were unduly delayed, the skipper would consider the necessity of returning directly to the starting line to avoid missing the start of a subsequent race. It hardly seems necessary or desirable to disqualify boats whose masts touch the water as is done in some English races. One other defect in self-rescue is the tremendous strain exerted on the rig of a boat held down by a load of water. Such strains should be prepared for at the design level, but should also be relieved as soon as possible by maximal efficiency in bailing and buoyancy apparatus and crew technique.

Bibliography

1—Wind

Blunt, G. W.   "Practical Weather Wisdom"   *Yachting* Magazine, March 1953
Chapman, Gale J.   "Weather for All"   *Yachting* Magazine, August 1955
Durosko, Ted   "Forecasting Boating Weather"   *Yachting* Magazine, March 1953
Emmons, Gardner   "Coastal Winds"   *Yachting* Magazine, July 1950
Ogilvy, C. S.   *Thoughts on Small Boat Racing*   Van Nostrand, N.Y., 1959
Proctor, Ian   *Sailing: Wind and Current*   Adlard Coles, Southampton, England, 1955
Watts, A. J.   "Sea Breezes and Offshore Winds"   *Yachting World* Magazine, June 1956

2—Tide and Current

Curtis, H. M.   "Sailing Across a Current"   *Yachting* Magazine, July 1953
Fisher, J. T.   *Better Small Boat Handling*   Adlard Coles, Southampton, England, 1955
Knapp, A.   *Race Your Boat Right*   Van Nostrand, N.Y., 1952

3—Sails

Argus, A.   "Spinnakers"   *Yachting Monthly* Magazine, September 1958
Bavier, R. N., Jr.   "Trim of Sails"   *Yachting* Magazine, May, June, July 1957
Besse, Arthur J.   "Sails Are Not Wings"   *Yachting* Magazine, October 1950
Grant, Howard P.   "Sails Are Not Jets"   *Yachting* Magazine, August 1952
Lingard, T. S., and Paine, J.   "Light on the Sailcloth Problem"   *Yachting* Magazine, April 1957
Morwood, J.   *Sailing Aerodynamics*   Philosophical Library, N.Y., 1954
Ratsey, E., and deFontaine, W. H.   *Yacht Sails: Their Care and Handling*   Norton, N.Y., 1957
Van Voast, J.   "Controlling the Boom"   *Yachting* Magazine, January 1958
Whiton, Herman F.   "Jet Theory of Sailing"   *Yachting* Magazine, October 1950

4—Hull and Rig

Argus, A.   "Centerboard Performance"   *Yachting Monthly* Magazine, February 1957
Argus, A.   "Balance and Weather Helm"   *Yachting Monthly* Magazine, January through July 1959
Blue, Peter   "Tuning for Dinghy Racing"   *Yachting Monthly* Magazine, March 1955
Crane, Clinton H.   "What Limits Speed Under Sail?"   *Yachting* Magazine, March 1957
Knapp, A.   *Race Your Boat Right*   Van Nostrand, N.Y., 1952
Knight, Jack   "Dinghy Masts"   *Yachting Monthly* Magazine, April 1956
Wells, Ted   *Scientific Sailboat Racing*   Dodd, Mead, N.Y., 1958

5—Crew

Fisher, J. T. *Better Small Boat Handling* Adlard Coles, Southampton, England, 1955
Hay, Doris D. "A Crew's Eye View of Racing Problems" *Yachting* Magazine, February 1956
Knapp, A. "Getting the Best Out of Your Crew" *Yachting* Magazine, December 1952
Ogilvy, C. S. *Thoughts on Small Boat Racing* Van Nostrand, N.Y., 1957
Proctor, Ian "Racing Dinghy Duet" *The Yachtsman* Magazine, Summer 1953
Somerville, Hugh *Yacht and Dinghy Racing* Adlard Coles, Southampton, England, 1957

6—Racing Rules

Bavier, R. N., Jr. *The New Yacht Racing Rules* Norton, N.Y., 1959
Hills, George E. "Burden of Proof" *Yachting* Magazine, November 1951
Ogilvy, C. S. *Thoughts on Small Boat Racing* Van Nostrand, N.Y., 1957
Successful Yacht Racing Norton, N.Y., 1951

7—Light Air Racing

Proctor, Ian "How to Win a Dinghy Race with No Wind" *The Yachtsman* Magazine, Summer 1956
Wells, Ted *Scientific Sailboat Racing* Dodd, Mead, N.Y., 1958

8—Starting in Moderate Air

Ogilvy, C. S. "Special Starting Tactics" *Yachting* Magazine, May 1952
Thoughts on Small Boat Racing Van Nostrand, N.Y., 1957
Wells, Ted *Scientific Sailboat Racing* Dodd, Mead, N.Y., 1958

9—Finishing

Knapp, A. *Race Your Boat Right* Van Nostrand, N.Y., 1952
Ogilvy, C. S. "Psychology in Yacht Racing" *Yachting* Magazine, March 1950
Successful Yacht Racing Norton, N.Y., 1951
Somerville, Hugh *Yacht and Dinghy Racing* Adlard Coles, Southampton, England, 1957

10—Beating in Moderate Air

Hasher, R. G. "Racing Close to the Wind" *Yachting Monthly* Magazine, February 1957
Jacobs, H. S. "Sail the Longer Course to Victory" *Yachting* Magazine, September 1959
Somerville, Hugh *Yacht and Dinghy Racing* Adlard Coles, Southampton, England, 1957

11—Beating in Varying Northwesters

Ogilvy, C. S. "To Windward in Unsteady Breezes" *Yachting* Magazine, November 1957
Trevor, C. S., Calahan, H. S. *Wind and Tide in Yacht Racing* Gabriella Pladt Shipshape Books, Washington, D.C., 1947

12—Reaching in Moderate Air

Curry, Manfred *Yacht Racing* Scribner, N.Y., 1948
Somerville, Hugh *Yacht and Dinghy Racing* Adlard Coles, Southampton, England, 1957
Wells, Ted *Scientific Sailboat Racing* Dodd, Mead, N.Y., 1958

13—Running in Moderate Air

Bavier, R. N., Jr. "Trim of Sails" *Yachting* Magazine, July 1957
Curry, Manfred *Yacht Racing* Scribner, N.Y., 1948
Fisher, J. T. *Better Small Boat Handling* Adlard Coles, Southampton, England, 1955
O'Day, G. D. "Downwind Sailing" *Yachting* Magazine, February 1959
Ogilvy, C. S. "Off the Wind" *Yachting* Magazine, August 1951
Wood, W. C. "The Element of Balance" *Yachting* Magazine, November 1947

14—Starting in Heavy Air

Knights, Jack "Half the Battle" *Yachting Monthly* Magazine, January, 1956

15—Beating in Heavy Air

Knights, Jack "Racing to Windward" *Yachting* Magazine, March 1959
Wells, Ted *Scientific Sailboat Racing* Dodd, Mead, N.Y., 1958

16—The Planing Reach

Bavier, R. N., Jr. "The Planing Sailboat" *Yachting* Magazine, January–February 1949
Fisher, J. T. *The Catamaran* Adlard Coles, Southampton, England, 1958

17—Planing with Spinnaker

Knights, Jack "Are Spinnakers Worth It?" *Yachting* Magazine, July 1958

18—Running in Heavy Air

Fisher, J. T. *Better Small Boat Handling* Adlard Coles, Southampton, England, 1955.

19—Race Management

Knights, Jack "Management of Dinghy Races" *Yachting Monthly* Magazine, March 1955
Munro, W. M. "Organizing for the Small Regatta" *Yachting* Magazine, August 1956
Ogilvy, C. S. *Thoughts on Small Boat Racing* Van Nostrand, N.Y., 1957
Roosevelt, J. K. "What is a Race Committee?" *Yachting* Magazine, May 1956

20—Rescue

Bavier, R. N., Jr. "Cure for Capsizing" *Yachting* Magazine, May 1951
Fisher, J. T. *Better Small Boat Handling* Adlard Coles, Southampton, England, 1955